Praise for *The Religion*

"Brian Cain's *The Religion of Witchcraft* stands as a seminal and immensely readable work, offering clear and concise insights into the profound depths of the Craft. As an ordained Alexandrian Priest, Cain's extensive knowledge and experience shine through, making this book an essential resource for both novices and seasoned practitioners. Cain takes you on a journey, guiding you along the path of Witchcraft's rich legacy, from the Mysteries of Egypt and Rome to the folk beliefs and mythologies of medieval Europe into the British Witchcraft Revival of the 1950s, through to the vibrant multifaceted expression of the Craft today. His sincerity and vast knowledge base is made captivating with his relatability, offering his wisdom in an often humorous way that engages and involves the reader. The meticulous exploration of Witchcraft as a religion, its historical timeline, and the rebirth of the Goddess Cult provides readers with a comprehensive understanding of the Craft's rich legacy. Cain's ability to demystify complex subjects like Neoplatonism, the Qabalah, and the Grimoire traditions, while weaving in the personal narratives of witches from around the world, creates an engaging and enlightening read. This book is not only a tribute to the Priests and Priestesses who have shaped the Craft but also a bridge between the old and new, offering a valuable perspective for anyone seeking to deepen their connection to this ancient and evolving spiritual path."

— **Fiona Horne**, author of *Living the Elements: Extreme Adventures for Witches*,

"Brian Cain's new book, The Religion of Witchcraft, is a crucial read for a time when the world needs Witchcraft more than ever. Our world is in turmoil and we are decimating the very land we stand on. Witches know that our gods and goddesses are actually our ancestors who reside in the otherworld and are conjured into this one through our sacred practices to help us change the world for good of all. Witchcraft stands uniquely as the only religion committed to refraining from harm, grounded in the profound truth that our ways are an actual science and that one does not need to do harm in order to manifest what one needs in life. We do not have a Devil or evil deity in our belief system and no Witch has ever started a war. In this enlightening book, Cain masterfully unveils the connection between the gods of witchcraft and its everyday practice, guiding you through what Witches do with a solid understanding of our principles and ideals, along with our roots in ancient practices and philosophy. Knowing—and defining—who we are as Witches in the world is so important, especially in an era where zealous and unscrupulous leaders seek to stifle our freedoms to practice our sacred ways. Witches recognize that our gods do not dwell in distant clouds but join us in actual existence. This deep connection makes our religion profoundly personal, offering a direct and intimate spiritual experience. Brian Cain's work stands as a fiery beacon, illuminating the path of Witchcraft and magic for those who seek to harmonize with the ancient wisdom and reverence for nature that is at the very heart of our religion."

— **Laurie Cabot**, The Official Witch of Salem, founder of the Cabot-Kent Hermetic Temple, and author of *Power of the Witch*, *Celebrate the Earth*, and *The Witch in Every Woman*

"In *The Religion of Witchcraft*, Brian Cain delivers a profound and insightful analysis of the vital role of initiation in the craft. With vibrant prose and unwavering honesty, Cain emphasizes the sanctity of one's oath, a commitment often overlooked in modern times. His dedicated and sincere exploration reveals the deep, spiritual significance of one's promises, underscoring the importance of maintaining integrity and devotion within the practice of witchcraft. This book is a must-read for anyone seeking a deeper understanding of the true essence and responsibilities of the Witch's traditional path of divine eloquence, offering a compelling reminder of the power and reverence of sacred vows and the incredible strength of the group mind."

— **Silver Ravenwolf**, author of *Solitary Witch: The Ultimate Book of Shadows for the New Generation* and *Poppet Magick*

"For those delving into the world of Witchcraft, *The Religion of Witchcraft* is an invaluable source to begin one's journey. Presented in the author's candid narrative, there threads a timeline of historical cornerstones, an illustration of the luminaries in the witchcraft landscape, followed by practical gems of basic working knowledge. This literary source provides a composite of the religious framework of witchcraft and will be a valuable resource on any witch's bookshelf.."

— **Sharon Day**, Alexandrian Priestess, Founder and Director of Rose Ankh Publishing (roseankhpublishing.com). and Founder and Trustee of Alexandrian Craft at alexandrianwitchcraft.org.

"Brian Cain brings together the rich history and myths of Witchcraft, creating a vibrant legacy that comes alive in his new book "The Religion of Witchcraft". From the ancient mysteries of Egypt and Rome to the folklore of medieval Europe and the revivalist movements of the 20th century, he takes us on a journey through time. His writing is both scholarly and inviting, making even the most complex concepts feel accessible and engaging. This book isn't just a historical account; it's a living story that celebrates the ever enduring spirit of Witchcraft and its deep influence on modern spiritual practices. His new work showcases the resilience of the Craft, its extraordinary ability to adapt and thrive through the ages, and its unbroken connection to the divine sacred feminine."

— **Karagan Griffith**, Author of *The Inner Circle, a Discourse About the Alexandrian Tradition of Witchcraft*

"Witchcraft as a religion is a concept that excites as many as it rankles and Brian Cain's new book is a bold and beautiful foray into the conversation. As Witchcraft has fascinated and ensorcelled a new generation of seekers, Brian's book is a clear and immensely enjoyable reminder that at the core of the Witchcraft Revival is a path filled with devotion, worship, transformative ritual, and (yes!) religiosity. Useful for new seekers as well as seasoned practitioners, this book is a clarion call rooted in the vision that spoke to the elders and formers of the revival of religious Witchcraft. Weaving together history, personal experience, ritual, and passion, Brian's book speaks to the very heart of why we would want to dive into the religion of Witchcraft. A must read for all who seek the deeper mysteries behind the renaissance of the Craft."

— **Levi Rowland**, author of *The Art Cosmic: The Magic of Traditional Astrology* and *Mother: Ecstasy, Transformation, and the Great Goddess*

"Brian Cain's *The Religion of Witchcraft* is a masterful exploration of modern witchcraft, grounded in deep historical research and enriched by his experience as an Alexandrian Priest. This book transcends the superficiality of social media sorcery, offering readers an authentic and profound understanding of witchcraft's core as a Goddess-centered spiritual path. Cain's insightful analysis reveals why witchcraft remains a compelling and genuine religion for those seeking to delve into the mysteries of the Goddess and occult spirituality. His eloquent writing and scholarly approach make this an indispensable guide for both novices and seasoned practitioners alike. *The Religion of Witchcraft* is a must-read for anyone serious about exploring the true essence of this ancient and evolving spiritual tradition."

— **Michael Herkes**, author of *The GLAM Witch*, *Glamcraft*, and *Glamstrology*

"Refreshing in its clarity and unyielding in its position, The Religion of Witchcraft by Alexandrian High Priest Brian Cain provides a generous window into the occult, specifically the sacred mysteries of witchcraft. By solidly framing witchcraft as religion, Cain dispenses wisdom while dispelling misconceptions. Pop culture and fascination with witchcraft as a statement of culture may recede, but devotees of witchcraft will endure. Steeped in the ancient but modern in its approach, Cain takes a deep dive into the implications, social, political, and otherwise of defining witchcraft as a religion. Cain writes with a definitive confidence, unafraid of dismantling popularly held beliefs, and Cain is both impassioned and fearless; a welcome voice on an increasingly crowded shelf. "

— **Judy Ann Nock**, author of *The Modern Witchcraft Book of Crystal Magick* and *The Modern Witchcraft Guide to Magickal Herbs*

"Brian Cain walks the walk and lives the life. As he says, he goes to bed each night and wakes every morning a priest. His words ring true because he lives those truths. There is a tremendous amount of well-researched information in this book. But what strikes me about all the knowledge Cain imparts is that he is writing from his own experience and passion for his craft and especially from the responsibility he bears for carrying its power and purpose and for inspiring and training other seekers. When the world finally tires of TikTok video bites, "The Religion of Witchcraft" will stand as an invaluable resource and repository of wisdom."

— **Sallie Ann Glassman**, Vodou Priestess, author of Vodou Visions, proprietress of Island of Salvation Botanica, and Director of the New Orleans Healing Center

The Religion of
Witchcraft

Brian Cain

Forward by Jimahl DiFiosa

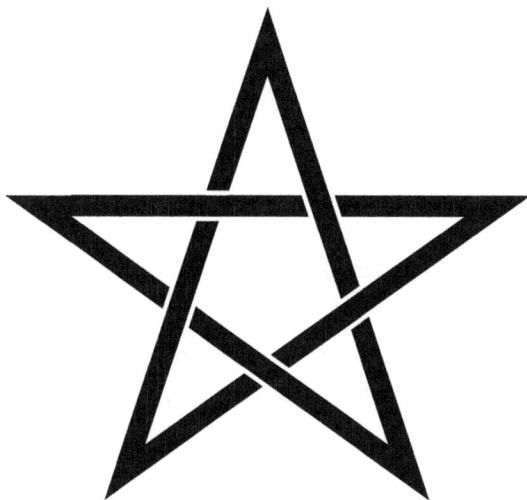

Warlock Press™

The Religion of Witchcraft

Brian Cain

© 2024 Warlock Press

Published by:
Warlock Press
1219 Decatur Street
New Orleans, 70116 LA, USA

Typesetting and Cover Design: Christian Day

Interior Illustrations: Lisa Ainsworth (founders of the Craft, Devil and Diana, interviewees, goddesses); Brian Cain with Christian Day (sigils and charts); Adobe Stock (botanical illustrations)

Photos: The New Orleans Coven and the Salem Coven

ISBN-10: 1733246682

ISBN-13: 9781733246682

I dedicate this book to one of the most devout High Priestesses I have ever known. My last Initiator, my teacher, and my friend, Val Hughs. We will share the wine again as we have shared the elixir of immortality. Blessed be.

Contents

Foreword

My typically idyllic and quiet life was pleasantly interrupted this week by the arrival of two unexpected messages. The first, a request from Brian Cain that I write the foreword to his new book *The Religion of Witchcraft*. This was a great honor for me as Brian's first book *Initiation into Witchcraft* remains one of my personal favorites.

The second message was from a friend sharing a rare 1950's essay on the subject of witchcraft by an American author named John Whiteside Parsons. Mr. Parsons was an occultist and self-defined witch, but is best remembered as the inventor of rocket propulsion technology.

More about "Jack" in a bit. First, I'd like to talk about the book you now hold in your hands.

The landscape of religious thought is a rich tapestry woven from the threads of countless traditions, beliefs, and practices. Among these, the religion of Witchcraft stands as a particularly vibrant and resilient strand, one that has endured centuries of suppression and misunderstanding.

In *The Religion of Witchcraft*, Brian Cain offers a comprehensive and insightful exploration into this ancient, yet ever-evolving faith, shedding light on its profound significance in the modern world.

Witchcraft, often misunderstood and misrepresented, is both a religion and a way of life. It is a path that embraces the divine feminine and honors the cycles of nature. In this book, Cain masterfully navigates the reader through the historical, spiritual, and practical dimensions of Witchcraft, providing a nuanced understanding of its role in contemporary society.

Brian's journey as an initiate and coven leader provides invaluable insight which imbues his narrative with authenticity and depth. His personal experiences and scholarly insights merge seamlessly, creating a work that is both informative and transformative - not an easy feat for a writer.

From the ancient mysteries of Egypt and Rome to the folk traditions of medieval Europe, Brian traces the history of Witchcraft with meticulous care, revealing both its roots and its many branches with equal reverence.

One of the most compelling aspects of this work is the emphasis on the living, breathing nature of Witchcraft. The author challenges the notion that Witchcraft is a relic of the past, instead presenting it as a dynamic and adaptive faith that continues to thrive and evolve. This perspective is particularly relevant in our current era, where the search for meaning and connection has led many to rediscover and reclaim ancient spiritual practices.

Consequently, *The Religion of Witchcraft* is not merely a historical account; it is a call to action. Brian Cain urges practitioners and seekers alike to embrace the full spectrum of Witchcraft, from its rituals and rites to its ethical and philosophical foundations. He emphasizes the importance of initiation, community, and the ongoing quest for knowledge and spiritual growth.

In a time when misinformation about Witchcraft abounds, *The Religion of Witchcraft* stands as a beacon of clarity and truth. It dispels myths and misconceptions, offering instead a rich and authentic portrayal of a religion that is deeply rooted in the human experience. By weaving together the strands of history, myth, and personal testimony, Cain creates a tapestry that is both beautiful and inspiring.

As you delve into the pages of this book, you will embark on a journey through the sacred and the mystical, guided by the wisdom of one who has walked the path of the Witch for many years. Whether you are a seasoned practitioner or a curious newcomer, *The Religion of Witchcraft* offers valuable insights and profound reflections that will enrich your understanding and deepen your connection to this ancient and powerful tradition.

As for the synchronicity of the Jack Parsons essay, a man who was clearly ahead of his time, this brief excerpt stands out as an unexpected parallel to Brian's work:

> *"We are the Witchcraft. We are the oldest religion in the world. When man was born, we were. We sang the first cradle song. We healed the first wound. We comforted the first terror. We are the guardians*

against the darkness. We are the witchcraft, and although one may not know the other, we are united with an indissoluble bond."

Brian Cain's work is a testament to the enduring power and relevance of Witchcraft. It is a celebration of the divine feminine, a homage to the ancestors, and a guide to the mysteries that lie at the heart of the Craft. May this book inspire you, enlighten you, and empower you to explore the rich world of Witchcraft with an open heart and an inquisitive mind.

— Jimahl Di Fiosa

Jimahl diFiosa is the author of four books about the Alexandrian tradition of witchcraft, most recently *A Place At The Table, the Human Legacy of Alex Sanders Continues.*

Introduction

Witchcraft is both a religion and a myth. It is a secret society, fertility cult, mystery cult, and a Priesthood. The Initiatory culture of Witchcraft spans generations, representing the lives of thousands of our forebears. After thousands of years of suppression, the Witch, the priestess reclaims her role returning that lost power and holy presence to Western civilization once again.

Witchcraft must be experienced as a way of life and a vocation, as it is the modern resurrection of the divine feminine, the Religion of the Mother Goddess. Today both men and women all over the world seek to reconnect to the ancestral current of Initiation into the way of the Witch.

In this book, you will be given a window to peer further into that world—a world filled with old gods and secret rites, forbidden practices, mystery, and magic. A world filled with Priests, Priestesses, Covens, Initiations, and Sabbatical ecstasy.

As the title suggests, this is a book about the religion of Witchcraft. The exact same words began the introduction to my first book, *Initiation into Witchcraft*. That book was well received by people all over the world—from new seekers to true elders of the Craft. It is in many ways a tribute meant to further the work of the many Priests and Priestesses that preceded me. But no one book is ever truly complete, and this book continues the work of the first book, but also begins with something new. It recognizes that Witches are not always Priesthood.

There are Witches around the globe that believe in our Gods, and recognize the priesthood and the sanctity and magic of Initiation. In time, some will become Initiates and others will carry on with personal pursuits, but this does not necessarily make them less sincere. Alexandrian and Gardnerian Witches are the two castes of Priesthood that descend from the original lines of succession. We are and will remain the North

Stars of the Craft. Yet, time is round, and today there is a large outer court of devotees all around the world, two separate paths that remain woven together in inspired worship. This book dares to serve as a bridge between these two worlds.

I have been a Witch, Initiate, and Coven leader for several decades. I am a member of the Alexandrian Priesthood of Witchcraft and work with Covens in both New Orleans and Salem Massachusetts. I embraced Witchcraft in my early teens and was first initiated into what is now called Traditional Witchcraft, running Covens within that system for about twenty-five years. I eventually moved to New Orleans where I was initiated into Alexandrian Witchcraft and formed the New Orleans Coven, which has been in operation for ten years to date. Through Maxine Sanders, I was privileged to meet High Priestess Val Hughes, who became my teacher and friend. I transferred into her lineage, Temple of the Mother, and through her guidance shifted the New Orleans group into the training Coven it is today.

In 2019, my first book *Initiation into Witchcraft* was published and two years later I began this book project which you hold in your hands, and which I intend to be my last book on the subject. However, as a good friend reminds: if you want to make the Gods laugh tell them your plans. In this book, I will take you on a journey, guiding you along the path of Witchcraft's rich legacy, from the Mysteries of Egypt and Rome to the folk beliefs and mythologies of medieval Europe into the British Witchcraft Revival of the 1950s.

In the chapter Interview with Witches, I ask the same questions to Witches around the world. Some of them are Initiates, and some are not. I've included varied traditions to give you, the reader, a pulse on the current movement and its diversity. With so much misinformation about Witchcraft being canonized and flourishing on social media (and even within some publishing companies) the truth has become a mystery unto itself.

Learn the truth about the word Wicca, what Goddesses we worship, who is the Devil, how to obtain the sacred Black Book or *Book of Shadows* and much more. In the back of this book, you'll discover the Grimoire Occultatum, Volume 2. This serves as both a sequel to Volume 1 and as a standalone tome of magic. I chose to include these tomes in my books to inspire seekers and to share some of my public ritual methods with Initiates. They are both safe and effective and have led many into the Mysteries.

It is vitally important that we do not cede the word Witch or our religion. There are religions and movements that would exterminate us, given the opportunity. Prejudice and persecution are never far around the corner. Allowing the word Witch to move into the secular also removes all legal protections. This would be great for corporations, not for Witches.

Historically Witchcraft was always religious, though it is true there was not an ancient singular religion called Witchcraft. But there is now. Thanks to pioneers like Gerald Gardner, Robert Cochrane, Sybil Leek, and Alex Sanders, Witchcraft is a living breathing Religion of the Goddess, and this book seeks to further that work into the world.

CHAPTER I

Witchcraft is a Religion

I am a Priest of Witchcraft, a High Priest of the Alexandrian Tradition, to be more precise. Declaring that my chosen faith is my religion is hardly unusual if I were a Catholic Priest, a Rabbi, or even a Priest of Voodoo. But in today's ill-informed magical community, the idea of being a Priest of Witchcraft is often met with prejudice, cynicism, and misinformation. There are individuals who have it firmly set in stone that my chosen faith does not exist, or that it must be Wicca.

Today there is a constant debate about whether Witchcraft is a religion. It is an erroneous debate, one that should never take place, because it is a fact that Witchcraft is a religion. And while there are individuals who simply dabble in spellcasting and identify themselves as Witches—or have a different narrative over what the word Witch means—it doesn't erase the fact that thousands of people around the world today identify Witchcraft as a religious faith. We have literature and history surrounding this movement.

The reality is that I go to sleep each night and wake every morning a Priest. My Priesthood has its own Gods, Holy Book, ethics, philosophies, laws, mythologies, rituals, culture, religious regalia, holidays, priesthood, and magical system. Yes, its own magical system. What other people think they know about it does not measure up to what someone who is fully involved knows. Likewise sharing, appropriating, or redefining our labels and beliefs for the masses does not imbue someone with real expertise. It is for some of these reasons that I have written this book and my first book, *Initiation into Witchcraft*. The world should know mimicking is not the same as knowing.

> ❝*The world should know mimicking is not the same as knowing.*

Some have adopted the modern usage of the word Wicca, perhaps because they are tired of this conversation. Unfortunately, in so doing they cede the word Witch to magic, Satanism, and a Christian narrative. Not at all wise. In today's modern, magical communities, there are many counterculture definitions that are used to define Witch. Sometimes these definitions are used in a broader sense, and sometimes they belong only in small subdivisions. For example, using the word Witch as synonymous with paganism, spell casting, or Satanism or using it as a label to empower the spiritual feminist movement. These are all fringe ideas and not common conceptions. Even the Witchcraft Priesthood, although more historic, could be considered less than mainstream as a concept.

First, let us define the word Witch. Who has defined it? Where does it originate? And why do we care about it today? Though we don't technically know the exact definition of Witch, there are four origin stories to the word, "Witch." These include language; its use in the lexicon of the Medieval Church; English colonization; and the Witchcraft Revival.

LANGUAGE
From Wicca to Witch

We can choose to believe Witches who came before us who say the word is derived from the old English word *wicca* or *wicce,* meaning wise.

The pioneers of the modern Witchcraft Revival presented the Witch or Witchcraft as a priestly cast following a pre-Christian cult or religion. Of course, we know that there was not a pre-Christian religion called Witchcraft. This is a medieval concept. The Church presented Witchcraft as a Cult often associated with perceived diabolical forces. We do not know if this had any merit or was pure fantasy inspired by fear and superstition. This is even true today when we approach Witchcraft as a religion. Historically Witchcraft was always religious. Today it is a religion.

The contemporary understanding of what constitutes a Witch is seemingly complicated. Some view Witches as practitioners of malevolent or harmful magic, known as Black Magic, intended to inflict damage or mischief. Others interpret the term more broadly to include anyone who engages in spellcasting, regardless of intent. Additionally, there exists a portrayal of Witches as purely mythological figures—creations of fiction and fantasy without real-world counterparts.

Most members of Initiatory craft identify as Witches and reserve the more mainstream Wicca for public dialogue, something I avoid at all costs. The common argument made today is that Witchcraft is a *practice* and not a *religion,* but that Wicca is a religion. This is a very silly argument, considering the fact that the word Wicca means Witch. Wicca was originally pronounced, *Witcha*, an old English word for a male Witch, and *wicce* was pronounced *Witchy* for the female counterpart.

Some may argue that words evolve. Sometimes this is the case, but it has also been the case that they devolve, in a sense, returning to their original usage. Even if you ascribe to the idea of the stereotypical Wiccan of the '90s, Wicca is still an alternative word for Witch.

Another fun argument that I like to put forward for those who want to stamp their feet and swear that the only religious Witchcraft is Wicca, is that Witchcraft is a legally recognized religion. And yes, the words Witch and Witchcraft are often lumped in with Wicca or paganism, but the current reality is that Witchcraft itself is either a fully recognized or partially protected religion in many countries including the United States, Portugal, Spain, the UK, and France. So, when someone says, "Witchcraft is not a religion," or "Witchcraft is not a religion but Wicca is," I'll tell you that is complete rubbish! It's a bit like shadowboxing with time or comparing Old English to modern English. They mean the same thing. However, some people are comfortable with this narrative because it speaks to their insecurities. Regardless this view flies in the face of current reality.

Back to what has historically defined what a Witch is, where the influence originated, and how it is used today. Its humble beginnings take place in merry old England and the original context is not used by most modern practitioners. The word Witch evolved in Britain with the birth of a new culture.

The Saxons and Frisians, arriving from the Germanic regions, brought their own customs, language, and societal structures. As they settled in the British Isles, they encountered the Romanized Celts, who had their own rich heritage shaped by centuries of Roman rule. This interaction led to a gradual assimilation and exchange of ideas, practices, and traditions.

The Roman influence, with its advanced infrastructure, legal systems, and cultural practices, left an indelible mark on the local Celtic population. The Celts, in turn, contributed their own unique traditions, folklore, and linguistic elements to the evolving culture. Over time, these influences melded together, creating a unique cultural landscape that was neither wholly Germanic nor entirely Roman-Celtic but a rich tapestry of both.

The resulting Anglo-Saxon culture was characterized by a distinct language that evolved into Old English, a vibrant mythology, and a complex social hierarchy. This culture laid the groundwork for the future development of English society, language, and identity, leaving a lasting legacy that continues to be felt in modern times.

A one-time obscure dialect that is now globally dominant, it was in this culture that the words wicca, wicce, wiccian, wiccan, Witch, and Witchcraft would gain popular use.

The question of who they were describing and to which ethnic group—if any—remains speculation. We do not know much about these old English Witches save that they were both male and female and that they practiced magic. We know that these words were not used interchangeably with words for magic, but rather describing a caste of people who used it. We also know that the Christian establishment of the time did not favor them in the slightest. Other than this information we do not factually know what they worshiped or how they practiced. A study of the early medieval people known as the Hwicce is a great place to explore for those curious about the subject. Unless the New Forest Coven was in some way connected to these Old English Witches this root origin has little to do with the subject of Witchcraft today save that Wicca is indeed an older word for Witch, something that Craft Elders stated from the beginning. It is my opinion that all our modern research and evolving theory still lead us to arrive at this same conclusion.

THE CHURCH
Witchcraft in Medieval Minds

The first great influence on the European mythology, history, and archetypes of the Witch remains the Church. Primarily the Catholic Church, but then later the protestants. First, let us be clear the Church did not view Witchcraft as magic. It was considered heresy; you were going against the religion of God in the form of some other worship. Traditionally, especially in the beginning, magic was a lesser crime than Witchcraft.

One of the earliest examples of how the Church viewed Witches is in the Canon *Episcopi* which states, "The Witches worshiped the Goddess Diana." Diana was often referred to as the last Goddess of the pagans:

"And the Witches flew at night with the Goddess Diana." So originally the Church was absolutely connecting Witches with an old pagan deity and perhaps a pagan cult, whether it existed in that time or not. This idea was so prevalent at the time it was recorded in the *Episcopi*. The Church believed the followers of the Goddess were the enemies of their God. [1]

> **❝By the Church's definition, Witches worshipped and made pacts and oaths with forbidden—and often infernal—entities in exchange for unholy powers.**

The deity of the Witches would eventually change in the eyes of the Church and become the Devil. Was this another Old God or simply Church propaganda? Regardless the Church always held the view that Witchcraft was a profane heretical religious practice—one that was contrary to that of God the Father. By the Church's definition, Witches worshipped and made pacts and oaths with forbidden—and often infernal—entities in exchange for unholy powers.

Was the Church's version of Witchcraft the fading memory of Europe's pre-Christian past coupled with hysteria and superstition? Or did the worship of the Goddess of the Moon and the many incarnations of the Old Horned Gods persist in the fringes of society long after the recorded end of such religious customs? I suppose we will never really know. Regardless, these beliefs have been so rooted in European culture that their impact is felt today.

---

[1]   Brian Cain: *Initiation Into Witchcraft*. New Orleans: Warlock Press, 2019. p. 93

ENGLISH COLONIZATION
Witchcraft As Malefic Magic

We must take note that we are looking through a very complicated cycle and through a British lens in most cases. The Church did not always use the word Witch. This was used by English-speaking Christians and took root in the King James version of the Bible. Many of us are in some way a product of British colonialism, and it's not an exaggeration to say the entire world has been impacted by the exploits of the British Empire, so much so that English is to date one of the most dominant and influential languages on the planet. Many of the pioneers of anthropology and archeology were British, white, male, and Christian. In their minds, Witchcraft was mere superstition—but at the same time evil. The British Empire was the largest empire the world has ever known. It had great influence over Europe, America, Africa, Australia, India, and parts of Asia. It not only possessed great wealth but dominated the fields of history and science. Because of this, the English language was often superimposed onto other languages, which doesn't always make for proper translation, especially when lack of cultural understanding was the norm.

In their grand exploration of the world, many Indigenous magical practices were dubbed Witchcraft—often mingled with superstition, fear, or even ignorance. An African tribal healer would become the Witch Doctor or someone who practiced Black Magic and Witchcraft. And where colonization took place, so too did cultural genocide, often in the form of a good Christian education. We can still see the results of its effects in the modern child Witch-hunts in Africa or the capital punishment of women in Saudi Arabia for the crimes of Witchcraft.

These academic pursuits coupled with the Christian British culture of the 1930s produced a definition of Witchcraft that can still be found in some dictionaries today—and there are many modern practitioners and magical people who are influenced by it. Witchcraft is malefic magic, which is equal to *any* form of magic in the eyes of a so-called "good" Christian. It is interesting to note that this terminology is considered incredibly outdated and inaccurate in academia today, and is no longer used, yet we still find it as a foundational school of thought by some self-proclaimed occultists.

Out of all the historical influences regarding the usage of the word Witch, this is perhaps the most unintelligent—not because it does not have a source, but *because* of the source and its unintended results. The idea that Witchcraft equates to magic has long been disposed of by the academic world that forged the definition, yet somehow it lingers on much in the same way people still believe the world is flat. From most perspectives, Witchcraft is not lighting candles, burning incense, making wishes, reciting chants, praying, setting up altars, or even casting spells. True, to some, it might be, but then again, I could be describing Buddhism.

THE WITCHCRAFT REVIVAL
The Religion of the Goddess

The last, and perhaps currently the most relevant place one can look to regarding the word Witch, is its active modern incarnation. Those like me, who practice the Religion of Witchcraft owe much of our beginnings to Gerald B. Gardner. In 1954, Mr. Gardner wrote *Witchcraft Today*, the first book about Witchcraft by an avowed Witch. [2]

He went on to appear on several media outlets to dispel the negative myths surrounding the craft and promote it as a positive, life-affirming Goddess faith. Yes, Gerald Gardner promoted Witchcraft as a religion—not only his religion but the religion of the Witches who initiated him into the New Forest of England in the 1930s. Gerald would eventually form his own Coven and go on to Initiate the founding members of today's Gardnerian Priesthood.

It is often stated that Gardner had created Wicca or invented the Witchcraft religion. It is true that Gardner re-introduced the word wicca to modern society, using it a total of two times in his public writings.

---

[2] Cain. *Initiation Into Witchcraft*, p. 5

He was far more responsible for introducing Witchcraft as a religion. He was also far from alone in the work as other Witches around Britain would make a similar claim. Many of these Witches had no connection to Gardner—or at times were even hostile towards him. Sybil Leek, Robert Cochrane, and Charles Cardell all publicly claimed Witchcraft as their religion. They had no connection to Gardner's groups, however there were striking similarities. They all worked in Covens, held Initiations, worshipped a Moon Goddess and a Horned God, and—of course— worked the arts magical. Witchcraft was a religion in full bloom. Today most credit is given to Gardner because the Witches he discusses in his book (Gardnerians and Alexandrians) would go on to become a pro- lific Priesthood across the globe, while the other trailblazers seemingly faded into obscurity. Though these two cousin Traditions both use the word Wicca interchangeably with its modern counterpart, it was not originally the rubber stamp that exists today. Wicca was a backseat word with little use outside of *The Book of Shadows*. Those who attempted to socialize Witchcraft often used it in public media, which eventually led to outsiders who could not connect the dots.

Many pioneer groups of the religion now exist only in the imagina- tion, but often this is enough to rekindle a new group or way of working. Then, of course, we have the Priesthood of the Goddess which remains intact in the magical Initiatory succession found within Alexandrian and Gardnerian craft, and perhaps a few other fringe groups that work from *The Book of Shadows* and its heritage. Still, other groups formed based on personal insights into Gardner's work, and today there are many published books on the subject.

This modern definition of the Witch put forward by the religion's pioneers is that Witchcraft is a magical Priesthood. Its adherents worship a monotheistic Moon Goddess whose consort had at one time been equated with the Devil of the Christians but was actually the archetypal Horned God of Europe. These Witches work in Covens which func- tion as individual cloistered orders and they have a sort of Bible called *The Book of Shadows*—a text that outlines the beliefs, laws, rituals, and works of magic within this Priesthood. Today this Priesthood exists in the Gardnerian and Alexandrian Traditions and continues to adhere to this definition in both form and function.

> **❝** *Our endless joy of diabolical festivals and sacred nods to Merry Old England also take place among the many practicing Covens today.*

Our definition can easily flow into that of the Church, in the way of Diana and the Devil. Our endless joy of diabolical festivals and sacred nods to Merry Old England also take place among the many practicing Covens today. If we go by the dictionary, religion is defined as the belief in a God or a group of gods; an organized system of beliefs, ceremonies, and rules used to worship a God or a group of gods; or an informal interest, a belief, or an activity that is very important to a person or group. I do not think I need to beat the proverbial dead horse any further in making the argument that Witchcraft is a religion and that there is a historical context to that very idea. Nor can its current existence be debated.

But what about contrary schools of thought? The one historical example has already been stated and is outdated. The other comes in the form of general modern paganism. Modern paganism is not a religion, but rather a collection of spiritual movements, ideas, and traditions that have been lumped together into a concept that doesn't hold to a meaningful practice, from my point of view. Paganism is an umbrella term that has had a cultural zombie-horde level of proliferation. Not only does it attempt to reconstruct a hundred dead cultures into one modern group, but its assumes that older traditions must kowtow to its ever-changing narrative. It is this group and its so-called prophets that have attempted to redefine modern Witchcraft. There is an unending desire for them to enfold our religion and its Priesthood into their agenda.

Gardner's work predates the modern pagan movement by at least 40 years. The many occult influences of Europe predate it even longer. As a Priest of the Goddess, I can only say that Witchcraft is not pagan. There is no evidence that the word is even pre-Christian. We are not an ethnic faith—we worship a monotheistic Goddess and believe in a form of reincarnation.

While we do hold and cherish some pre-Christian ideas, we must remember that even the old English wicca existed in a Christian world. The modern pagan movement was inspired and influenced by the Priesthood of Witchcraft, but this form of paganism has long been forged by individuals who were never initiated, trained, or belonged to the Craft. Today's paganism is also more of an American construct. In the U.K. it was all about the festivals and local customs and was more cohesive with Craft versus a conglomerate attempting to be a movement. Over time the idea that Witchcraft was a form of paganism has increasingly taken root. America took the reigns as it does most things through the power of consumerism. The company at the forefront of this movement was Llewellyn. In 1988, they published one of their best-selling books of all time: *Wicca: A Guide for the Solitary Practitioner* by Scott Cunningham. For many, this book would be their introduction to spiritual counterculture, and with no reason to doubt the author, they would be indoctrinated into concepts that had not existed within the religion of Witchcraft for the previous forty or so years.

For those of us already in the know, it was a disturbing turn of events, but even we had no idea how problematic it was. I still recall seeing that book on the shelf at the Open Door bookstore for the first time. I was not overly familiar with the word wicca, having only seen it briefly mentioned in the books I had read, and I was not at that time initiated. I asked a Witch Priestess working in the store about the book, "What is this wicca book?" "The beginning of the end," she replied. Thankfully, she was only partially correct.

Llewellyn was hugely successful in the 'nineties and though they have put out some good books over the years, I personally think the publication of that particular book by Cunningham may well be the worst thing that ever happened to Witchcraft. I commonly refer to it as the Book of Lies. An actual Craft Priestess did not Initiate Mr. Cunningham. He was not honest about his lack of credentials, and I believe it was unethical for Llewellyn to misrepresent a British-born religion in the way that they did. It's fair to say, that I did read it, in sheer horror, and although at the time I was not initiated I still knew it was rubbish. Sadly, this was not the case for many. This book along with a few others would begin to form the narrative that wicca was one of many modern pagan religions. This idea has persisted and even exists within the Priesthood, particularly in America. It however remains incorrect.

> ❝*The Craft is alive and well it's the living incarnation of the religion of the great Goddess we call Witchcraft.*

Simply put, each of us is following one of these narratives—both publicly and in private—and they often blend or blur in some cases. So here we are, as I begin to write this book in 2021, and I meet Witches and Covens from all over the world who have received their Initiations, worship the Moon Goddess and Horned God, keep to the Old Laws, and work the rites and magics of *The Book of Shadows*. The Craft is alive and well it's the living incarnation of the religion of the great Goddess we call Witchcraft. The history of Witchcraft is both obscure and well documented and although this is not a history book —nor attempting to be— it is important that we know where we come from.

CHAPTER 2

A Simple Historic Timeline of Witchcraft

Before delving deeper into the religion of Witchcraft, I want to provide a basic overview of its historical timeline. This is not meant to be an academic study of Witchcraft's history, but to help understand the concepts discussed here. The following is a concise history of Witchcraft. Tribal practices, mystery cults, and the rise and fall of cultures have all played a role in shaping the mythology and religion of the modern-day Witch. These moments in history are significant because each has contributed to the contemporary Witchcraft Revival of the 1950s and continues to influence the present. They form the backbone of our religion.

ANCIENT/CLASSICAL PERIOD
(700 BCE - 476 CE)

─(THROUGHOUT) Magic and polytheism thrived with tribal religions and established castes such as the Druids.

─(CA. 700 BCE) The rise of city-states led to priesthoods and the mystery cults of Greece and Egypt.

─(336) Alexander the Great's empire and Hellenization led to the spread of mystery cults, like those of Isis and Serapis, into the Greek world.

─(27 BCE) The Roman Empire rose, assimilating Greek legacies, while suppressing conflicting cults, diminishing the Druids' political power.

─(323 – 32 BCE) Mystery cults, including those of Isis, Magna Mater, and others, spread as the Roman Empire became a Hellenized culture.

─(380 CE) Rome declared Catholic Orthodoxy, leading to the closure of pagan temples.

─(550 CE) The last pagan temple, the Temple of Isis at Philae, closed in 550 CE.

MIDDLE AGES
(476 - 1450)

─(476 CE) The fall of Rome ushered in the Dark Ages; the Catholic Church began consolidating power.

─(THROUGHOUT) Pagan beliefs were rebranded as devil worship; suspicion around magic grew.

—(THROUGHOUT) Witchcraft evolved into a feared concept, associated with devil worship.

—(CA. 1020 CE) The Canon *Episcopi* declared Diana as the last Goddess of the pagans and condemned harmful magic.

—(CA. 1231 CE) The Papal Inquisition targeted heresies, including Witchcraft.

—(1258 CE) The Knights Templar were accused of heresy.

—(1346 – 1353 CE) The Black Death heightened superstition; the Cathars were condemned.

LATE MIDDLE AGES TO RENAISSANCE (1450 - 1600)[1]

—(1486 CE) The publication of the *Malleus Maleficarum* marked an era of Witch hunts.

—(1542 CE) English law criminalized Witchcraft with the Witchcraft Act of 1542.

—(1584) Reginald Scot's *Discoverie of Witchcraft* showed skepticism while documenting beliefs about Witches.

—(1611 CE) The King James Bible included references to Witches.

—(1580 –1660 CE) Europe experienced the peak of Witchcraft cases.

—(1692 – 1693 CE) The Salem Witch Trials occur.

---

1   Jone Johnson Lewis, "A Timeline of Witch Hunts in Europe," *ThoughtCo.com*, Feb. 20, 2020.

MODERN PERIOD
(1700 - PRESENT)[2][3]

—(1717 CE) The last Witch trial in England was recorded in 1717.

—(1833 CE) A Witchcraft prosecution took place in the United States.

—(1862 CE) Jules Michelet's 1862 work *La Sorciere* called for a return to Goddess worship, portraying Witch hunts as religious persecutions.

—(1888) The esoteric society The Hermetic Order of the Golden Dawn was established in 1888.

—(1897) *Aradia, Gospel of the Witches* by Charles G. Leland appeared in 1897.

—(1903) Order Templi Orientis was founded.

—(1921 –1929) Publications on Witchcraft and pagan religions increased with works by Margret Murray (1921) and R. Lowe Thompson (1929).

—(1939 – 1959 CE) Gerald Gardner was initiated into the New Forest Coven in 1939, and later published key texts on Witchcraft in the 1940s and 1950s.

—(1951 CE) The Witchcraft Act of 1735 was repealed in England in 1951, signaling a change in societal views.

---

² Charles Godfrey Leland, *Aradia or the Gospels of the Witches,* 1899, Accessed via *Sacred-Texts.com,* 2021.

³ Caroline Oates and Juliette Wood. *A Coven of Scholars: Margaret Murray and Her Working Methods,* published by Folklore Society of Britain, 1998, p. 14

CHAPTER 3

The Rebirth of the Goddess Cult

When discussing Witchcraft as a Goddess Cult, both in the past and present, we can begin with the occult orders, and even masonry, to find mention of several Goddesses, the most predominant usually being Isis. We can even look at the notorious Hellfire Club, where it is said that they worshipped Aphrodite during their nightly debaucheries. The most famous order is that of the Hermetic Golden Dawn, where such members as MacGregor and Moina Mathers believed that the Cult of Isis would emerge to mankind in the New Age as its primary religion.

In the story of Witchcraft, as has already been mentioned, Gerald Gardner was influenced by the current literature at that time. He had also been a member of several occult orders and a sincere believer in past lives. In Jack Bracelin's biography of Gardner, Witch, and later in Philip Heselton's works, we get a glimpse of Gardner's life in Cyprus and his work there with the Goddess Aphrodite. I have been told he wanted at one point to resurrect her Cult in Cyprus while he lived there in the

1960s. Of course, we have no way of knowing if that is actually true, but from what we know of him, it is certainly likely.

Although all the pioneers of Witchcraft had a similar belief in the supreme maternal, it was Gerald Gardner's work as the first spokesman of modern Witchcraft who could be said to be primarily responsible for dethroning the Devil and giving Diana back her seat.

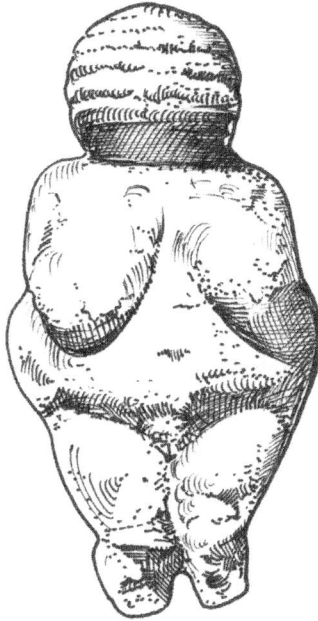

Venus of Willendorf

Today we have a Goddess women's movement, we have spell-casting Witches on TikTok, and pagan reconstructionist gatherings at every park across the nation. There seems to be an endless supply of female Goddess cohorts to choose from, at times treated like action figures—but then again, we also have a magical reemergence of real divine female power. The modern contemporary Witchcraft Revival was the gateway for European or Western Goddess worship to return to this world, and we Witches remain her custodians today.

The rebirth of the Mystery Cult known as Craft is also sometimes referred to as the Old Religion. A title that critics refute—when only taking occult associations into account, they ascertain that the Craft can only be traced into the early 1930s or perhaps earlier. This is a fair observation, but one must consider that there is nothing new under the sun. They are correct in that there is no evidence that the Craft in its current form is pre-Christian. The modern Craft's traceable roots exist in operative folk magic, festival customs, occultism, and what has been preserved from the classic works such as the philosophies of Plutarch, Plato, Socrates, and Aristotle. This is not to say for certain that our roots as Witches of the Craft are not older; however, apart from these customs and teaching and the living mythology of the Dianic Cult of Witchcraft, it must be left to theory and imagination. Regardless of the antiquity of Craft, our ideas and the Gods we worship are with the origin of mankind, so the title Old Religion is very appropriate from a certain point of view.

In my previous book, *Initiation Into Witchcraft*, I discussed the many similarities between the Cult of Isis and modern Craft. Indeed, the Craft functions much like the Mystery Cults of old.[1] Before the Church gained full supremacy, much of Europe, including Britain, was Romanized. The religions that the Church had to compete with were not that of the Druids or people of Odin, many of whose practices had fallen out of favor long before the Church rose to its great political power. The Church initially had to deal with the ever-so-popular Mystery Cults that flourished in the Roman Empire, even during its decline.

The Cult of Isis was one of the most widespread and prominent. Modern historians correctly ascertain that this could have indeed been called the Cult of the Goddess. This Roman Isis was the Goddess of 10,000 Names. She was given the epitaph, Queen of Every Land, and had at that point merged with several Egyptian, Greek, and Roman deities. She was a monotheistic Goddess who ruled over the moon, the waters, and the realms of magic. Her Initiates were both male and female. And according to *The Golden Ass*[2], also called *The Metamorphoses of Apu-*

---

[1]   Cain, *Initiation Into Witchcraft*, pp. 87–90

[2]   Lucius Apuleius, *The Golden Ass* by Lucius Apuleius. London, U.K.,: Penguin Random House, 1998 and "The Golden Ass." *Britannica.com*. Accessed June 19, 2022.

leius—a Roman version of a novel that retains details of beliefs revolving around the Cult of Isis—had three degrees of Initiation. She had particularly merged with the Goddess Diana and was even worshiped in her localized places of Nemi and Benevento. It is not hard to imagine that as Rome withdrew, their Imperial Mystery Cults went with them, and the more local Goddesses would begin assuming her role. The Goddess Diana was much more relatable to most of Europe and did not require grand temples to be worshiped by the common people. The Cult of the Goddess may have lived on—perhaps in a new incarnation.

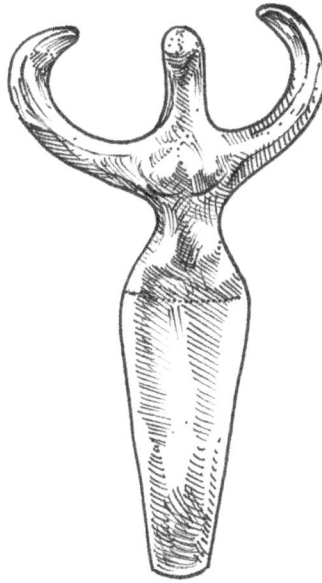

Nile River Goddess

This Cult of the Goddess could very well be responsible for the Church giving Diana the title, Last Goddess of the Pagans. Is it possible the old Cult of Isis lingered on in Christian times, and transformed into her more European counterpart, Diana? Or was it just a memory of an old, almost forgotten rival? [3] Regardless, the myth of the medieval Witch cult, whether based on reality or fantasy, has a direct impact on our religion today. Aside from the Church, there are a few primary sources for this.

---

[3] Cain, *Initiation Into Witchcraft*, pp. 90–97

One being *The Golden Ass*. This book was massively influential in the study of the subject of both Goddess worship and European customs, both inside and outside of the occult world.

Another source we have is *The Discoverie of Witchcraft*, 1584, by Reginald Scot. In this book, Scot gives descriptions of the Sabbath, in which the Witches revel with fairies, Diana, and the Devil. It must be noted that Scot's work was written from the perspective of a skeptic who was trying to prove that Witchcraft was a mere fantasy and that supposed Witches were being accused unjustly. Still, this book remains a window into the deep fears of Witchcraft and the ideas of its practice at the dawn of the enlightened age. Scot describes assemblies at which the Witches bring forth new disciples called novices. The novice must swear fidelity and partake in certain rituals, such as denouncing Christianity, making packs or an oath, receiving instructions in magic, and receiving the Witches' Mark. [4]

> **❝*Diana is Queen of Witches, teacher of sorcery, mother, lover, sister, Goddess of the moon, wine, the oppressed, and other worlds.***

Another extremely important work is *Aradia: Gospel of the Witches* by folklorist Charles Godfrey Leland. First published in 1899 [5], it is in this book that the Goddess Diana is the Goddess of the Witches. Her brother is Lucifer, and she has a daughter called Herodias or Aradia. Any student of Witchcraft will benefit from a deep dive into this book. The Goddess Isis is not mentioned; however, Diana has certain qualities never revealed in her older Roman incarnation: she's not a virgin; she turns into a cat to seduce her brother, Lucifer, and together, they have a

---

4 Cain, *Initiation Into Witchcraft*, , p. 93

5 Ibid, p. 45

child with whom they form a sort of trinity. From my perspective, both the Egyptian and Christian influences are clear—Lucifer is a strong mix between the Christian Devil, Apollo, and Serapis. Diana not only takes on Isis but also Hecate and the God Dionysus. Diana is Queen of Witches, teacher of sorcery, mother, lover, sister, Goddess of the moon, wine, the oppressed, and other worlds.

The gospel lends credit to the theory that there may have been a merging of cults within this Cult of Diana. Carlo Ginzburg and his work *Ecstasies* has great research on the subject, using church records that demonstrate the Church's belief in the Witch Cult of Diana. The primary book held most responsible for Gardner's ideas of Witchcraft is *The Witch-Cult in Western Europe*, by Margaret Murray. In this book, Murray refers to Witchcraft as a Dianic Cult. True or imagined, the idea of a secret magical Goddess cult known to many as Witchcraft persisted in the Western mind from as early as the 10th century to the present. Fact or fiction, it remains a powerful religious mythology. It has bubbled under the surface for hundreds of years and in the 1930s, in a small New Forest town in England, it began to overflow onto the surface.[6]

---

6   Ibid, p. 95

CHAPTER 4

The Pioneers of Witchcraft

When addressing the subject of the modern Witchcraft Revival and its history, we look to the many personalities that formulated the religion. These trailblazers often held the same viewpoints and had the same general beliefs about the Craft, no doubt being influenced by the books available at the time. Then, of course, there was the influence of the occult world from which the Witchcraft Revival did indeed emerge.

These early Witches all proclaimed to inherit the secrets of the Witch Cult, be it through family, Initiation, or as the case often was, both. In this book I will not attempt to prove or disprove their many claims, nor will I focus on useless information about their lives, as many books have (and no doubt will continue to do so). I will submit facts and claims, only giving my feelings and opinions about them when I deem it necessary. In truth, even with reasonable deduction, no one can prove or disprove most of them anyway; we humans do not like to admit how much we do not know. What is important in keeping with this subject is what these pioneers formulated, contributed, and inspired in others. What mark have they made and what legacy did they leave behind?

Although avoiding information about Gerald Gardner's time on a tea plantation may make me less of a historian, it is a risk I am all too happy to take, as this book is about the religion of Witchcraft and not his mundane world. I will also repeatedly point out that the many personalities are not all connected to Gardnerian Covens. Often, they were at odds. I hope this point will help put to rest the idea that the Old Religion of the Witch Cult was the invention of Gerald Gardner or his idea. As you will see below, the founders, leaders, and original teachers of the Witchcraft Revival had an overall shared concept regarding the subject of the Craft. Whether we credit this to Murray, Leland, Reginald, or others, it seems at least at some point in time the Witch Cult was, and is, a reality.

When looking at Craft as a mystery cult and religion it is important to recognize what these Witches collectively did believe. We shall begin with the Gods. All these early Witches had a chief Goddess and God. Not just Gardner's groups, but also Cardell's, Cochrane's, and Leek's. The Goddess was associated with the moon and the God was horned and linked with the folk beliefs regarding the Devil.

These Witches were also never solitary. They all worked in Covens and had some sort of Initiatory process, even when family claims for hereditary status ensued. Initiation was still deemed necessary regarding officially belonging to the Cult. Magic and all sorts of sorceries, of course, were also a shared skill, as was the concept that Witches had a special power that did not belong to the magicians or conjurors of old. This of course implies a magical system unto itself. These Witches also all conducted Esbats and generally some, if not all, eight Sabbats, something also adopted by the modern Druids of Britain. This makes perfect sense when one considers shared geography and history. The Sabbats however are not the subject at hand.

Reincarnation, a type of karma, other worlds, spirits, and general occult philosophy were also all common to varying degrees. The major difference being those who followed *The Book of Shadows*. We can call these Witches the Witches of the Book. As far as we know only the Gardnerians and Alexandrians worked from it in the early days—though it is certain that the others were at least aware of its existence.

This is, of course, because the Gardnerians and Alexandrians come from the same religious line of succession or Priesthood. An actual link between us and the others has never been revealed and most likely does not exist. The ideas about Witchcraft and our ways, however, seem to predate us all, and these concepts are alive and well today in a myriad of forms.

THE PIONEERS OF THE CRAFT

GERALD BROSSEAU GARDNER
Craft Name: Scire
Birth: June 13, 1884
Death: February 12, 1964
Became public: 1954

Occult credentials: Master Mason, member of the Ancient Druid Order, charter member of the O.T.O, Initiate of Witchcraft (New Forest Coven,1939). [1]

Publicity: Perhaps it all began on the Isle of Crete, where Gerald Gardner had a vision of the Goddess Aphrodite. So inspired, that he wished to build a temple for her there. Alas, he would have to settle for writing one of his first books, *A Goddess Arrives*, in 1939, which would be followed in 1949 by *High Magic's Aid*.

---

[1] Doreen Valiente: *An ABC of Witchcraft Past and Present*. Blaine, WA: Phoenix Publishing, 1986. pp. 183–190 and Cain, *Initiation Into Witchcraft*.

This was the first book written about modern Witchcraft though at first it was released under his pen name, Scire, and published as fiction. He would then go on to write the first two books in modern history about Witchcraft written by an avowed Witch, *Witchcraft Today* in 1954, and *The Meaning of Witchcraft* in 1959. Gerald Gardner took over the Museum of Witchcraft and Magic on the Isle of Man in 1949 with Cecil Williamson, taking full ownership in 1955. Gardner continued to run the museum until his death. [2] Gardner continued his public education about the religion of Witchcraft, becoming the world's first publicity Witch. He appeared in newspapers, articles, on the radio, and was even the first Witch to broadcast on television in 1957. At the Museum—now also called the Witch's Mill— he was interviewed by Daniel Farson on AZTV.[3]

Esoteric work: Gerald Gardner started his first Coven, the Bricket Wood Coven in 1949. He was responsible for the Initiation of several key figures of the Witchcraft Revival, Doreen Valiente, Lois Bourne, Arnold and Patricia Crowther, Eleanor Ray Bone, Monique Wilson, and Rosemary and Raymond Buckland, just to name a few. These Priests and Priestesses formed their Covens in Sheffield, Perth, Cumbria, London, and Long Island, New York. Other Covens were indeed formed, but are less well known. Alex Sanders was most likely a product of one, working in Gardnerian Covens in both Derbyshire and Nottingham. Gardner had at the very least, a brief correspondence with him. He also had associations with Aleister Crowley, Rosaline Norton, Ross Nichols, and Margaret Murray,[4] [5] along with many other noteworthy occultists. Perhaps Gerald Gardner's greatest accomplishment was heralding the Witchcraft Revival. In many ways, he's responsible for

---

2 Steve Patterson. *Cecil Williamson's Book of Witchcraft.* St. Paul, MN: Llewellyn: 2020. pp. 131–133.

3 https://www.youtube.com/watch?v=WN0fUikv88g.

4 Cain, *Initiation Into Witchcraft*, pp. 46–48.

5 Phillip Carr-Gomm. "Gerald Gardner & Ross Nichols." Published on *phillipcarr-gomm. com*.

almost the entirety of the Craft today and much of general paganism. Thanks to him, the modern Priesthood of the Goddess has been reborn in Western Civilization. Most Witches who descend from Gardner's line of succession or the succession of his more well-known priestesses are referred to as Gardnerians. Today, Gerald is most remembered for the Gardnerian Tradition of Witchcraft, though his contributions far exceed this one endeavor. For Gerald Gardner's goal was not to start a singular Tradition, but a religion. A religion he brought forward to the feet of the great Mother Goddess.

Teachings and beliefs: Gerald Gardner clearly believed in magic but a great deal more than that. He did not fully dedicate himself to the work of the magician nor the modern Druid but to the Religion of the Great Goddess and her Horned Consort. Witchcraft was his passion and in the end his life's work. Gardner taught that Witches believed in a form of reincarnation with certain ethical standards and laws. "An it Harm none, do what ye will," otherwise known as the Witches' Rede, would become the most well-known of these codes, with implications that have been compared to Karma. Gardner embraced many of Margaret Murray's ideas. She wrote the foreword to one of his books. They disagreed on the origins of Witchcraft however in Murray's opinion it originated in Egypt whilst Gardner firmly believed it to be Celtic. They both shared the idea that it was an old fertility cult that did exist within Christianity and had pre-Christian roots. Gardner and his prodigy worked from *The Book of Shadows*. This book was received in part from the New Forest Coven, but the rest was his design—often borrowing from other occult sources to which he had been exposed. Later Doreen Valiente would contribute her poetry to many of the rites replacing some of the O.T.O. material. *The Book of Shadows* is still hand-copied today and passed on to each new initiated Witch giving them the basic structure of the Craft as well as the beliefs of Gardner himself.

Summary: Although I have no emotional connection to the man named Gerald Gardner, I have great admiration for him and a religious belief that he was chosen as a messenger of the Gods. One cannot help but picture Yoda—unassuming, comical, easily underestimated. But in truth, powerful and wise. He was a trickster. By his peers was said to have a sense of humor, intelligence, and an intangible something an old soul. He was a colorful character with a curiosity about people. And perhaps, Patricia Crowther coined it best, "The mercurial herald of the Old Religion."[6]. Whatever one's opinions of Gerald Gardner and the religion of Witchcraft may be, the people who knew him have stayed fiercely loyal to the end. The Priests and the Priestesses who worked with him loved him and admired him. And even Doreen Valiente, one of his biggest critics, adored him for the reasons that matter most. Anyone who practices Witchcraft today in any form or imagining, or is a part of some tangled pagan movement, even many magicians owe a great deal of gratitude to him. In many ways in his time, he was Witchcraft.

DOREEN VALIENTE

Craft Name: Ameth

Birth: 1922

Death: 1999

Became public: 1962

Occult credentials: Initiate of the Bricket Wood Coven, Coven of Atho, and Tubal Cain. Gardnerian High Priestess and occultist,[7][8] Witch.

---

6 Patricia Crowther. *Lid Off the Cauldron*. Somerset, England, U.K, Capall Bann Publishing, 1998. pp.26 – 33.

7 Buckland. *The Witch Book*. Canton, MI: Visible Ink Press, 2002. pp.485 – 486.

8 Doreen Valiente's Witchcraft for Tomorrow. Marlborough, U.K, Crow Wood Press 1993.

Publicity: Doreen Valiente is best known to many as the author of several Witchcraft books, her first being *Where Witchcraft Lives*, 1962; followed by *An ABC of Witchcraft Past and Present*, 1973; *Natural Magic*, 1975; *Witchcraft Tomorrow*, 1978; and *The Rebirth of Witchcraft*, 1989. Like Gardner, Doreen appeared in the press to a lesser extent, including in the 1971 documentary *Power of the Witch* and 1989, *Earth Magic*.

Esoteric work: Doreen contributed her poetry to *The Gardnerian Book of Shadows* from 1954 to 1957. She was initiated into the Coven of Atho by Ray Bowers in 1963 and then Tubal Cain by Robert Cochrane in 1964.[9] Doreen was also a self-proclaimed occultist and student of Witchcraft both of which she did appear to have a strong understanding. Unfortunately, she was never satisfied in any of her groups, as can be seen in the evidence of her many falling outs.

Teachings and beliefs: Like Gerald Gardner, Doreen had a genuine belief in the Old Gods. She also held Murray's view that despite Britain's Celtic influence, Witchcraft was in part connected to an old Dianic cult.[10] In her public Grimoire, *Liber Umbrarum,* she uses Pan and Diana as her principle God forms. Doreen also believed in spirit communication, having received contact with the spirit of a Witch named John Breakspear between 1964 to 1966.[11], which inspired some of the public rituals within her grimoire. Doreen embraced most Gardnerian tenets, sharing Gardener's views on ethics, reincarnation, and a form of Western karma. Although, like many Witches, she was a bit relaxed in these philosophies.[12] Doreen was also influenced by her work with Robert Cochrane and Raymond Howard. However, this seemed to broaden her viewpoints versus changing them. It is clear that Valiente

---

9   *Doreenvaliente.com*

10   Valiente*: An ABC of Witchcraft Past and Present.* pp. 113–116.

11   Doreen Valiente. *The Rebirth of Witchcraft.* Marlborough, Wilshire, U.K, Crow Wood Press, 2007, pp. 99–116

12   Valiente, *Witchcraft for Tomorrow,* pp. 36–46

did indeed believe in the antiquity of the Old Religion, and personally held the view that it was older than Gardnerian Craft.

Summary: Doreen is one of those pioneers who, in my opinion, is both given too much credit and not enough. She did contribute a great deal of magically inspired poetry to *The Book of Shadows* and the Craft in general. However, she did not write *The Book of Shadows* and some of her rituals were not entirely of her own making, despite popular opinion. She did not create the Charge of the Goddess. She reconstructed it. The Charge of the Goddess was originally created by Gardener using Charles Godfrey Leland's *Aradia* material with Aleister Crowley's poetry.

Doreen disliked the idea of Crowley being associated with Craft and talked Gerald Gardner into replacing Crowley's poetry with her own, which she proceeded to write. Doreen's greatest contributions were her many publications and her role as a public spokesman. She did run two Gardnerian Covens but does not have a downline to the present like her contemporaries, perhaps because she did not persist in that work. She referred to herself as a student, and indeed she was, being initiated into not one, but three different branches. Of her three teachers, Gardner seemed to be the one that left the greatest impression on her. Doreen is most well-known and remembered for that association today. Her later work was within a pagan framework as she had all but retired from Craft.

Doreen Valiente is my favorite Craft poet, and, in my opinion, this was her greatest service to the Goddess. Sometime in 2015, I met a man named John Payne who proclaimed himself to be Doreen Valiente's last acting High Priest. Perhaps this is the closest I would ever get to that iconic Priestess who had inspired me since my early teens. I was able to visit with John Payne and get to know him. I found him to be delightful and sincere. I do believe that it is true that Doreen did leave her legacy to him. I do not believe it was done in a Gardnerian manner. You see, Doreen had mixed her drinks at that point. Her view on Witchcraft was not purely Gardnerian, and how she passed things to Payne was probably not either. Regardless Mr. Payne kept good his word and in a few short years established her foundation before he himself slipped into the wood between the worlds.

ROSALEEN MIRIAM NORTON

Craft Name: Roie
Birth: October 2, 1917
Death: 1979
Became public: 1949

Occult credentials: Occultist, trans medium, High Priestess of the Coven Pan-Hecate in Kings Cross Sydney, Australia.

Publicity: Rosaleen's public association with Witchcraft began with her arrest in 1949. The charge was obscenity regarding her artwork which depicted pagan and sexual content. Rosaleen would continue to appear in the press and local magazines up until 1957, earning her the title Witch of Kings Cross, a title she at first disliked but eventually thoroughly embraced. In 1952, she published *The Art of Rosaleen Norton* in which she sent a copy to Gerald Gardner. The two continued a brief correspondence of unknown content. Norton's publicity would continue long after her death with various books and documentaries about her such as *Pan's Daughter* by Neville Drury; *Pagan* by Inez Baranay; and *Thorn in the Flesh*, *The Magic of Pan* and *Three Macabre Stories*, all by Keith Richmond. In 2020, the documentary *The Witch of Kings Cross*, directed by Sonia Bible, was released and at the time of this writing can still be viewed on Amazon.

Esoteric work: Rosaleen Norton's greatest contributions to the occult world are her many beautiful paintings and, to a lesser known degree, her poetry. In 2000, an exhibition of her paintings was held in Kings Cross, Sydney, Australia by local enthusiasts of the Australian Order Templi Orientis. And it seems one of her poems found its way into some Gardnerian Covens through Doreen Valiente. Doreen shares it with us in her book *The Rebirth of Witchcraft* though she had corrected the grammar in parts:

> *"The Craft is only part of the Way and must not be mistaken for all of it. But in itself it is important, for it can be used to lighten burdens and to help in the Great Work. It is not for the weak. Had you been such, you would not be here. Therefore, know this. Some have the power, most have it not. If you have it, it springs from within you, from the will, the mind and the spirit; and it can be joined to external symbols. It must grow through practice, as you gain knowledge and skill. The implements, words, symbols, and spells are your working tools. You must be guided by the gods who dwell in the mind and body. The Officers of the coven will tell you of the Gods, for this knowledge is too secret to be written. Always remember that you must be stronger than the powers you evoke. Knowing how this is done is one of the signs of mastery. Therefore to the work, and to the knowledge that is joy and strength and light and life everlasting."*[13]

Teachings and beliefs: Rosaleen Norton clearly believed in the Witch Cult. She worked with a God and a Goddess, primarily Pan and Hecate although she also worked with many other different facets including Lilith, Lucifer, and an entity she referred to as The Master. Rosaleen claimed her branch of Witchcraft was Welsh in origin and was known as The Goat Fold. She worked in a Coven and held a single Initiation rite. They utilized both ritual nudity and, at times, robes or ritual masks. Her Coven had only one degree of Initiation and focused heavily on the astral worlds, teaching that there were two: one for man and one for the elementals. They practiced Qabalah and most forms of general occultism. Like the Witches of Britain, they held eight Sabbats, a feast of cakes and

---

13 Valiente, *The Rebirth of Witchcraft*, p. 157.

wine, and used ritual tools—namely the Athame, cup, censer, pentacle, and cords. It is curious to wonder how Rosaleen Norton's Witchcraft is so similar to Gardnerian Witchcraft, which, at the time, was not public in its practice in any way, unlike today.

CHARLES CARDELL

Birth: 1895
Death: 1977
Became public: 1961

Occult credentials: Coven leader of his Tradition which he called Wiccen or the Old Tradition.

Esoteric work: Cardell's greatest impact came from the work of one of his former students, Ray Howard, who led the Coven of Atho into which Doreen was initiated in 1963 after taking his correspondence course. It is really from her publications and painting of the famous head of Atho that Cardell is known today. Cardell may also be responsible for both the propagation and mispronunciation of the word Wiccan, which he spelled W-I-C-C-E-N-S, and which predates anyone else's use of the word publicly.

Teachings and beliefs: Cardell's group worked with a Horned God calling him Pan or Atho. Atho was the name of the idol used. Incidentally, Atho is also a name for Zeus. The Goddess they worked with was Diana. In their rituals, a horn and long bow were used which was unique when compared to other forms of Witchcraft at the time.[14]

---

14 Melissa Seims. The Wica: "Charles Cardell." *www.thewica.co.uk*

The head of Atho may hold the key to the Coven's system of magic which can be found in Doreen Valiente's book, *An ABC of Witchcraft*. The head reportedly was made of oak and is the symbol of the Horned God. Upon it are various astrological symbols, symbols of the Zodiac, triangles, pentagrams, a chalice, the moon, circles, an eight-spoked wheel, twin serpents, the elements of nature, and other curious and occult symbols. The number seven featured heavily in the Coven. Cardell was the propagator of the 7 'D's which are: Humility - Dalen (moon); respect - Donna (Saturn); trust - Dello (Jupiter); kindness - Doven (Venus); truth - Dessa (Mercury); honor - Dorran (Mars); and dignity - Deth (Saturn).

Five of these 7 'D' words are found in a list of Witch words that exist in correspondences between Gardner and Jack Bracelin. It is believed that these words originate with Charles Cardell. In Howard's material from Doreen Valiente, we find this list had been changed to presence, truth, kindliness, tolerance, awareness, strength, and perception.

Summary: Charles Cardell and his partner Mary Cardell had a mutual exchange of information with other occultists and Witches. Cardell, having had at least some correspondence with Gerald Gardner, with whom he, as well as Doreen, had a falling out, thus beginning the first modern Witch war. According to Doreen, Gardner's Initiator, Dafo, knew Cardell and warned her about him. I find this curious indeed. What previous experience or knowledge did Dafo have?

It is clear from Cardell's shenanigans that at one point in time, he acquired *The Book of Shadows*, either from Gardnerian Priestess Olive Green or perhaps during an Initiation in the 1950s. Regardless, we know that a feud did ensue between Cardell, Doreen, Gardner, and other members of the Craft resulting in the publication of Cardell's pamphlet *Witch* that both attacked Doreen and published snippets of *The Book of Shadows*. Charles Cardell by all accounts and Witchcraft standards, was not someone to be admired. However, I think it is important to bear mention of him in the subject of this book for he did indeed run a group and practice a religious form of Witchcraft as early as 1961. We know that Gardner and he exchanged information—how it was put to use and by whom is mostly unknown. Was Cardell the individual who introduced Gardner to the Old English word for Witch, jumbled, spelled wrong, and mispronounced as it was? Perhaps so, or maybe it was the other way around. We also know that Cardell worked with several other individuals, some of them well-known to the occult communities at that time. One must wonder how these individuals went on to do their work, and if Cardell's influence seeped into other areas of the Craft. [15]

ROBERT COCHRANE

Birth Name: Roy Bowers.

Birth: 1931

Death: 1966.

Became public: 1963.

Occult credentials: Folk magician; Magister of Clan Tubal Cain.

Publicity: He was featured in the 1963 article in the *Psychic News,* "Genuine Witchcraft Is Defended." He also cooperated with Justine Glass in her book *Witchcraft: The Sixth Sense*, published in 1965. [16] [17]

Esoteric work: *The Clan of Tubal Cain*: A series of letters distributed to several people, including Bill Gray and Joe Wilson.

Teachings and beliefs: The Cochrane Tradition observed the same Sabbats and Esbats as Gardnerian Witchcraft. They wore black robes. The

---

15 Jonathan Tapsell. *Ameth: The Life & Times of Doreen Valiente*. London: Avalonia Press, 2014, pp. 61–64.

16 Shani Oates. *The Robert Cochrane Tradition*. Published independently, 2018.

17 Valiente, *The Rebirth of Witchcraft*, pp. 117–136

Coven primarily worked outdoors. They held a single Initiation and, like other Covens of the day, worshipped the Moon Goddess, who had a secret name, and the Horned God, whom they called Tubal Cain. The tools used by Cochrane were the knife, staff, (also called a stang—a term he coined), cord, cup, and a stone. They held a ritual meal of cakes and wine. Like other Witches, he also created a circle and acknowledged the four quarters. Robert Cochrane also taught reincarnation as a part of Craft philosophy.

Summary: Robert Cochrane certainly has influenced modern Craft. Most of what we know about him comes from the works of Doreen Valiente, who had once been a member of the Clan Tubal Cain. Robert Cochrane practiced the religion of Witchcraft, worshiping the Horned God and Moon Goddess of the Witches by names he gave them. In my opinion, he was a self-starter. Though rumors abound about his association with Gardnerians and even Charles Cardell, I think that these exist in the realms of fantasy. What is certain is that Robert Cochrane did interact with many occultists and Witches of his time period, some of whom were Initiates of Gardnerian Craft, and there is evidence that there was a crossover between these two Traditions via Initiates leaving one camp for the other. It is said Robert Cochrane was so hostile towards Gardnerian Witchcraft that he actually first coined the name Gardnerian as a form of abuse to note that they were not really the old Traditional Witches that he claimed to be. Robert Cochrane's legacy exists as a myth. Today, there are several groups and Traditions claiming association with him. I view them as reconstructionists. They have studied his handful of letters and what history we know of him, and they've tried to capture the spirit of the kind of Witchcraft that Cochrane practiced.

As Doreen Valiente states in Evan John Jones' book *Witchcraft: A Tradition Renewed*, Robert Cochrane's Tradition could not be recreated, nor could its rituals be written down. For they were sporadic and, in Valiente's opinion, something that Cochrane made up as he went along. However, she does state that some of her most magical Sabbats were held with him.

Today, I believe "Robert Cochrane: Magister of Clan Tubal Cain," is used by people who wish to assert that Traditional Craft is older than Gardnerian Witchcraft. Gardnerian Witchcraft is the modern upstart and so are all its contemporaries who follow Wicca. However, the fact remains that Robert Cochrane was not practicing a form of folk magic devoid of religion. He was practicing—as were his followers—religious Witchcraft in such a compatible way that they were able to sidestep between his own tradition and the Gardnerians. The spirit of Robert Cochrane certainly lives on, and I believe that this is his greatest impact. But regardless of his origins or his contributions, he makes one believe that he was a sincere Priest of the Old Religion of Witchcraft.

SYBIL LEEK

Birth: February 22, 1917,
Death: October 26, 1982
Became public: 1962 to 1963

Occult credentials: Leader of the Horsa Coven; Initiate of Witchcraft; general occultist, worked Golden Dawn rites with Israel Regardie.

Publicity: Leek first became known from her multiple antique shops, one of which was located near where she created her Coven of Witches in the New Forest. She did research for the TV show called *Southern Television*. In 1963, the *Daily Herald* published a feature article about Sybil and her shop. The article was titled, "Yes, I Am the

Forest Witch." A television program titled Circles of Power aired on the Canadian Broadcasting Corporation featuring Sybil and other Witches, including Doreen Valiente. She did a lecture tour in the United States, which was very successful and eventually led her to relocate to New York, then later Los Angeles, and then eventually to Houston and Florida. Sybil Leek wrote over 60 books on the occult along with numerous magazine articles. Her most famous book is *Diary of a Witch*, published in 1968. Sybil was also known for being a member of the Witchcraft Research Association from which she eventually resigned. [18][19][20]

Esoteric work: Sybil Leek is not especially known for her contributions to the body of esoteric work, though she did spend a brief time studying with Israel Regardie working the rituals of the Golden Dawn, and was considered an occultist. There are claims that members of her Horsa Coven still practice today, though they seem to have made no impact on the larger Craft world. Her contributions go hand in hand with publicity and public education.

Teachings and beliefs: Sybil Leek was a known occultist and claimed that her family was filled with psychics, mediums, and astrologers, and she wrote many books on these subjects. She believed in a God and a Goddess and worshiped them as Diana and Faunus. However, she held the philosophy that there was a higher creative force behind all the human icons. She taught Reincarnation, believed in Initiation, and claimed herself to have been initiated in France. In her book, *The Complete Art of Witchcraft*, She lists the Witch's working tools as being those used by other Initiatory British Traditions. She also published pieces of Gardnerian ritual materials, demonstrating that at one point, she had gained access to them.

---

[18] "Ordinary Witch from New Forest Dies at 65." New York Times obituary. nytimes. com/1982

[19] Valiente, *The Rebirth of Witchcraft*, pp. 144–150

[20] Melissa Seims: The Wica. "Other Witches of the 1950s and '60s." *www.thewica.co.uk*

Sybil Leek's personal Witchcraft teachings consisted of a series of philosophies. She taught the tenant of balance. The tenant of balance was seeking harmony with all life and the self in connection with nature and the divine. Her other philosophies included the practices of avoidance and pursuit, desire and aversion, and delusion and apprehensions. Whether Sybil really received these teachings from her forebears or constructed them herself, they helped navigate her belief about the religion of Witchcraft.[21]

Summary: What most of us know about Dame Sybil Leek comes from her iconic book, *The Diary of a Witch,* where she makes fantastic claims of belonging to a hereditary Witchcraft family of Russian and Irish descent. She states that she received her Initiation in France and became the High Priestess of a New Forest Coven connected to many other Covens in the region. She also claimed to have known Aleister Crowley as a child, and that he spoke to her of Witchcraft and magic. It is from this source that many people believe that Aleister Crowley indeed belonged to the Witch cult. Whether one believes Sybil Leek's claims, or she was just another iconic Witch who created fantastic stories, may be irrelevant. Her personality was of great presence in both Britain and America and the myths surrounding her inspired many people to pursue the deeper meanings of the Goddess, the Craft, and the world of magic.

---

21 Sybil Leek. *The Complete Art of Witchcraft.* New York: Signet, 1971, p. 110

LOIS BOURNE
Craft Name: Tanith.
Birth: April 10th, 1928
Death: December 22nd, 2017 [22]
Became public: 1961

Occult credentials: Initiate of Witchcraft, Gardnerian High Priestess of the Bricket Wood Coven; Claimed to be Magistra in another form of Witchcraft.

Publicity: Lois Borne was the subject of several articles appearing in *Psychic News* in 1961; *Saga Magazine* in 1966; *The People* in 1969; and *Voices from the Sixties* in 1967. She wrote several books: *Conversations with a Witch*; *A Witch Among Us*; *Dancing With Witches* and *Spells to Change Your Life*. Prior to any of this, back in 1946, she published a pamphlet, *Witchcraft and Manningtree*, as Lois Hemmings.

Esoteric work: Lois worked for many years in Gardnerian Craft, but would go on to join an unknown form of Craft. [23] She eventually received the title Magistra and led a Coven in St. Albans. She discovered her later Tradition through a fellow Gardnerian Initiate she called Margo. Margo was currently the Magistra of the group, with her partner being the Magister. In the Tradition, they were the de facto Coven leaders although they answered to an older couple known as the Lord and Lady. Margo's Coven was presided over by the Lord and the Lady, who were seated on chair-like thrones overseeing the rituals. The Coven was very

---

22 Melissa Seims. The Wica: "Elders of the Wica" www.thewica.co.uk
23 Lois Bourne. *Dancing with Witches*. London: Robert Hale, 2006, p.89

agricultural in nature. They worshiped a God and a Goddess, although the God was viewed as the primary source of power. Many of the rituals were conducted in silence but remained sophisticated. There was also a great focus on meditation. [24]

Teachings and beliefs: Lois believed in the God and the Goddess, magic, reincarnation, Initiation, and Coven Witchcraft, and merged her two Traditions.

Summary: Lois Bourne is a curious figure to me, as I have received personal reports of her activities with Alexandrian Priesthood in her later years. Although secondhand, I was informed by more than one source that she was aware of Alex Sanders' Initiator and his Initiation into what would later be called Gardnerian Witchcraft.

She disagreed with the posturing and attitudes of her Gardnerian peers regarding Alexandrians at the time. To quote a statement, "We know they are of us. We should bring them in." Whether this story is true or not—and I am leaving out details—it echoes a sentiment I have often heard. Lois was grateful to Gerald Gardner and her time with the Bricket Wood Coven. She had a love and loyalty towards him. She did, however, join another Coven after his death. This Coven is an unknown Tradition but claimed to be older by 300 years. Her work does appear to lean towards this Craft in her later years, although she also always identified as a Gardnerian High Priestess. In one of her last interviews, Lois, speaks with great love of the God and the Goddess and about their love for all of mankind. It exudes her role as Priestess. [25]

---

24   Ibid. pp. 98–100
25   Liz Williams. "Lois Bourne, 1928 – 2017." Jan. 11, 2018. *wildhunt.org*

ELEANOR "RAY" BONE

Craft Name: Artemis.
Birth: 1910.
Death: 2001.
Became public: 1964

Occult credentials: Initiate of Witchcraft, She claimed to have been initiated into a Coven in Cumbria in 1941, and would later become Gardnerian in 1960.

Publicity: Much of Bone's publicity was through print media, as she is the subject of several articles, including those printed in the *Sunday Telegraph* in 1964; *Life Magazine,* 1964; and *The Weekend Telegraph*, 1965. She also makes an appearance in the 1970 documentaries *Witchcraft '70* and *The Power of the Witch*, 1971.

Esoteric work: High Priestess of a Coven in South London. She developed a large downline, particularly through her Initiates Madge and Arthur Worthington. She also was known for developing the healing arts within her Coven, which was a primary focus of her work. [26][27]

Teaching and beliefs: Eleanor Bone followed the teachings of Gerald Gardner, who she remained a staunch supporter of. Believing deeply in the Goddess and being an advocate for the Craft and its healing work was her primary focus.

---

26   Buckland. *The Witch Book*. pp. 56 – 57.
27   Melissa Seims. The Wica: "Elders of the Wica" *www.thewica.co.uk*

Summary: Bone was one of three High Priestesses initiated by Gerald Gardner who would go on to develop their own lineages of the Craft. The lineage most associated with Bone is known as the Whitecroft Line, although there is another lesser-known line—referred to as The Bone Line. Bone claimed to have met Dafo and stated that Dafo had told her that Gardner had only been initiated to the First Degree by the New Forest Coven. Bone knew many Initiates, including Patricia Crowther and Alex Sanders. She has been rumored to have visited Sanders and worked with him in London. Bone was a Priestess who marched to the beat of her own drum. She is difficult to research as she never wrote any books and mostly kept her practices private, despite her many activities in the arena of publicity.

PATRICIA CROWTHER

Craft Name: Thelema
Birth: 1927. Still living
Became public: 1965

Occult credentials: Initiate of Witchcraft. Gardnerian High Priestess.

Publicity: Crowther was the author of several books including *The Witches Speak* (1965); *Witchcraft in Yorkshire* (1973); *Witch Blood: The Diary of a Witch High Priestess* (1974); *Lid Off the Cauldron* (1981); *The Zodiac Experience* (1992) *Witches Were for Hanging* (1992); *The Secrets of Ancient Witchcraft with the Tarot* (1992); *High Priestess: The Life and Times of Patricia Crowther* (2001); *From Stagecraft to Witchcraft: The Early Years of a High Priestess (2002);* and *Covensense* (2009). In addition, she had considerable press, primarily print media, including *Far Out* in 1990, *the Weekend Telegraph,* and many more. She also appeared on a BBC Radio show episode called *A Spell of Witchcraft* in 1971.

Esoteric work: Patricia Crowther is responsible for the Sheffield line and, in a way, the Alexandrian tradition. Despite her disdain for Mr. Sanders, it is clear they had a connection—at the very least through her Coven maiden Pat Kopinski [28] Kopinski allegedly worked with Alex under a Priestess named Medea in the Derbyshire Coven, and then later in the Nottingham Coven that she herself ran. Patricia has confirmed publicly that the Alexandrian *Book of Shadows* is identical to hers. Regardless of the many mythologies surrounding the issue, the two lines have many other shared practices that are not found elsewhere. Patricia Crowther has set up several Covens. Her work within astrology has also been a foundational source for many Witches today, and at the time of this writing, she continues to help guide the Gardnerian Tradition.

Teachings and beliefs: Patricia Crowther is a staunch supporter of Gardner and believes in the antiquity of Witchcraft, fostering it as a priesthood of the Old Gods. Patricia believes Witchcraft is a religion from the Stone Age and for the Space Age.

Summary: Patricia Crowther is the last living Initiate of Gerald Gardner. She has been a guiding light and at times the voice of reason for the new generation of Witches. Her lineage, dubbed the Sheffield Line, is one of the smallest, but perhaps most reflective of Gardner's work. Although the result of conflict, Crowther is a reluctant ancestress of the Alexandrian line, although publicly this remains unrecognized. [29]

---

[28] In his book *A Coin for the Ferry: The Death and Life of Alex Sanders*, author Jimahl di Fiosa notes that there are three spellings for Pat's last name: Kopinski; Kopanski; and Kasprzynski. Kopinski was the one most often used by Pat herself.

[29] Buckland. *The Witch Book*, pp. 111 – 113.

MONIQUE WILSON
Craft Name: Olwen
Birth: 1928
Death: 1980
Became public: 1961

Occult credentials: Initiate of Witchcraft and Gardnerian High Priestess [30] [31]

Publicity: Monique Wilson is mentioned in several articles during the 1960s, including *News of the World*; *Sunday's Mail*; (1961) *The Daily Express,* 1964; *The Observer,*1968; and *National Geographic,* 1972. She inherited the Witchcraft museum on the Isle of Man in 1964. [32]

Esoteric work: Monique ran a Coven in Perth, Scotland, and helped to establish the Craft in that country. Perhaps her greatest contribution was the Initiation of Raymond Buckland at the behest of Gerald Gardner. Buckland would become the first Witch to establish the Craft in America alongside his more silent partner, his wife, Rosemary. Today, the Kentucky, California, and Long Island lines are descended through him, although honorary credit is given to the work of Monique Wilson. Monique only trained Buckland for a total of 12 days. She claimed the title Queen of All the Witches, much to the chagrin of other British Witches, something that appeared in the papers in 1964. [33]

---

30   Melissa Seims. The Wica: "The Scottish Wicca" www.thewica.co.uk
31   Buckland, *The Witch Book*. pp. 351 –352.
32   Melissa Seims. The Wica: "The Scottish Wicca" www.thewica.co.uk
33   Cain, *Initiation into Witchcraft*, pp. 51–56

Teachings and beliefs: Monique's teachings and beliefs are a bit obscure and are most likely best reflected by the Gardnerian Kentucky Line prior to the influence of the Long Island Line. At that time, it was more in line with her and Buckland's actual practice. Her downlines have greatly changed in the way they practiced when Buckland first brought her teachings to America. These changes have been attributed to the massive influence of Theos and Phoenix of the Long Island Line.

Summary: Monique Wilson is among the strangely problematic figures in modern Witchcraft. On one hand, she has a rather massive downline in America, the newest branch of the Priesthood. On the other, she was less than popular in the UK, being disliked by most other elders, including Alex Sanders. This was due most likely to her sale of Gardner's estate to Ripley's Believe It or Not, and to her self-proclaimed title as Queen of All the Witches, which she claimed to have received in Gardner's will. Despite all the negative stories, I believe she had a real connection to the Goddess. From her earliest childhood, she was exposed to the worship of Quan Yin, and I believe it had an impact on her. The result of her Initiation to the Craft speaks volumes on its own, as do her many descendants.

ALEX SANDERS

Craft Name: Verbius

Birth: 1926

Death: 1988

Became public: 1962

Occult credentials: Initiation into Witchcraft, Alexandrian High Priest, Magician, trans-medium.

Publicity: Alex Sanders was the subject of much press during his lifetime, and even after his death. Earlier articles about him were published in such mainstream publications as *The Manchester Evening Chronicle,* 1962; *Manchester Comet,* 1965; *American Publications,* 1966; *Reveal,* 1970, and *Brighton Evening Argus,* 1988. Alex advised on several films including the 1966 film, *Eye of the Devil.* The 1970—movie, *Legend of the Witches* was based on June Johns' 1969 biography about Sanders, *King of the Witches.* He also appears in *Witchcraft '70 (1970)* and *Secret Rites (1971).* Sanders wrote one book himself, *The Alex Sanders Lectures,* which was published in 1984. [34][35]

Esoteric work: Alex Sanders was the co-founder of the Alexandrian Tradition of Witchcraft. Without any doubt, Alex Sanders spent years as a student of both Witchcraft and the occult. His family was involved in mediumship, and he did indeed practice it in his formative years. His work as a magician was in the role of a research student influenced by such works as the *Abramelin the Mage, The Key of Solomon, The Magus,* and the writings of Franz Bardon and Éliphas Lévi.

In 1963, he was initiated by a Derbyshire High Priestess named Medea. While working with Patricia Kopanski (or Kopinski, or Kasprzynski) and Sylvia Tatham, Alex met his future wife, Maxine Morris—later Sanders. Alex and Maxine would eventually move to London in 1967 and together founded the Alexandrian Tradition. Their line, with its roots entangled with the Gardnerians and other branches of the occult, is now one of the world's foundational Craft Priesthoods with its current Initiates numbering thousands all over the world. Alex was very much responsible for the training that now takes place within many Covens. He introduced weekly meetings at the same time, at the same location, and on the same day. He introduced Hermetics and lectures and tied the occult and Witchcraft together in a way that still continues, He limited control and never retained the measure; overuse of the scourge

34 Valiente. The *Rebirth of Witchcraft.*,163,177.
35 Cain, *Initiation into Witchcraft,* pp. 57 to 64.

was done away with and only used when the magic called for it; likewise with ritual nudity. He established the Alexandrian Tradition of giving the Second and Third Degrees at the same time, ending the carrot-and-stick approach to teaching.

Teachings and beliefs: Alex Sanders was initiated into Gardnerian Witchcraft before the label Gardnerian had come into use, so in actuality, it was just called Witchcraft at the time. He worked from *The Book of Shadows* and his beliefs revolved mostly around it. Through both ritual and media, he became known as the King of the Witches, a reflection of the title Witch Queen and the mythologies of the Sacred King of the woods or the land. His Witches would come to be called Alexandrians and have a greater focus on the occult and training than their Gardnerian cousins. Alex also introduced philosophy to his interpretation of *The Book of Shadows*, expressed best by the words freedom, beauty, and power.

Summary: As I have mentioned elsewhere, the smear campaign against Alex Sanders continues. He is often overlooked by writers with Gardnerian bias. Despite this, his work and legacy continue to flourish around the world. Although Gerald Gardner was the Craft's first spokesman, Alex carried that task forward, and with greater results. He was a brilliant showman. Alex did correspond with Gerald Gardner. He had also known Patricia and Arnold Crowther, Eleanor "Ray" Bone, Monique Wilson, Fred Lamond, and many others. What is very clear is that Alex had two versions of *The Book of Shadows*. He knew and worked with several Gardnerian Witches. He knew how to execute the rites and had oral lore that was passed down only through in-person training. What is important, however, is not speculation on history or magic, but the results and, in this, Alex Sanders was plentiful. But I will give you my current theory. Medea was the craft name of a secret Initiate known to Gerald Gardner. Alex received his First Degree from her. Alex later received his Second and Third Degrees from Patricia Kopanski or Sylvia Tatham, although other candidates are equally possible.

MAXINE SANDERS

Craft Name: Veda.
Birth: 1946. Still living.
Became public: 1965

Occult credentials: Initiate of an Egyptian Mystery Tradition, Initiate of Witchcraft, High Priestess, and co-founder of Alexandrian Witchcraft.

Publicity: For Maxine, publicity began in 1965 and hasn't really stopped. Articles about her appear in the *Manchester Comet*, 1965; *Newspaper Daily Star*, 1979; *Sunday People*, 1977; *News of the World*, 1975; and *The People*, 1965, to name a few. She is prevalent in the 1969 book about Alex Sanders, *King of the Witches,* by June Johns, 1970. She is also mentioned in Stewart Farrar's 1971 book *What Witches Do* and is the subject of Richard Deutch's 1977 book, *The Ecstatic Mother: Portrait of Maxine Sanders, Witch Queen.* In 2007, she wrote *Fire Child: The Life and Magic of Maxine Sanders, Witch Queen.* Maxine also appeared on an album cover for the band, Black Widow in 1968.

Esoteric work: Maxine Sanders was initiated into the Egyptian Mysteries at an early age, and perhaps this is where she began her occult journey. She would later become an Initiate of Witchcraft and, eventually, the co-founder of the Alexandrian Tradition. She helped establish the philosophies of Alexandrian Craft and its core concepts: beauty, power, and freedom. She elevated the discipline of the Alexandrian Witches through exercises in consciousness. In her work with the Temple of the Mother in London, she further developed many Hermetic practices and healing arts and also introduced the angelic practices often associated with Alexandrians. Maxine continues her work today by guiding several Alexandrian Covens in the training process as well continuing her many appearances and public lectures. [36]

Teachings and beliefs: Like Alex Sanders, Maxine was initiated into Witchcraft before the labels Gardnerian or Alexandrian had come into use and her original training was probably more in line with those who would later become known as Gardnerian. Once Alex and Maxine moved to London, she would help Alex to develop the tenets and practices that Alexandrian Witches are known for today. Maxine is a Witch of the Book as well as an occultist with a strong emphasis on the Priestly vocation and its virtues of discipline, service, dedication, consciousness, and the compassion necessary to wield the power properly.

Summary: Alex and Maxine created a strong emphasis on training that did not previously exist in Witchcraft Covens. The teachings passed within our Tradition are both highly developed and multifaceted. They include Hermetic exercise, ritual theory, and discipline, Qabalistic and angelic practices, a broad spectrum of occult knowledge, and the wielding of power. Alex and Maxine's contributions to modern Witchcraft cannot be overstated. Without their perseverance, commitment, and love for the arts magical, I do not think that the practice of Witchcraft would be as widespread or accepted as it is today. [37]

After Maxine and Alex parted ways in 1973, divorcing several years later, Alex went on to live in Bexhill-on-Sea and formed a new Coven there. Maxine continued the work of the London Coven, which eventually evolved into her own group, the Temple of the Mother. The Temple of the Mother further developed the magical systems that are still utilized within the Alexandrian Tradition today. With more considerable attention given to occult science, angelic magic, and hermetic practice, the Temple further honed the structure of the Alexandrian ritual and placed

---

36   Cain, *Initiation into Witchcraft*, p. 63.

37   Cain, *Initiation to Witchcraft*, pp. 63–64

a stronger emphasis on the importance of training than ever before. A large focus of the Temple of the Mother was healing, including working with the poor and dying in the London community.

Since Alex's passing in 1988, Maxine Sanders remains a North Star for those practicing the Tradition. She has, since that time, assisted hundreds of Initiates in both their training and journey into the Mysteries of the Goddess. Today, she continues to lecture, write, attend conferences, and guide Covens in their pursuit of the Inner Mysteries. In my own words, I will say that Maxine Sanders exudes both the Witch and Priestess she is: first and foremost a servant to the Circle.

CHAPTER 5

The Providence of Witchcraft

Reading any basic book on the religious beliefs of Witches, you will discover that we do not worship Satan and that the devil of the medieval period is a folk figure believed to be related to the Old God, specifically the Horned One. The description given by the Church describing our God is in all actuality taken from pre-Christian Gods of nature, such as Pan, Faunus, Dionysus, Serapis, Cernunnos, and many more—of course this is a simplification of a greater truth.

> **❝The devil worshiped by the Witches is in all actuality the old primordial God of hunting, death, resurrection, and preservation.**

The devil worshiped by the Witches is in all actuality the old primordial God of hunting, death, resurrection, and preservation. He is the first warrior who would eventually go on to become a symbol of agriculture. We also worship a Goddess who is associated with the moon, fertility, life, love, and magic. Therefore, the basic concept is anchored in nature. We worship a God and a Goddess whose archetypes are connected to magic, the cycles of nature, the elements of earth, air, fire, and water, the sun, the moon, life, death, and rebirth.

Initiates have both secret and sacred names for these Gods. However, as Witchcraft continues to be developed in the outer court of the public eye, many choose their own sacred divine couple from various pantheons to represent them such as Osiris and Isis, Dionysus and Ariadne, or Pan and Diana. This cosmopolitan idea has given rise to the idea that Witches practice duotheism, while others—more influenced by the modern American pagan movement—favor the idea of polytheism, perhaps in a misguided attempt to be more authentic than their predecessors.

One year, during a panel at WitchCon, the online conference I host with my husband, I had a woman advocating for the idea that we were all polytheists. She went on and on and tried to play the Devil's advocate. When I simply stated, "I am not a polytheist, I am a monotheist," the wrench that it threw into the wheel of her mindless gymnastics was breathtaking. She simply stammered and had nothing to say. She knew I was Alexandrian and an Initiate, and she knew she did not have keys to my kingdom. So, therefore, she realized at that moment that she didn't know what she was talking about, and everyone else realized it too. Of course, I was being a bit naughty because, in truth, Witches are not simply monotheists, nor are we polytheists.

Witchcraft, as a historic mythology, modern Mystery Cult, and misunderstood anthropological footnote, has never been pre-Christian. We have pre-Christian beliefs and philosophies. Witchcraft was born out of the occult world, which itself drew heavily from Greco-Roman and Egyptian sources. Although the genius loci of Britain and various folklore traditions do influence the Craft, the core of the Priesthood has more in common with the Roman Cult of Isis or the Mysteries of Eleusis than it does with modern interpretations of polytheism.

Of course, there are elements of Witchcraft and its beliefs that may indeed be older than the occult world. It is not necessary for us to continually point out that some of our religion is modern, nor do we have to buy into the academic narrative. After all, academia often proves itself wrong given time. The fact remains that although our Priesthood may be a revival of sorts, many of our beliefs and practices are ancient, including our Gods.

Contrary to what some skeptics believe, most Witches today have a somewhat literate understanding of ancient history. We know where we come from and are fully aware that our beliefs have roots in movements like Neoplatonism and the occult orders that would transmute Platonic beliefs into what is now the Western Qabalah. Our religion does not have direct origins in any one culture aside from modern Britain. We are not necessarily pagan. Nor are we hard polytheists, animists, duotheists, or monotheists. One could say we practice polytheistic monism. However, the Craft is actually a bit unique in its approach.

It is vital to examine the concept of the One regarding Craft because it highlights a fundamental core of our Religion. Witches do not claim to have all the answers about God, the afterlife, or the nature of the universe. The great work of the Initiate of the Mysteries is to undertake the quest perilous—to go beyond the veil and transcend the limits of human understanding. Witches, like our predecessors, work theurgic magic. The divine is both necessary and desired in our magics.

Initiates, or Witches of the Book, do worship a God and a Goddess but philosophically we also believe in the One. Sometimes this is expressed as the Primordial Goddess who existed before the God and sometimes it is thought of as a formless power beyond our understanding. The Gods are either born out of this power or viewed as its manifestation through human perception. The One is not worshiped or invoked—it is an occult idea that is in keeping with the running theme in the belief of Witches: room for the unknown. Unlike many religions, we never claim to have all the answers.

The occult author and magician Dion Fortune may have coined our belief system best, "All Gods are one God. All Goddesses are one Goddess, and there is one great initiator."

The concept of one unknowable source can be found in many esoteric traditions. The basic idea is that God is fractured like the sun through a prism. We can only know God or connect to it through its emanations. This concept is as old as Egypt and may have originated from its first mystery cults. Those beliefs spread to Greece and eventually to Rome through its Priesthoods. Western occultism slowly adopted these ideas through Neoplatonism, the Masons, and later Theosophy, being further developed into Qabalistic teaching by the Hermetic Order of the Golden Dawn. It is interesting to note that African diasporic religion and even Catholicism retain elements of this concept.

THE EGYPTIAN ONE

In Ancient Egypt, the divine hierarchy began with a single primeval entity sometimes called Nun, Atum, Amun, or later Amun Ra. For the sake of simplicity, we will use the Heliopolitan Tradition of Nun and Atum.

In the beginning was the dark waters of Nun, from Nun emerged a mound, and upon that mound was Atum. This was the creation of order out of chaos. Atum then created the first Gods: Tefnut, the lion-headed Goddess of moisture, and Shu, the God of air—believed to represent time and space. Atum then created the eye of Atum to watch over its children and in so doing wept tears of joy creating humans and the eye would become the sun to watch over them. Tefnut and Shu gave birth to Nuit and Geb who begot Osiris, Isis, Set, and Nephthys—the first of the Gods. This is just one of many examples of the Egyptian creation myths in which the divine One unknowable propagates the Gods.

Egyptian Heliopolitan Divine Hierarchy

The primeval God, embodying creation, awareness, chaos, and order.

Nun   or   Atum

The First Gods. Shu is the God of air (space), and Tefnut is the Goddess of moisture (time).

Shu   Tefnut

Shu and Tefnut's children. Geb is the Earth, and Nut is the sky. Together they represent the biosphere of our planet.

Geb   Nut

The children of Geb and Nut become the first of the Egyptian pantheon of Gods, giving birth to all the other Gods.

Osiris   Isis   Set   Nephthys

[1] [2] [3]

---

[1]   Richard H. Wilkinson, *The Complete Gods and Goddesses of Ancient Egypt*. London: Thames & Hudson, 2017. pp. 63–65

[2]   Korwin Briggs. "An Almost Historical Egyptian God Family Tree." Nov. 23, 2015. *veritablehokum.com*

[3]   Wim van den Dungen, "Amun, the Great God: Hidden, One and Millions." 2016. *sofiatopia.org*

NEOPLATONISM

Neoplatonism is a philosophical movement that emerged in the 3rd century BCE, drawing heavily on Plato's doctrines. Originally just called Platonism it has developed a more religious nature after the rise of Christianity and several waves of pagan revival. Neoplatonism today is not just an esoteric or academic subject; it has found its place within various religious and magical traditions, including Judaism, Islam, Catholicism, Greek Orthodox, Western occultism, and modern Witchcraft. This continuity reflects its relevance within religious studies.

The Great Chain of Being is a concept that exemplifies the idea of a structured universe, an uninterrupted hierarchy that begins with the absolute, or the One. Though often associated with Plotinus, this idea has its roots in the philosophies of Plato, Aristotle, Plotinus, Iamblichus, and others who developed the concepts of a divine hierarchy, emanations, and transcendence. These concepts would go on to influence the idea of divine Kingship in Western Europe: the belief that Kings were chosen by God. An idea that once again comes from Egypt, but was transmuted through the Greeks and later Romans. [4] Some of the notables of Platonism and Neoplatonism include Plato, Socrates, Aristotle, Plotinus, Euclid, Pythagoras, Iamblichus, Isidore, Hypatia, Damascus, Proclus, and Iamblichus. Perhaps regarding pre-Christian Hellenic religion and the occult, the three most influential to the religious Neoplatonic movement were Damascus, Proclus, and Iamblichus. These teachers developed beliefs far more religious in nature than their predecessors and these beliefs exist today within the Priesthood of Witchcraft and other occult orders. Let us examine a few quotes and examples.

DAMASCUS

Damascus, 480 BCE to c. 550, was the pupil of Isidore of Alexandria and head of the Athenian Academy until its closing by Emperor Justini-

---

[4] Editors of Encyclopaedia. "Great Chain of Being." Encyclopedia Britannica, December 10, 2021. *www.britannica.com/topic/Great-Chain-of-Being.*

an. He explored the work of Proclus and genuine mysticism. He believed mankind could not make contact or understand the One or ineffable first principle. He believed the One existed in the hierarchy of reality. And that we require intermediaries to have a connection or union with it. [5]

Proclus of Athens

Proclus of Athens, 412-485 CE, was the most prominent philosopher of late antiquity to the Middle Ages. He was not only in charge of the Platonic Academy in Athens but also an exceptional writer. He wrote commentary on Aristotle, Euclid, and Plato, as well as works about religious traditions such as Orphism and Chaldean Oracles. Proclus, like Iamblichus, opposed Christianity and passionately defended the Old Gods and Mystery Traditions. He was influential in spreading Neoplatonic ideas throughout the Byzantine and Roman Empires and even influenced early Islam and Christianity.

"Every good tends to unify what participates it and all unification is good and the good is identical with the One."
—Proclus [6]

Iamblichus

Iamblichus, 242 – ca. 325, was a Syrian Neoplatonist and editor of Plotinus. His work was more religious in nature, and he was a true theologian of the Old Gods. He was an advocate of salvation by ritual known as theurgy. [7] The concepts put forward by Iamblichus are influential even today in the foundation philosophy of Western Occultism. Even with the final conquest of Christianity, Neoplatonic tradition never died out

---

5   Editors of Encyclopaedia. "Damascius." Encyclopedia Britannica, February 26, 2024. *www.britannica.com/biography/Damascius.*

6   Christoph Helmig and Carlos Steel, "Proclus", The Stanford Encyclopedia of Philosophy (Fall 2021 Edition), Edward N. Zalta (ed.),. *plato.stanford.edu/archives/fall2021/entries/proclus/*

7   Gregory Shaw. *Theurgy and the Soul: The Neoplatonism of Iamblichus.* University Park, PA: Penn State University, 2003. p.88

among the educated elite. During the Middle Ages, it survived in three distinct traditions, European, Byzantine, and Islamic. [8] Iamblichus states the Gods share a single unity as emanatory manifestations within Their singular divine source, the One. [9]

Divine hierarchy of Iamblichus

Example One

Gods
↓
Archangels
↓
Daimons
↓
Heroes
↓
Archons Sublunary
↓
Archons Material
↓
Human Souls

Example One

The One
↓
The Gods
↓
Archangels
↓
Daimons
↓
Heroes
↓
Purified Souls
↓
Humans
↓
Animals
↓
Matter

8 Gary Zabel. "Philosophy 108: Moral and Social Problems" Spring 2017, syllabus. Baltimore, Maryland: University of Maryland, published online at *faculty.umb.edu*.

9 Riccardo Chiaradonna and Adriend Lecerf, "Iamblichus", *The Stanford Encyclopedia of Philosophy* (Winter 2023 Edition), Edward N. Zalta & Uri Nodelman (eds.). *plato.stanford. edu/archives/win2023/entries/iambilichus*

THE LADDER OF ASCENT

All emanates from the one, all transcends back to the one. Initiation is the process of transcendence.

The Ladder of Ascent

The One
or Absolute

Mind
(nouse)

Psyche

Material
Reality

THE CONCEPT OF THE GREAT CHAIN OF BEING

Continuity: The Chain of Being is continuous. Every intermediary between the highest and lowest forms of life exists, creating a seamless gradation from inanimate matter to God.

Plenitude: The universe contains every form of existence. God, in His infinite wisdom and generosity, created every being, filling the universe with a vast diversity of life.

Gradation: There is a hierarchical structure to the universe, where beings and objects are ranked according to their degree of perfection. The more divine or form something possesses, the higher its place on the chain; the more matter it possesses, the lower its place.

Interconnectedness: All parts of the Chain of Being are interrelated. The well-being of one part depends on the well-being of the others.

THE QABALAH

First, we should make a distinction between Western occult Qabalah and Jewish Kabbalah. Although both retain some Neoplatonic influence, the Jewish Kabbalah is focused on interpreting the Torah and has very little to do with the occult. In the Renaissance, philosophers like Marsilio Ficino [10][11], Giovanni Pico della Mirandola [12], and other Christian mystics and occultists integrated Neoplatonic and Qabalistic concepts, further blending and adapting these ideas within the context of Western esoteric traditions [13].

This fusion contributed to the development of Hermeticism, Theosophy, and various occult philosophies. It is most evident in the concept of the Tree of Life, which continues to express the Ladder of Ascent and the Great Chain of Being. Occultists such as Cornelius Agrippa, A. E. Waite, Éliphas Levi, and MacGregor Mathers furthered the development of Western Qabalah by weaving it into several magical systems, developing a sort of universal correspondence between astrology, tarot, divine hierarchies, and the grimoire traditions. Occult lodges like the Hermetic Order of the Golden Dawn and the Ordo Templi Orientis cemented these ideas and eventually influenced many of the pioneers of the Witchcraft Revival, such as Gerald Gardner, Doreen Valiente, and Alex Sanders. It is most likely that members of the New Forest Coven and other early groups shared in this broad occult influence. Most occultists today are very aware of the influence of the Qabalah, but perhaps not as aware that the system they are embracing is repackaged Neoplatonism. Aside from the Tree of Life, another example of this is the concept of Ain Soph Aur. Ain Soph Aur is the emanation of The One or Absolute, also rep-

[10] Editors of Encyclopaedia. "Marsilio Ficino." Encyclopedia Britannica, March 1, 2024. *www.britannica.com/biography/Marsilio-Ficino.*

[11] "Marsilio Ficino, 1433–1499." Internet Encyclopedia of Philosophy. Acessed on Aug. 11, 2023. *Iep.utm.edu/ficnio*

[12] Ron Cacioppe. "Marsilio Ficino: Magnus of the Renaissance, Shaper of Leaders." Medievalists.net, 2009.

[13] Boaz Huss. *Academic Study of Kabbalah and Occult Kabbalah*, May 25, 2021, published *in Occult Roots of Religious Studies.* Boston/Berlin: Walter de Gruyter, 2021. pp. 104–105

The Tree of Life

Ain (Nothing)
Ain Soph (Limitless)
Ain Soph Aur (Limitless Light)

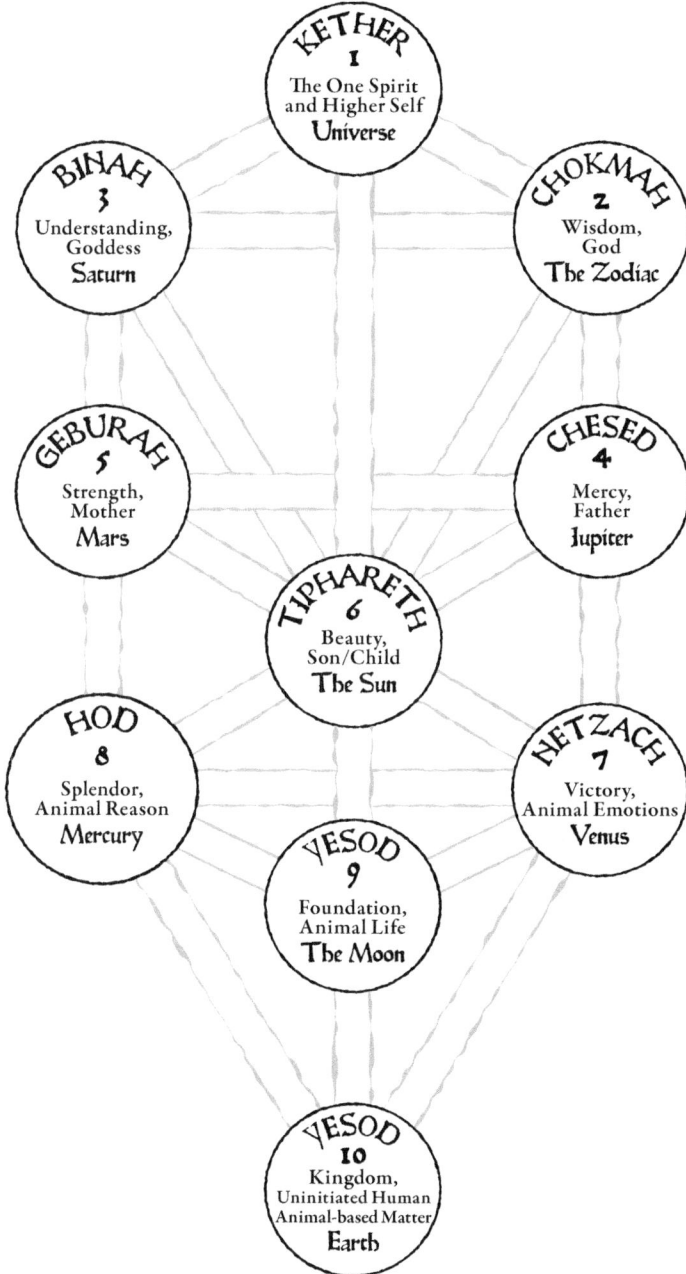

KETHER
1
The One Spirit
and Higher Self
Universe

BINAH
3
Understanding,
Goddess
Saturn

CHOKMAH
2
Wisdom,
God
The Zodiac

GEBURAH
5
Strength,
Mother
Mars

CHESED
4
Mercy,
Father
Jupiter

TIPHARETH
6
Beauty,
Son/Child
The Sun

HOD
8
Splendor,
Animal Reason
Mercury

NETZACH
7
Victory,
Animal Emotions
Venus

YESOD
9
Foundation,
Animal Life
The Moon

YESOD
10
Kingdom,
Uninitiated Human
Animal-based Matter
Earth

resented as Kether on the Tree. Like Nun in Egypt, Ain represents nothingness. Ain Soph represents the limitless, like Atum in Egypt. And Ain Soph Aur represents limitless light, as with Atum Ra in Egypt. In Western Occultism, we have a marvelous blending of both modern and ancient concepts that are equally important to the revival and practice of the Witch.

THE GRIMOIRE TRADITIONS

The Celestial and Infernal Hierarchy of Dionysus

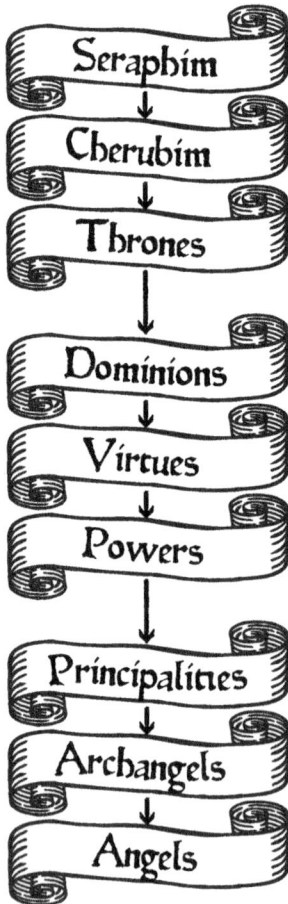

Seraphim
↓
Cherubim
↓
Thrones
↓
Dominions
↓
Virtues
↓
Powers
↓
Principalities
↓
Archangels
↓
Angels

Grimoires, or magical books, can find their origins in Ancient Egypt, with many Egyptians having been buried with their own magical spell book to help them navigate the afterlife. The rise of Christianity saw the fall of many magical manuscripts while simultaneously some members of the clergy saw to their preservation, often giving birth to new systems with a Christian veneer. At a certain point, the Grimoire Tradition had been formed right alongside Christian mysticism. Many grimoires would be attributed to biblical figures, Popes, and even saints. Some of these include the following: *The Grimoire of Pope Honorius*, or *Le Grimoire du Pape Honorius*, a 17th to 18th-century grimoire which claims to have been written by Pope Honorius III. We have the *Grimoire of Pope Leo*, or *The Enchiridion of Pope Leo*, a French grimoire and textbook of magic attributed to him. *The Clavicle of Solomon* is reported to have been written by King

Solomon. This mythos had already been circulating in the Eastern Mediterranean during the first few centuries A.D. By the 15th century, hundreds of copies were in the hands of Western academics and clergymen. Other writings of note include The works of Cornelius Agrippa, the French Petit Albert, and *The Magus*, published in 1801 by Francis Barrett.

Perhaps one of the most important considering the subject of this chapter is *The Celestial Hierarchy* by Dionysius the Areopagite. This book categorized angels into nine orders across three hierarchies. [14] This structured view of celestial beings profoundly influenced Christian theology and the development of Western occultism. Grimoires and other magical texts from the medieval period onwards, often drew upon the angelic hierarchies outlined by Dionysius.

The Keys of Solomon, the works of Agrippa, *The Magus*, and many other grimoires were poured over by

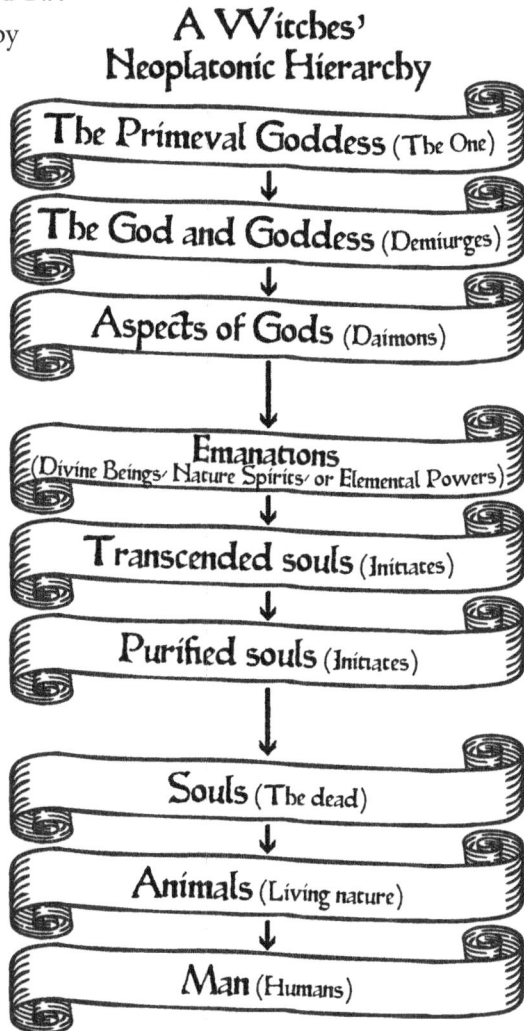

A Witches' Neoplatonic Hierarchy

The Primeval Goddess (The One)

↓

The God and Goddess (Demiurges)

↓

Aspects of Gods (Daimons)

↓

Emanations (Divine Beings, Nature Spirits, or Elemental Powers)

↓

Transcended souls (Initiates)

↓

Purified souls (Initiates)

↓

Souls (The dead)

↓

Animals (Living nature)

↓

Man (Humans)

---

14 "The Celestial Hierarchy: Dionysius the Areopagite" from Esoterica, published on *esoteric.msu.edu*. Accessed on March 1, 2023.

both the pioneers of the occult and those of the Witchcraft Revival. The weaving of Neoplatonic and Qabalistic philosophies with the Grimoire Traditions created the backbone and foundation of many lodges, including the Hermetic Order of the Golden Dawn. These traditions created the divine hierarchies of both angels and demons and further preserved the wisdom eventually influencing the modern Witchcraft Revival. [15]

---

[15]   Owen Davies. "Top 10 Grimoires." April 15, 2009. Oxford University Press blog. *blog. oup.com/2009/04/grimoires/*

CHAPTER 6

Diana and the Devil

Diana and the Devil are the most historical figures associated with Witchcraft by the Church historians, folklorists, and modern-day Witches. In my previous work, Initiation into Witchcraft, I do address these figures and how they evolved from old traditions into modern Witchcraft figures. The Roman Goddess Diana would be transformed into various folk figures, such as Herodias, Habundia, and the Queen of fairies. Likewise, the Devil of the witches is believed to be a folk figure made up of gods such as Hades and Pan. These figures may encapsulate a lingering living memory from our pre-Christian past, heavily influenced by the mystery cults that directly competed with Christianity during its rise to power. Although by then, in just a few generations, the mystery cults of Isis, Magna Mater, and Dionysus had seemingly been forgotten, being replaced by these figures.

Early Church letters indicate concerns that the old Gods, whom they believed to be devils, lingered on as a religious opposition to the church. The Gods of this religion were Diana and the Devil, and its adherent witches. Whether this held any truth or was just paranoia has little bearing on the outcome. One of the most cited passages comes from the 10th-century Catholic document, Canon *Episcopi*:

> *It is also not to be omitted that some wicked women turning back to Satan seduced by illusions and phantasms of demons believe and claim that in the hour of night, they ride on certain beasts with Diana, Goddess of the pagans, and an innumerable multitude of women.*

A century later, Bishop Burchard of Worms (ca. 952–1025 CE) added the phrase, 'Or with Herodias,' to the passage, which not only merges a biblical New Testament figure with the Diana myth but also plays into another more mysterious Witch Goddess. I think it is interesting to note the phrase, "Wicked women turning back to Satan." Is this a clue that the Church was talking about older religions? Or are they implying women naturally gravitate to the archfiend? [1]

The persistent association that Diana, Herodias, and the Devil have with Witchcraft or its subsequent Witch cults cannot be overstated. This belief was not regulated simply by any church or trial records but deeply ingrained into the cultures of medieval Europe up to the present day. Modern Witches view this as the natural evolution of the Old Gods who continue to survive in the subconscious inner planes until the time was right and perceptions could be changed.

The European aristocracy maintained an interest in the classical deities and the principles of Neoplatonism, which contributed to the development of what is now known as the occult. Meanwhile, the general populace kept the older Traditions and myths alive through various forms of art, woodcuts, music, poetry, storytelling, and folk practices, including magic. This cultural preservation led to a gradual shift in the perception of figures such as Pan, Serapis, and Cernunnos, as well as Isis, Diana, and Hecate. These ancient Gods and Goddesses were reimagined as the Devil, or as various demons, spirits, or supernatural entities, effectively morphing from divine to diabolical figures.

---

1   Cain, *Initiation into Witchcraft*, p. 93.

The medieval archetype of the 'Witch' frequently featured a dominant female figure, as chronicled in historical accounts and folklore. This figure often had a male partner. Over time, however, the prominence of the female figure began to diminish, and her male counterpart started to take precedence. Eventually, he transformed into the figure commonly identified as the Devil or Satan, taking a central role in the conceptualization of Witchcraft as a satanic or antichristian religion. While there is no precise chronology of this transformation and its occurrence was not uniform but rather varied by region, there are significant cultural indicators spanning from the classical religious era up to the 1950s. From antiquity and the classical age, we can trace the decline of pre-Christian religions alongside the ascent of Christianity and the systematic suppression of pagan practices.

In the medieval period we see the continued domination of Christianity and the emergence of folk figures in what today would be deemed as folklore. In the early modern period and Renaissance, we can see the birth of the occult taking place. And of course, in the modern era, we have a resurgence of Witchcraft through the Witchcraft Revival of the 1950s.

The Witch's Sabbat, or Sabbath, was a key theme in how society perceived the Devil and his worshipers.[2] It was a weaving of fairy gatherings, the nocturnal flights of Diana, and perhaps the old pre-Christian festivals that lingered on in certain communities. The Witches Sabbath was said to be held on the old Druid festivals and the solstices but was most likely seen as a mockery of the many Christian seasonal festivals and saint days.

The Church had completely erased the memory of the divine outside of its cosmologies. Fairies became familiars or demons, the Old Gods of nature, the Devil, and the Goddess, a succubus or Witch. As far as most were concerned, the Witch was now a Satanist who practiced the religion of the Devil, their God. The religion of Witchcraft was the religion of the Devil, and it was real.[3]

The Devil or Satan are Christian concepts and certainly, the pictures painted of the Witches on their Sabbath are not likely to have been actual events or gatherings.

They're either (A) complete fabrications that do indeed draw on memories of pre-Christian revelries, like those that at one point did compete with the Church, or (B) a twisted version of a real event. Perhaps a village May Eve celebration through the eyes of a paranoid and superstitious Christian. And of course (C), that there was actually a medieval Satanic cult. Although I'm in favor of option (B), it is also possible that all of these things could have contributed, and the truth cannot be easily pinned down. Delusion and paranoia as well as a lack of education fueled beliefs that were simply untrue.

Some of this was a Church strategy, particularly in its early conceptions. However, in the later period, most clergy believed in an anti-Christian revival. It is also a fact that folk festivals and customs continued, which could have been easily labeled or perceived as proof of Witchcraft. And I think it is very likely that small cults and practices did develop based

2   Britannica, T. Editors of Encyclopaedia. "Witches' sabbath." Encyclopedia Britannica, March 1, 2002. *www.britannica.com/topic/Witches-sabbath*.

3   National Archives. "Early modern Witch trials." October , 2020. *nationalarchives.gov.uk/ education/resources/early-modern-Witch-trials*

on popular ideas and religious beliefs, just as they do today. If people can commit mass suicide to be beamed up into a mothership, the medieval possibilities are unimaginable.

I think believing we have a full understanding or that we know every story is ridiculous. What we know to be a fact is that the Church, the common people, and even kings believed in Witchcraft and believed that Witches practiced an evil religion. We know that this shared European mythology consisted of pre-Christian ideas, propaganda, and delusion. We also know the mythology of Witchcraft has persisted into the present day. We modern Witches still practice a religion that Christians still find contrary and evil. We worship a Goddess and a Horned God who absolutely have connectivity to these early ideas. You see, the Diana of Witchcraft is somewhat unique compared to her old Roman incarnation. And the Devil of the Witches seems to be more pagan than biblical."

THE GODDESS DIANA

The Goddess, Diana Artemis, is the only Goddess mentioned in the New Testament of the Bible. Referencing Diana of Ephesus, Acts 19:35, the Church, as we have already made mention, also gave her the title of the Goddess of the Pagans. Beginning her early associations with medieval Witchcraft. Before this time, Diana had been a Goddess of the hunt and the woods, eventually evolving into a moon Goddess governing fertility and childbirth. Her connection with the fairies or the nymphs is very old, but how did we make the leap to Witches? Surely, Goddesses like Hecate would have been a more appropriate candidate for a Witch Goddess in our modern minds.

It is well known that Diana, in typical fashion and like all popular Goddesses, merged with or absorbed her counterparts, with the Greek Artemis, Luna, and Selena being the front-runners. However, by the time Christianity had become her rival, Diana had also been prominently tied to both Hecate and Isis. In the late Roman periods, the Cult of Isis had spread across the empire, and emperors like Caligula and Hadrian had become Initiates and supporters of the Cult. Caligula played a major role in this, having supported the Cult of Isis in Nemi, where the sacred lake, forest, and temple to Diana, had been. He went so far as to build two barges on the lake dedicated to Isis, further cementing the association between Diana and Isis. [4]

Diana had already begun to have associations with Hecate, adapting the names and titles Trivia, Three-Faced Diana, Triple Hecate, and the Threefold One. Caligula helped to merge Diana and Isis and was an Initiate of the Cult of Isis, worshiping her at Nemi, one of the oldest Latin centers.

Isis was the only Goddess in that time to achieve global superiority in a very real sense. In her syncretic bond with Isis, Diana was no longer the virgin huntress, but a fully realized queen of nature, fertility, and magic. In a way, she had come full circle, having predated herself throughout Europe and perhaps even India and Asia Minor.

It is also worth stating the Greeks had identified Artemis with Isis during the Ptolemaic Empire. After the fall of Rome and the rise of Christianity, the cults would seemingly disappear into obscurity. Christianity at one time had been a Roman mystery cult, rising into supremacy, fully bent on having no competition. Seemingly gone were Mithra, Cybele, Dionysus, Sol Invictus, and Isis. And indeed, the Church made mention of none of these rivals. It is claimed that it was Diana who faced off with them one last time. Some historians speculate that the Church used Diana as a simple placeholder for the Goddess or any Goddess from antiquity, and it was not literal. However, that is just a theory and perhaps somewhat irrelevant to this conversation. Whether factual or fabrication, it is documented. In modern Witchcraft lore, Diana is an iconic name for the Queen of the Witches, and we draw from history, church records, folklore, and even fairy tales, in our religious belief. Mythology in every form shapes both culture and dogma.

[4] Margaret Stenhouse. *The Goddess of the Lake: Legends and Mysteries of Nemi*. Press Time Editions, 1997, pp. 77–108

"*Diana had begun to transform into the leader of night flights, perhaps fusing with other European Goddesses on the same trajectory. The Lady had arrived.***

The medieval Diana, in many ways, became the personification of Hecate under her epitaph as Herodias. Herodias is the name used in the Bible in connection with John the Baptist's execution. This association aided in demonizing the figure. Her name, however, predates the New Testament and most likely means Queen Diana. In some myths, she's the daughter of Diana, also called Aradia, Herodiade, and Erodiade. Whether or not Herodias was another pre-Christian title for Diana or a biblical folk fusion, the association is clear. Diana had begun to transform into the leader of night flights, perhaps fusing with other European Goddesses on the same trajectory. The Lady had arrived.

In a very real way, Diana represents the bridge between ancient times, medieval mythology, and the modern Witchcraft Revival. Diana and her secret cult have been a powerful myth in modern Witchcraft. Anthropologist Margaret Murray believed Witchcraft to be the cult of Diana in her 1921 book, *The Witch Cult in Western Europe*. This idea may have originated not only from church documents and trial records, but from folklorist Charles Godfrey Leland, who in 1899 published *Aradia, or the Gospel of the Witches*.[5]

Leland's collection gives us a unique perspective of both Diana and Herodias. Leland claimed to have received the manuscript from an Italian Witch named Maddalena, who he claimed to have retained the practices of the Old Cult.

Regardless of one's view, it does seem, to me, to contain authentic materials, partially due to the undeniable Christian influences, but also to the fact that this Diana of Leland is very different than her standard Roman incarnation. She very much embodies several Gods of the mystery

---

5   Cain, *Initiation into Witchcraft*, pp. 93–96.

cults, which rather brings to mind the "Last Goddess of the Pagans." I discussed this from a more historical point of view in my book *Initiation into Witchcraft*. Here I wish to focus on the attributes of Leland's Diana.

First, she has several Egyptian attributes. In antiquity, her twin brother was Apollo. They have no romantic inclinations, and in fact, she was a virgin. In the gospel, her brother is called Lucifer. A name, like that of Herodias, easily demonized, yet has pre-Christian roots. It could have been a name for Apollo before its association with the Christian Satan. Diana and Lucifer are lovers, and together they have a daughter, Herodias, forming a triad, something very popular in Egyptian religion. The Diana of Leland's *Aradia* is a mother and has an established consort who she pursues in the form of a cat. Perhaps it is my fanciful imagination, but it has an Isisian ring to it all.

The historic connection between Isis and Diana had been firmly established in places in Italy like Benevento and Nemi. Both were sacred centers with temples to the Goddess Diana and would later be usurped by the Cult of Isis. In the medieval period, these temples would belong once again to Diana and her Witches. Perhaps this is a bit of genius loci. Diana of *Aradia* also has a strong association with wine and agriculture, going so far as to refer to the wine as her blood. This is not only very Dionysian but could serve to be seen as adversarial to the Church in the form of a Black Mass. Throughout the manuscript of the Gospel, she is also very much representative of the Lady of the Night Flights and the Queen of Fairies. In this one manuscript alone, you see Diana as a classical Goddess and as a Goddess who had clearly merged with other Gods, absorbing their attributes to the manifestation of her as a folk figure with demonic inclinations. The last feature of Leland's document is what would go on to be called the Charge of the Goddess. As a Witch and an occultist, one must acknowledge the persistent power of Leland's *Aradia* in the world of modern Witchcraft.

The Charge in Aradia

"When I shall have departed from this world, whenever ye have need of anything, once in the month and when the moon is full, ye shall assemble in some desert place or in a forest all together join, to adore the potent spirit of your queen, my mother, Great Diana. She who fain would learn all sorcery yet has not won its deepest secrets. Them my mother will teach her. In truth, all things as yet unknown, and ye shall all be freed from slavery. And so ye shall be free in everything and as a sign that ye are truly free, ye shall be naked in your rites, both men and women also. This shall last until the last of your oppressors shall be dead and ye shall make the gains of Benevento extinguishing the lights and after that shall hold your supper thus."

—*Aradia, Gospel of the Witches* by Charles Godfrey Leland

I believe that the Goddess speaks through time and space in the Gospel and that aside from *The Book of Shadows* it is the most important book one can find on Witchcraft. Even if it was a fabrication, the power and results are undeniable. But—as it is often said—the Craft will use anyone to survive.

THE DEVIL

In the tapestry of classical religions, sorcery frequently found its embodiment within the revered figures of Goddesses throughout Europe, such as Isis and Hecate. These divine archetypes persist in the guise of figures like Diana and Herodias, along with other folklore personas. However, their prominence gradually waned in Western Witchcraft literature. The Lady was dethroned by—quite literally—the demon of patriarchy. The pioneers of the modern Witchcraft Revival worked to educate the public about the religion of Witchcraft. We worship a Goddess and not the Devil. In fact, the imagery surrounding the Devil, through the lens of Western Europe, was a twisted version of our God, who we called the Horned One. He has, over time, simply been mixed up or fused with the biblical Satan.

The devil associated with Witchcraft, as recorded in art, folklore, trial records, and church documents, has very little in common with anything in the Bible. This diabolical devil God of the Witches hosted parties in forests, offered magical powers to his followers, and promoted sexual promiscuity in his worship. The sin of dancing, drinking, and nocturnal revelry sounds very similar to the stories of the Dionysian festival rites and other pre-Christian gatherings. The descriptions of the Devil as a cloven-hoofed, horned, pitchfork-wielding demon also do not originate from the Bible. Older Gods such as Pan, Faunas, Serapis, and Cernunnos are a more suitable source. The only anti-Christian aspect of this folk figure is that he demanded that the Witches worship him and give him fealty. When one thinks about it, this could be said about many historic Gods and religions.

Other than the occasional accusations of murder, cannibalism, and baby sacrifices—allegedly carried out in his name—he does not seem to be diabolical. The figure of the folk devil had many names—we have already discussed Lucifer. Another version, mentioned by Carlo Ginzburg in his examination of the Witch Cult of Diana, is that during the games of Diana she at times had a companion or consort they called Lucifello. I highly recommend Ginzburg's works, *The Night Battles* and *Ecstasies*, to all those who wish to know more about the subject.

Lucifello reminds me of another of the Devil's titles, Robin Goodfellow. Robin Goodfellow's artistic portrayal is pan-like holding a broom surrounded by dancing Witches. He has also been associated with the Fairy King and Puck. Robin as a name for the God of the Witches was extremely popular in Britain. The red-breasted robin features heavily in folklore and superstition, often being associated with luck, fertility, and the spring. In late Christian festivals, the robin was prominent, particularly in the Christmas season, symbolizing the promise of spring. Some believe that it is Celtic in origin.

Other variations of the God or Devil are Cock Robin, Robin Artisson, Robert, and Robin Hood, another important folk figure. The name Robin or Robert means famed, bright, or shining, so to be speculative, Lucifello and Robin Goodfellow both imply that they're Gods of Light.

Other names for the Devil are Old Nick, Old Scratch, Barrabon, Hammerlin, Peterlin, Christsonday, Hou, and my personal favorite, Old Horny. In the religion of Witchcraft, we have a God and a Goddess. The folk figures of the devil generally do not have a female consort; rather, he works alone. In many cases, the Goddess is replaced by a mortal Witch in this role, copulating with the Devil in exchange for her powers.

The exception to this is the occasional association with the Fairy Queen, Dame, or Lady. In some cases, they become one and the same. In an Aberdeen trial in 1598, Andrew Mann allegedly confessed that he worked with the Queen of Elfhame and a spirit by the name of Christsonday, who appeared as an angel clad in white. [6][7]

The folklore figures associated as being the master and mistress of Witches generally had common running themes. He was dark or black, a horned beast or man, often associated with light. She was nocturnal and associated with fairies, the moon, and night flights. Both were perceived as being capable of bestowing magical powers.

At times they appear as a couple, such as Diana with her Lucifer or Lucifello, or the Queen of Elfhame with Robin Goodfellow or Puck. The pioneers of the modern revival tapped into the myths and powers in a very real way. The Old Gods did survive as fairies, folk figures, fantasies, saints, delusions, and demons. Never far from the human psyche, we are ready to receive them.

Witchcraft as a European myth or reality is, for all intents and purposes, not pre-Christian or Christian, nor can it properly be classified as pagan. Instead, it seems to be a bit original and born out of all the above.

6   Charles Sinclair. "Andrew Mann, 1598." From *Scotland's Wicked Witches*. Cockenzie, Scotland: Goblinshead Books, 2011, accessed via goblinshead.co.uk/bogles.
7   Cain, *Initiation into Witchcraft*, 171–177.

A sort of counterculture folk religion whose Gods either were demonic or perceived as such. The evolution of these supernatural entities represents the missing link for modern-day Witches. Not content to be just a modern occult echo, we continue to reach back into the past, drawing on these powerful archetypes. I think it is a mistake to overlook them and simply try to recreate pre-Christian religions. Fortunately, academia does have a vested interest in this era and, along with modern-day Witches, continues to explore it.

Twentieth-century Witchcraft scholars believed that pre-Christian beliefs not only survived alongside Christianity but sometimes permeated it so subtly that the Church became a mere facade for these older traditions. Folklorists have since identified numerous modern customs as remnants of such ancient belief systems. A few academics, like Sir Stephen Runciman, Sir George Clark, Christopher Hill, and notably, Margaret Murray, went further to suggest that Witchcraft represented a continuous thread of classical paganism.

However, by the 1990s, a consensus had emerged in historical academia, refuting the idea of enduring paganism across Europe beyond a few centuries post its official conversion. This new scholarly agreement firmly dismissed the existence of formal pagan practices, Witch Covens, or hidden cults. The figures from the medieval era defy clear classification as strictly Christian or pre-Christian, and in most instances, their origins as pre-Christian entities or abstract saints remain unverifiable.

Take, for instance, the concept of Mother Earth or Mother Nature, a figure still resonant in Western culture, rooted in the concept of Earth Goddesses like the Roman Terra Mater. Despite her significance, Mother Earth was not formally recognized with tangible evidence of worship or cultic centers, except for the occasional preserved poem or prayer in Old English.

Mother Nature's image would later inspire the notion of the cosmic Great Mother among poets, philosophers, and artists. In the early modern period, Platonic teachings would help propagate these concepts, which persisted into the 19th century, where the romanticized Goddess symbolized an undercurrent in the collective social conscience—a thoroughly modern conception.

In medieval Britain and Western Europe, Goddess figures took various forms. In Britain, the Fairy Queen, possibly a mix of Celtic-Saxon origin, came to be associated with the elves from Germanic lore. She became a staple in literary chivalric romances. By the 1300s, this Fairy Queen was referred to as Proserpine. As the 14th century waned, the church began condemning those who were thought to consort with fairies and their Queen of Witchcraft.

By the 1450s, the Fairy Queen had ingrained herself so deeply in British culture that she was acknowledged by criminal gangs and folk magicians alike, becoming a part of the common people's reality. While fairies maintained their image as capricious tricksters, the Fairy Queen was seen as a benevolent figure.

In parallel, a comparable figure was emerging in Western Europe, possibly predating the Fairy Queen—known variously as Diana, Herodias, Holda, Perchta, Bensozia, and Nicnevin. This figure, connected to the ancient tradition of the Wild Hunt, was venerated, or acknowledged chiefly by the lower classes and folk magicians, like the Fairy Queen. It is difficult to ascertain when the European Lady first materialized, or how the belief in her spread across the continent. Many modern Witches view both the Fairy Queen and The Lady as continuations of a singular ancient Goddess, a subject that remains contentious among historians and academic pagan authors. From the perspective of this book, the debate is of little consequence.

The essence of the Goddess, whether through literal or mystical means, found a way to endure even in the most inhospitable environments, influencing subsequent generations and contributing to the Witchcraft Revival of the 1950s. The elusive link between pre-Christian Goddesses and their later incarnations as folk figures is best exemplified by Diana and Herodias. Diana is an established deity, while Herodias, also mentioned in the Bible, is tied to her, yet perhaps distinct in origin. Some speculate that the Church may have labeled The Lady as Diana or

Herodias rather than the people, though there is no definitive evidence for this. Should this be the case, it could imply that the Church and the laypeople viewed The Lady as synonymous with the ancient Goddess. Herodias as a name is Greek in origin and does predate the New Testament; it may have simply been a coincidence that the title Queen Diana shared space with the enemy of John the Baptist.

In Gaelic traditions, the Hag, often associated with Witchcraft, emerges as a third cultural icon, separate from the Fairy Queen and The Lady. She epitomizes what would become the archetypal Witch of Halloween. The Hag's lineage likely traces back to British figures like the Irish Goddess Cailleach or the medieval Welsh Cerridwen, both regarded as folk figures and possible vestiges of older Celtic Goddesses. The Hag or Crone remains a powerful image in today's Craft and has its origins in these folk figures whose iconography was used by the Church to further demonize the Witch. [8]

The Gods of Witchcraft indeed take us on a journey from the Stone Age tribes to the Mystery Cults that once dominated Europe, only to be plunged into the Dark Ages and persist as folk figures, demons, and fairy phantoms. They rested in the human consciousness through the classics and Romanticism, until brought back into a state of reality by occult invocations and the modern Witchcraft Revival. Today, Diana has been fully re-embraced as both the Goddess and the Queen of Witches, and the Devil has returned to his original form, the Old God of Fertility and nature. In magic, myth and reality often merge as one, becoming manifest in the very world around us, and Diana and the Devil are no exception.

---

8   Ronald Hutton, lecture "Were their pagan goddesses in Christian Europe?" via Youtube, accessed on Jan. 12, 2024. *www.youtube.com/watch?v=Pr0m6z2r-kQ&t=71s*

CHAPTER 7

An Interview With the Witches

12 Witches Speak About Their Craft

QUESTION ONE

How did you get involved in the Craft, and how long have you been practicing?

ANSWERS

Elie Barnes, Alexandrian High Priestess

The wiring of my brain and my energy field is the wiring of a natural psychic, shaman, animal and plant worker, healer, death speaker, and mystic. There was nothing I could do to avoid Witchcraft. I was born into an unusual southern family who were interested in subjects of the paranormal and the occult. There was nothing I could do to avoid exposure to the world of the occult. I was born into an age where alternative religion and esotericism were becoming mainstream subjects with books being published on all these topics.

My natural instincts and passions were unchecked, and I read hundreds of books and studied widely in the fields of Witchcraft, operative and religious, even studying it in college. There was nothing I could do to avoid becoming a High Priestess of an Initiatory British Witchcraft Coven. There was nothing that took me away from my true path and glory.

SOLARIS BLUE RAVEN, GARDNERIAN WITCH

Since I was a young girl, I was always drawn to magic and Witchcraft. I would find whatever books I could and read about magic, ritual, astral projection, and circle work. I had gifts of seeing energy or knowing who was calling or knocking before they showed up. You can say I had a supernatural life yet figured I was like everyone else. I remember a Beltane ritual I was invited to in my teens, which was in the middle of nowhere. It could have been dangerous to go off with strangers, yet for some reason, I trusted spirit and participated with a large group of Coveners. The High Priestess was truly a beautiful Goddess in form. I remember the energy and how the timelessness of the moment was beyond magic. As I stood in circle, I received the blessing of the High Priestess. She passed her hand over my crown and third eye and looked at the friend who brought me to this celebration. She then said, "She is one of

us." That always stuck with me as I realized yes, Witches are everywhere, and they are quite lovely and magical people, and as it would appear, I was one as well. I then continued studying and practicing solo until my mid-thirties when I joined my first Gardnerian Coven. The rest is a progression of Initiation, dedication, service, and a more alchemical approach to Witchcraft today.

CHRISTINE STEPHENS, ALEXANDRIAN HIGH PRIESTESS

Like many, I grew up within a major organized religion. I was baptized Catholic and loved the mysterious Latin words, the incense smoke, and the rituals and celebrations that occurred on high Holy Days. These spoke to my soul, as did the folk magic and remedies practiced by some of the women in my family—everything from removing (or returning) the evil eye to dealing with ailments physical or emotional. The natural world also played a part. I saw people and animals be born and die and watched flowers wither only to return once again in the spring. And all of these things spoke to divine duality—to male and female both playing an equal part in the circle of life. I did not see that in the Catholic Church. Women were revered, but not equal.

So, I began to explore and was drawn to British Traditional Witchcraft because of its attunement to the natural world and especially because of its divine duality. Like many at the time, I read everything I could find and began solitary magical practice. It was not Witchcraft as I know it today, but it was a start. I continued down that path and attended some "outer court" type events with a few groups over the years. Most were lovely people, but we simply did not connect in a way that I knew was possible. And then I met my first Alexandrian. The person who would become my High Priest, working partner, and beloved friend—Brian Cain. Brian held a gathering of a few seekers and the connection with him and another in the group was instant and powerful. Although I was unsure what I could bring as a solitary who practiced scrying, herbcraft, and folk magic, I found the courage to ask for and receive Initiation. I studied and wrote. I worked the magics and learned the ritual, the ecstasy, and how to raise and use the power of Alexandrian Witchcraft. After a few years, I once again asked for—and received—Initiation and became the High Priestess of the New Orleans Coven. I am forever thankful for the honor and the opportunity to care for and be of service to my Coven and my community. Although I had to leave New Orleans two years ago, I continue to honor the vows made to my God and Goddess during those Initiations to this day.

Fiona Horne, Rock Star Witch

At the time of writing this, I am entering my 39th year as a devoted practicing Witch.

I grew up in the Australian bushland, which I intrinsically experienced as magickal. Earth, air, water, fire ... I crawled into caves to be held by the earth, climbed up the trees to be closer to the flying birds, stood in the river as it flowed rapidly through me, and stood in awe of bushfires when they roared towards our home.

This reverence was further ignited during the '80s when I stumbled upon the book, *The Way of The Goddess* by Ly Warren-Clarke— its teachings anchored in Wiccan practices which opened me up to the religion of Witchcraft. It was almost impossible to meet other Witches

back then; I remember I suggested to a street press magazine that I write an article about Witches so that I could somehow meet others that might be like me.

Ultimately, when my music career took off in the '90s, I became a solitary eclectic as I travelled the world with the band and could not have committed to an initiated tradition. The opportunity to write 15 published books spanning 26 years has kept me regularly interacting and communicating with the exploding international magickal community and I love where the Craft is evolving. I choose to prioritize enlightened discussion and practice in my personal Craft, and I do service work to assist others in magickal crisis when it is presented. I like to stick with the Witches who make me smile, not frown, as much as I can.

TRACY FRASCHE, GARDNERIAN HIGH PRIESTESS

My sister, who was eight years older than I, would research anything and everything on the paranormal, ghosts, hauntings, and poltergeist activity, and eventually, she began exploring Witchcraft. She would leave her books lying around, and I would sneak them into my room and read them while she was out. My best friend and I would pretend we were casting spells in our garage. We were terrified that they would work!

I realize I may be dating myself, but I absolutely lived for shows like *Bewitched* and *I Dream of Jeannie*. While my other childhood interests waxed and waned, my interest in Witchcraft was an enduring presence in my life. It was part of who I was. When we purchased our first home computer, the first thing I researched was Witches, which led me to Wicca. I was shocked that there was actually a religion whose tenets mirrored the way I had been living my life. I found the first Coven I ever practiced with, Daughters of the Moon. I knew absolutely nothing, but they were accepting and patient. The first Sabbat I attended was Samhain, and yes, I pronounced it just that way and was corrected with a resounding "Sow'en." I remember returning home after that first ritual, and it felt as if there was Witchcraft running in my veins. I didn't sleep at all that night, and I knew at that point there was no turning back, and so began my journey.

I have been practicing for about 35 years, give or take a year and a day. I was initiated into the Gardnerian Tradition 15 years ago and am a 3* HPS in the Tradition. We run an Outer Court training group called Circle of the Awakened Forest as well as a Coven here in North Carolina.

MICHAEL HERKES, THE GLAM WITCH, ECLECTIC SOLITARY

When I was a child, I was deeply fascinated with femininity, serpents, and the moon. As I grew older, my interest in the Craft piqued with the rise of Hollywood Witchcraft. It was that gateway that led me to exploring at the age of 11 back in 2000. While "real" Witchcraft was much different than the "reel" Witchcraft I was watching, I was completely overcome by it in that it not only embraced a feminine form of divinity that was linked to snakes and the moon, but also offered a sanctuary for me as a Queer person. In my early readings, I was heavily influenced by the work of Fiona Horne and over time developed my unique path. Centering my Craft around magical aesthetics and adornment, I use fashion and makeup to cultivate inner and outer makeovers—inspiring

others to tap into their personal power and creativity to create positive change in their own lives and the world around them.

LEVI ROWLAND, ALEXANDRIAN HIGH PRIEST

My background is in Catholicism, but after leaving the Church, I explored a lot of esoteric and occult communities. It was the power of the Goddess that drew me to Craft, above all else, and I have been devoted to Her for almost ten years at this point. Joining an Alexandrian Coven felt like coming home in a way no spiritual experience ever has. In the work of the group, the raising of power, the worship of the Gods, I never had that feeling of discomfort and spiritual illness that came from so many patriarchal religious groups I had tried before. I knew I was home.

CARIE EWERS, ALEXANDRIAN PRIESTESS AND ELDER

My journey with Craft began when I was 10, and I just turned 50, so it has been a 40-year journey so far. I have seen ghosts and spirits since I was 3 and always felt there was a way to communicate with unseen energies that always flow around us and harness those energies as well. I have always felt a connection to magic and the occult. I have been an Alexandrian Priestess for nine years, and I am an elder in my Coven and one of the founders.

SILVER RAVENWOLF, BLACK FOREST CIRCLE AND SEMINARY

Entering the Craft was a process of self-exploration for me. It began as a child when I realized I could "make things happen." On a hot summer day when visiting relatives in West Virginia, I distinctly remember empowering a finger puppet to bring myself and a childhood acquaintance ice cream and pretzels. I can remember our mutual astonishment when, an hour later, we were presented with the goodies.

When I was 16, my mother became terminally ill. Sick and dying, she was not treated well by the traditional religion of her choice, and I felt worthless because I could not save her. The same callous religious behavior had happened with both of my grandmothers. This nonchalant attitude toward the spiritual needs of the sick and elderly infuriated me. When my mother passed, I seized the opportunity to think and discover unfettered. I began an exploration into alternative religions, magick, science, and human psychology that has never stopped. At seventeen, the book that set me on the path of the Craft as we understand it was *Diary of a Witch* by Sybil Leek. When I read it, I said, "Oh my gracious, this is me! It is okay to believe this way!" And so, it is! Spiritually, I have been practicing since my childhood. Traditionally, I entered the Craft in the late '80s through Initiation by Lady Bried FoxSong and have met many exciting, good souls since then in various traditions and practices.

ROZI JAMES, ALEXANDRIAN HIGH PRIESTESS

Since I was a young child, growing up in the countryside, I've always felt there to be something mysterious and sacred about the natural world. I sometimes used to play on my own in the woods and was always mesmerised by mountains, the sea, log fires, and the wind—it felt like they held some power beyond my understanding, and I was intrigued to know what that was. As a teenager, I became curious about the spiritual practices of my Scottish ancestors and I started looking into Paganism, which led me to books on Witchcraft. The more I read, the more it felt like I was re-learning something I already knew, and I began to develop some basic solitary rituals and spells, observe the Sabbats, and engage with nature in a more conscious way, especially trees and the moon.

At 18, I started attending the local May Day festival and eventually got to know some Alexandrian Initiates, although I wasn't aware of who they were at the time; they just seemed like interesting people. In 2009, when I was 25, I went to a soirée at the temple in my town, which as it happened was literally around the corner from my house. Although I had been resistant to the idea of receiving instruction when it came to my spiritual development, I quickly realised that the people in that group were connected to the mysterious 'something' in a way I hadn't been able to access on my own. So, I requested Initiation and began the process of preparation for the First Degree, and I've never looked back.

POPPA CAPP, ALEXANDRIAN WITCH

My fascination with magic and all things esoteric began early in my childhood. At the age of 14, I acquired a deck of tarot cards, which catalyzed my lifelong exploration of the occult, religion, and philosophy. I had the pleasure of growing up in the culturally rich milieu of the San Francisco Bay Area, and I availed myself of the abundant resources and vibrant communities devoted to the occult and spirituality. Over time,

I engaged deeply with various occult organizations and religious affiliations, but despite those involvements, I found myself perpetually dissatisfied, compelling me to continue my quest for spiritual fulfillment.

In 2019, driven by an inexplicable impulse, my partner and I divested ourselves of nearly all possessions and embarked on a journey to New Orleans. Upon arriving in New Orleans, I was again searching for a spiritual home, which landed me at an Alexandrian Soirée. Soon after, I had a tremendous revelatory experience with the Goddess and chased after religious Witchcraft with great enthusiasm. In July of 2021, I was initiated into Alexandrian Witchcraft, marking the culmination of my protracted spiritual quest. As I continue with my fourth year of involvement with the Craft in the latter half of 2024, I anticipate an enduring commitment to it throughout the remainder of my lifetime.

REV. JACQ CIVITARESE, CABOT HPS, ELDER

I was born in Salem, Massachusetts, and grew up mostly in the next city over in Beverly throughout the 1980s and 90s. Every person I knew, knew that Witches were real people and that they truly practiced their Craft, especially Laurie Cabot. She was still a regular guest on the radio, offering astrology and simple spell crafting ideas to all listening.

The family on my mother's side gravitated towards Laurie and the notion of being a "natural Witch;" without a doubt, my family has a long history of being psychic and "just knowing." We are completely Celtic in our lineage: Welsh, Irish, Scottish, British, French, and Basque. Anyways, the best place I can start with my involvement with the Craft is the first spell I did with my mother and sister while listening to Laurie on the radio at six years old... a Jupiter Spell.

All during my childhood, we three daughters experienced many psychic or otherworldly phenomena, and my mother and aunts were always open to discuss and offer explanations for these occurrences, explanations that I thought were common knowledge until 5th grade. It was when I was nine that the nickname "Wacky Jackie" came about... this is when I stopped sharing my experiences and family-given answers with most, except a few true friends who shared the psychic gift and openness to it that we had.

Jumping ahead, my dear friend Krystal announced herself as a Witch in 7th grade, and to deflect the ridicule, she outed me. Krys, a bookworm, supplied me with the missing material needed, the part of the Craft that is ritual, devotional, and guiding. I have been a practicing Witch since then. When I was 27, I started to work with Laurie Cabot at ..... ALL THIS IS TOO LONG I'm not sure how to answer this with my history. MEOW!

QUESTION TWO

In the 1950s, Gerald Gardner and other pioneers of the Craft began a campaign to dispel popular misconceptions about Witches. Through books, interviews, radio, and television, the public was introduced to the Religion of Witchcraft as a Goddess-oriented fertility cult focused on a form of positive, life-affirming magic. Witches were not evil. They did not worship Satan, eat babies, or sacrifice animals. It was not just something of fairy tales, but a living, breathing belief system complete with its own Gods, rituals, literature, ethics, and priesthood. Today, public Witches are often known for wanting to make a buck, be famous, or simply seeking attention found in social media. Yet the work continues with a handful of Priesthood. How important do you think public education about the Craft is today? Is it still needed? Why should it or should it not continue??

ANSWERS

ELIE BARNES, ALEXANDRIAN HIGH PRIESTESS

If we look at human nature, we will notice that the less informed seem to have the loudest voices. Those who are seriously working on an ideal will not have as much time for chit-chat. I think it is best if we have a balance of intellectual and academic education to counter the constant stream of opinion, emotion, and misinformation that comes from the general population. Personally, I think less is more. For those who have ears to hear and eyes to see, we will know the value in education presented by others because they have personally worked on the subject matter for a period of time. At best, it is circumnavigations.

For those who lack formal introduction, Initiation, or more informed education, and deem themselves seekers, they will search to the ends of the earth to find anything no matter its value. Education about the religion of Witchcraft is a necessary evil..

SOLARIS BLUE RAVEN, GARDNERIAN WITCH

Know thyself and know your Craft. I think it is critical that serious-minded practitioners of Witchcraft respect the art and its origins. I have observed a watered-down, almost careless approach to Craftwork these days, which in my opinion is a disservice to how sacred and powerful the art of Witchcraft is. As it is said, "Never summon anything you are unable to banish," which goes for a reckless and uneducated approach to the intimacy of the sacred circle. Have an educated teacher and Witch who respects you, inspires you, and truly shows you this powerful path to alchemical transformation. These days, there is a thin line between how much magic one should share in the public arena. In my opinion, the seeker will find the teacher. The true teachers should shine bright regardless of how distorted the Craft community and misperceptions become. I would also say there is a time in the illusion to conceal that which is most sacred, like a precious-gem Grimoire, and share with very few serious Initiates.

Christine Stephens, Alexandrian High Priestess

Craft education is as vitally important as it has ever been. Maxine Sanders, the co-founder of the Alexandrian Tradition of Witchcraft, is fond of saying, "Magic will have its way." I believe this to be true. The Gods have always used whatever means were available to reach seekers of occult teachings. Today, social media, Internet classes, and a plethora of flavors of magical knowledge are available at the click of a button. There are myriad messages, and Craft education needs to be among the options available to seekers. As these seekers continue, some will be content with the aesthetic and the idea of proclaiming themselves Witches, and for them, this is sufficient. Some will begin the quest for knowledge only to lose interest once the trendiness passes, or to run for cover when the world begins to persecute Witches once again. And others will find that traditions such as Voodoo or Santeria resonate more strongly with them, and they will follow those paths. None of these

are wrong answers, as we are all on our own journeys. Finally, there are those who continue to seek Craft knowledge that cannot be easily obtained on the Internet or social media. For these, the Priesthood must remain ready to Initiate, to teach, and to protect these fledgling practitioners of Witchcraft.

FIONA HORNE, ROCK STAR WITCH

Witchcraft will always be occult (secret/hidden) at its core and in its most enriching mysteries. That doesn't mean that it should be exclusive to only the very few, though. True seekers will ultimately earn this knowledge. Public education allows for spirited debate and co-creative learning experiences, which keep the Craft vibrant, alive, and relevant in the present moment. This is where its most positive attributes of healing, positive empowerment, and reverence for the Natural World are so needed in these rapidly changing times.

TRACY FRASCHE. GARDNERIAN HIGH PRIESTESS

I have always been a great proponent of education when it comes to the Craft. In 2007, I was living in an affluent village in New Jersey (translate that into beyond the very definition of snobbery). I was doing some publicity work for a Witches Ball event that was raising money for St. Jude's Children's Hospital. I reached out to our local newspaper and jokingly signed my letter, "The Un-Official Witch of Ridgewood." The next thing I knew, I was being asked to do a "People and Places" article in which they interview residents who are doing something interesting or worthwhile for the community. The first thing they asked, however, was, "Do you have a black cat?" I told them, "No black cats, no black hats, no brooms," or I wasn't interested. It had to be respectful to the Craft community as well as educational for the reader.

But good Lord (no pun intended), did I agonize about whether to do it or not. I had two children in the public school system, and a husband who was a music director in a local church as well as a high school teacher. I worried about the impact it would have on our family. Would the kids be bullied? Would my husband lose his job? I hoped I was just being overly dramatic, but I knew the possibility existed. I've known people who have been investigated by child protective services and threatened to have their children removed from the home for peacefully living their lives as Witches. A beloved friend's estranged husband is currently using her being a "white Witch, who holds bizarre rituals in my home" as grounds for divorce. So, what would make me decide to do an article that would draw me out into the bright light of day? I thought it was an awesome opportunity to educate people who probably never give Witches a second thought except on Halloween! Let's face it, we're like turkeys on Thanksgiving. Everyone pretty much ignores us unless there's a reason not to, like when the news reports of a ritual sacrifice, but then it's usually the Satanists that get blamed. Time to shake things up a bit!

I have to say, the article was amazingly very well received. As I skulked around the neighborhood, hoping that no one would recognize the "Unofficial Witch," I was surprised when more people than I expected, snobs included, came to me to tell me how much they enjoyed it and how much they learned. My husband kept his job, and my kids weren't bullied. Their friends thought it was "so cool," and the bullies were too scared to mess with them afterward. Admittedly, I did get the stink eye from some of the A-list mothers on the playground. That was more than enough for me!

We recently moved to a state that isn't as nearly as progressive as New Jersey. I was somewhat trepidatious about wearing my pentacle in public for fear there might be repercussions. I envisioned a mob showing up on my front lawn with torches or slinging a noose around our majestic oak. So, I stopped wearing my pentacle for a while as I settled in, and it was awful! I felt that I was denying who I was just to fit into the local culture. "Fuck this!" I thought. "This is not who I am!" It also prevented any chance for the opportunity to educate those who might be harboring the more typical fear-based misconceptions about Witches and the Craft. I see absolutely no reason why we shouldn't continue trying to finally put an end to these. And may the Gods preserve the Craft.

LEVI ROWLAND, ALEXANDRIAN HIGH PRIEST

The Craft has gone through so many phases when it comes to its relationship to the wider culture. The proliferation of "Witchy" culture in the current climate has done a lot to reduce the concept of Witchcraft to an aesthetic, or a rebellious political phase. I believe public education does a lot to dispel this harm, but frankly, it is too late, in my opinion, to completely counter the image of Witchcraft that youth culture is currently creating. Priesthood, in Craft, can best respond to the commodification of Witchcraft by the religionification of Witchcraft.

We should absolutely be educating others about our path, but only in the sense that we make it known that we are available; that we truly believe in the Gods and the power of magic to transform lives; and that we exist for earnest seekers who are willing to put in a lot of work; and that we are much more than a specific "look" or ragtag collection of New Age ideas. We must educate within the language of religion. We need to hold back the experiential aspects of Craft and only teach the foundational principles. The lived religion itself only happens within a Coven, and keeping it that way preserves a lot of what really matters in Craft. We must simultaneously be more open, and more closed. We become more open by being more public, more available to students and open about our existence. We maintain our closed nature by refus-

ing to sell our Mysteries for a dime, and refusing to water down what we believe is the central rite of Craft: Initiation.

CARIE EWERS, ALEXANDRIAN PRIESTESS AND ELDER

I think it is important now, more than ever, to get back to educating the public about Witchcraft and the occult. It often gets overlooked that it is a religion to many Witches and practitioners and always has been. Witchcraft has been practiced in many, many forms since time began. It is not about a quick fix or notoriety. Power and results are lovely, but sacrifice and humility are equally important.

MICHAEL HERKES: THE GLAM WITCH, ECLECTIC SOLITARY

I think that education on the Craft is only going to enrich and help Witches on their path. Education on any subject is always essential for growth and mastery. After all, you can cook a meal without knowing the proper methods involved in the practice, correct ingredients, instruments to use, timing, etc., but the question then is, does it taste as good as someone who is seasoned with training? That's also not something for me to decide—sometimes a little diner meal can hit the spot better than a Michelin Star restaurant. Similarly, I'm sure that there are a handful of Witches who are less interested in promoting education on the Craft's history, and if that works for them, it works for them. That history is always going to be available for those seekers who wish to enrich themselves. I tend not to get too caught up in worrying about social media Witchcraft and the inaccuracies that come from it because I believe that anyone who is serious about wanting to practice the Craft will come to find the truth in their own time. Social

media was just starting with MySpace back when I started practicing. Nothing has really changed, and I was misinformed on certain things back then too. But my dedication and genuine desire to become a Witch led me to what I needed.

SILVER RAVENWOLF, BLACK FOREST CIRCLE AND SEMINARY

I believe ongoing education about the Craft is vital for the survival and peaceful enjoyment of our belief systems for ourselves and our families. And I say "systems" plural because of the diversity of groups under the Wiccan/Witchcraft umbrella. I agree that misinformation from a plethora of sketchy sources inside and outside our community continues to negatively impact our practitioners. The suffering of others created for personal gain or ego gratification is unconscionable, whether it is in person, on social media, or otherwise. Such condemnation through misinformation campaigns is not relegated to our religion — it is worldwide, covering a host of issues. Our best defense is to continue to educate the public. Education does not just protect the individual — it encompasses their friends, families, groups, and organizations.

ROZI JAMES, ALEXANDRIAN HIGH PRIESTESS

I'm always in favour of sharing any concept or perspective that presents an alternative to the mainstream narrative, whether that's a narrative about religion, politics, history, social norms, or anything else. Craft is still an 'alternative' religion in comparison to the major religions most people are familiar with, so in that sense, I think it's a worthwhile endeavour to let them know that there are other – equally viable – options, even if it's just with the intent of broadening their minds.

Added to that, I believe that for anyone who has experienced trauma as the result of an abusive upbringing where religion was used as a means of exploitation or control, but who still feels the need to connect with a spiritual tradition, Witchcraft – with its emphasis on the balancing forces of Goddess and God and its roots in nature – can be incredibly healing and empowering. So, in that sense, it feels important to raise awareness and potentially enable someone to access their own spirituality in a way they might not have done otherwise.

In other words, I think public education about Witchcraft is important if its purpose is to help and empower people, but I don't honestly think that Craft itself would suffer at this point if we didn't make any more effort to educate the wider world about it. Thanks to the work done by our predecessors in the 20th century, the majority of Witches today are safe to go about their business without fearing violence or discrimination, at least in the Western world. There will always be misinformation and misinterpretations out there, like with any other subject, but the tenets at the heart of Craft have a way of reaching those with the eyes to see and the ears to hear, and I don't necessarily think it's a bad thing if seekers have to put in a bit of effort to separate the true Mysteries from the rest of the noise.

Of course, Craft is benefited whenever a sincere seeker contributes their life experience and energy to the Work, so I'm in favour of all ongoing efforts to let people know what we're about. But I believe that those who are drawn to Craft will always find their way to it, one way or another, so in that sense, we don't need to concern ourselves with bringing it to people's attention..

POPPA CAPP, ALEXANDRIAN WITCH

Public education about the Craft will always be imperative, and it is incumbent upon the priesthood to actively contribute to advancing the pioneers' advocacy while disseminating the correct narrative. Despite the growing popularity of Witchcraft, a substantial number of individuals, societies, and traditions persist in adhering to their stark misconceptions and unfounded fears revolving around our religion. We must build upon the groundwork laid by our predecessors to rectify these erroneous perceptions, thereby fostering a heightened global understanding and acceptance of Witchcraft as a benign and benevolent faith.

While the prioritization of the pioneers' campaign remains indisputably crucial, Initiates should consider another significant reason to perpetuate education regarding Witchcraft—to sufficiently counter the increasingly rampant proliferation of false and misleading narratives surrounding our religion. In recent years, much of this misinformation has been spread via social media by individuals falsely claiming to be Witches. They are motivated by a desire for attention, to adhere to a particular aesthetic or trend, or the inflation of their egos, among other purposes.

Particularly pernicious among these misconceptions are assertions that equate Witchcraft solely with spellcasting and beliefs proclaiming that one can undertake the Craft as an eclectic or solitary endeavor. The Priesthood should impart knowledge regarding the true nature of Witchcraft upon those who have been egregiously misinformed and misguided. Initiates should emphasize that Witchcraft transcends the narrow confines of mere spellcasting. Instead, we should assert the Craft's status as a comprehensive religious system, stressing the necessity of Initiation for individuals to identify as Witches. By refuting these escalating misconceptions on social media, where falsehoods are rife, the priesthood can adapt and enhance education regarding the Craft to address contemporary sources of confusion.

REV. JACQ CIVITARESE, CABOT HPs, ELDER

In this time of social media and trending topics, the correct history, message, and application of the Craft, told by those who have truly studied, practiced, and most importantly, devoted themselves to the Goddess, is needed now more than ever before. With "Witchcraft" on the rise, we see a plethora of detached practices and eclectic shareable memes passing off as true wisdom. I feel this trend has added to the fairy tale/ not real belief that Witchcraft has endured since children's literature and movie depictions.

Perhaps it's the Priesthood side of the Craft that hasn't stepped up enough to fill in the misconceptions around both the uninformed voices of today's Witches and those who still deem Witchcraft as a form of devil worship. Ultimately, I feel Witchcraft as a Religion will not be taken seriously as long as those who undermine the importance of honoring the Goddesses and Gods of old persist. We are not in a time where Witches are fully understood, free to practice in public spaces, and recognized as an established belief system by others in the religious and political spheres. Greater public education and other modern campaigning could ease this. Of course, my mind goes right to Laurie Cabot's "Witches' Do's and Don'ts" pamphlet from 1986, which is still free to copy and distribute, and which answers many misconceptions that the common person has about Witches and Witchcraft.

QUESTION THREE

The women and men who led the Witchcraft Revival of the '50s and '60s worshiped a monotheistic Goddess of the Moon, alongside her consort, the Horned God. This included, but was not limited to, Gerald Gardner, Alex Sanders, Robert Cochrane, Charles Cardell, and Sybil Leek. Today, there is an increasing endeavor to dethrone this Goddess, replacing her either with the Devil or a pagan ideology of many less important Goddesses, generally in the form of a chosen polytheistic culture or cultures. What are your thoughts on this subject?

ANSWERS

ELIE BARNES, ALEXANDRIAN HIGH PRIESTESS

After reading and thinking about various models for the creation and function of the Multiverse, I tend to follow a Qabalistic, Neoplatonic, Hermetic system. So, the Limitless Light condenses into the One, Kether, and in turn manifests itself as Chokmah and Binah, the Eternal Couple of Polarity. Forever participating in the One and simultaneously projecting, by their electrical impulsive co-manifestation, a holographic Universe which reflects the One and the Many, in Four Worlds.

Humans create the philosophies and ideologies of religion, and they tend to use ideas that benefit their own needs, ideals, and politics. Changing the main deity of religion away from a male God and towards a female God serves the needs of the people who wanted to worship a female deity. That seemed to correspond with the emergence of the women's liberties movement. And now the pendulum swings back toward a male God focus, and probably swings back in response to political and cultural change on the ground, in human lives. This corresponds to how we are rethinking gender and sexuality on a large scale, for instance with the transgender and the nonbinary movements. Currently, we also are experiencing a direction change, away from democracies and globalization and towards oligarchic power and rekindled strong national identity.

My answer is that humans are always swinging back and forth on a pendulum of ideology and identification. We have archaeological evidence from thousands of years that depict forms of Gods, forms of Goddesses, and images of the supreme Godhead. I expect that we will continue to go around and around on how to represent Gods, ever-changing, as humans are ever-changing. Current stress being placed on a male God figure for the religion of Witchcraft is illustrating how people who practice the religion of Witchcraft are becoming more male-power oriented.

SOLARIS BLUE RAVEN, GARDNERIAN WITCH

I am a firm believer in respect and honor to the Goddess. It would appear these days that terminology becomes clouded and somewhat hijacked to accommodate a different belief system or perhaps a comfort zone. If you are a Priest or Priestess Witch, you know how powerful and sacred Drawing Down the Goddess is. Honor this gift and respect the ancient wisdom passed down through many magical generations. The concept of worshiping lesser entities is, in my opinion, a contaminated wellspring that can lead to less clarity in areas of scrying and magickal arts in general. Once again, it boils down to education. I do honor the free will of the Witch, yet as they practice, so too will their fruits be shown by their beliefs.

CHRISTINE STEPHENS, ALEXANDRIAN HIGH PRIESTESS

Those who do not learn from history are doomed to repeat it. I believe in the Goddess of the Witches. I believe that people in general—Americans specifically—tend to get hung up on the sexuality of the person and not the roles of the Divine duality in the circle of life, death, and rebirth.

Both aspects of this duality are vital, and it is often the human experience, politics, and/or environment that cause magical practitioners to diminish or even exclude one aspect of this duality in their practice. For me, it is right and necessary to worship both The God and the Goddess of Witches. Each has their place, each has their power, and each has their lessons to teach and wisdom to share..

FIONA HORNE, ROCK STAR WITCH

I do not know of one Witch who does not honor and revere the Goddess of the Moon—but their interpretation and choice of worship for this Deity may be different from those who led the Witchcraft Revival of the '50s and '60s. I humbly offer, in my experience of honoring the Divine, different Gods and Goddesses have resonated with my practice at different linear times—or probably more accurately, I have resonated with them.

The nature of everything is change—it is the one inescapable fact of existence. Everything evolves. That doesn't mean the origins are not to be honored and methods of worship enacted upon with reverence and expertise by those who choose to. But I would offer that a significant strength of the evolving Craft lies in its diversity, with all anchored by a sincere intention to venerate the divine (even if that divine is of atheistic principle—a reverence for the universe itself), work magick with sincere intent, and remember that our origins are born of a time when humans lived with the Earth and not on top of it.

TRACY FRASCHE, GARDNERIAN HIGH PRIESTESS

The Devil? In the Craft? Isn't this the myth we've been trying to dispel for decades? And here is a perfect example of why, in some circles (no pun intended), the word "Wicca" has become an insult. Since the Devil is a Christian construct, replacing the Goddess with such a deity would be contrary to our beliefs and wouldn't be recognized in Traditional practice, but the world is a twisted place.

There is a deep and timeless connection between us as Witches and the quintessential Goddess of the Moon. She is the embodiment of the divine feminine, ever-present and palpable. She, in her aspects of Maiden, Mother, and Crone, is the flame that empowers women during every phase of their lives and leads them away from the oppression of patriarchy. I don't believe she can be replaced without losing an integral part of our connection to what defines us as Witches.

The sacred couple, the Goddess of the Moon and the Horned God, are part of the very foundations of Wicca. For some of us, they are the first Deities we were introduced to when we were called to the Craft. They are, in essence, the "power couple" of all creation. They are infinite..

LEVI ROWLAND, ALEXANDRIAN HIGH PRIEST

I believe the backlash against the Goddess movement is rooted in nothing more than misogyny. Goddess literature and pioneers in the revival of Goddess worship in predominantly Christian cultures have been retroactively branded as less serious, more "New Agey," and duped into believing faulty anthropology and dishonest history. The male pioneers of the occult revival, as guilty as anyone when it comes to historical revisionism and bad information, are forgiven all their academic sins and are often labeled as lovable cads or misunderstood geniuses. The women of these movements, however, are often labeled as frauds, charlatans, or ignorant. I often think of the different treatments received in the current climate by Blavatsky versus Crowley, for example.

Serious academic work on the Goddess is given short shrift in comparison to male-dominated mystical and magical traditions such as ceremonial magic, the Grimoire Tradition, Norse paganism, and other paths. When a woman is central, critics come out of the woodwork to label it as weak, "fluffy," silly, or less serious-minded. I truly believe that many people have an extremely difficult time breaking free of patriarchy and its hold on religious expression.

Until the seeker can shake off patriarchy, they are never going to truly understand Witchcraft.

CARIE EWERS, ALEXANDRIAN PRIESTESS AND ELDER

I feel like that comes from a fear of the power of the Goddess and the Divine Feminine as a whole. The honoring of the Goddess has always been part of my magical journey.

MICHAEL HERKES, THE GLAM WITCH, ECLECTIC SOLITARY

On one hand, the Goddess, and even the Horned God for that matter, have slanderously been replaced by the Devil in modern interpretations such as TV and movies due to other religions' ignorance and attempts to assassinate belief systems that are different from theirs. These stereotypes have existed for many years in the world and, as a result, unfortunately bleed into representations of Witchcraft. That being said, there are a vast number of different Goddesses that have existed throughout the course of history. I believe that the Goddess, or any form of divinity, will show themselves to the seeker in whatever way the seeker needs to see them. It is perhaps possible that more and more Witches share this idea because believing that there is one true right and only Goddess, and/or God, often feels synonymous with the patriarchal religions which many seekers are trying to escape from. Personally, I am devoted to one specific Goddess only. However, I see all expressions, names, and archetypes as relevant and alive in their celebration and worship.

SILVER RAVENWOLF, BLACK FOREST CIRCLE AND SEMINARY

The answer to this question is difficult because our community is continuing to grow and change. Some people seem to be more worried about personal acceptance rather than the group mind, and clarity of who is in the community, who is on the fringes, and who does not practice but chooses to lend an opinion is sketchy. Additionally, you have the blend of Wicca, Witches, Pagans, Druids, Heathens, etc., which all have their own choices; yet many of us communicate freely and absorb each other's practices, seeking the ultimate continuous spiritual experience.

Many other religions have constantly dethroned the Goddess, and if you look at the big picture, it has harmed the rights of women for thousands of years. This same process continues and, like other negative habits, can bleed into our community. People choose deity based on their past experiences as well as their current needs. Perhaps we should be looking at both aspects to determine why these choices are being made in today's practice. At the moment, the theme of accepting diversity is foremost for many people. What is beautiful about the Goddess is that She speaks to all in a language they will understand. Her energy is powerful, compassionate, and encompassing. She is birth. And She supports the birth of new ideas because She is the Mistress of Constant Change. The better we know ourselves, the better we know our Goddess.

Rozi James, Alexandrian High Priestess

For me, all the Goddesses are one Goddess, all the Gods are one God, and both Goddess and God are representations of the dualistic aspects of the Divine, so it doesn't matter what name you give them: they're all just different facets of a single universal whole.

In a way, I find it strange that people insist on one pantheon being more legitimate than another or believe that different pantheons somehow exist in competition with each other, because surely, we're all talking about the same thing, just with different words. A tree is a tree, no matter whether you use the English word or the

Greek word or the Arabic word or the Hindi word; why are we arguing over whose language is the most appropriate to describe the same thing?

Having said that, it seems as though some religious traditions have emerged as a kind of reaction to earlier belief systems; their practices seem to be directed more at disrupting or discrediting other people's beliefs than at creating a new system for themselves. And that's totally fine, people are free to believe whatever they want, but I do wonder how much merit there really is in a religious tradition that has to define itself in opposition to another one. If the main driving force is to tear something down rather than build something new, I don't know if it's really serving anyone. It seems a bit of a waste of energy.

POPPA CAPP, ALEXANDRIAN WITCH

I am confident that we can all discern the apparent correlation between endeavors to impose the Devil as the central figure in the Craft, or the dispersal of the Goddess into many lesser goddesses, and the entrenched presence of misogynistic patriarchy. Still, I do not believe that most individuals undertaking these substitutionary efforts harbor malicious intent behind their actions.

Many individuals turn to the occult as a response to their traumatic experiences with Abrahamic religions. For them, the attraction lies in embracing a form of spirituality that actively opposes the belief systems that caused them harm in the past. Their resulting eclectic magical practices, often mislabeled as "Witchcraft," are not a genuine pursuit of seeking or experiencing the religion of the Goddess. Instead, their practices represent an endeavor to construct a spiritual framework divergent from prior religious experiences. A great irony arises when considering that the concept of the Devil itself originates from within the Abrahamic traditions.

Thus, individuals who integrate the Devil into their occult practices inadvertently undermine their intended objectives of expressing adversity and excommunication from Abrahamic influences. On the other hand, the fragmentation of divinity into expansive pantheons is often a cognitive necessity for the human mind to apprehend the Goddess's ineffable nature. Our minds inherently seek to restrict intricate concepts through the imposition of boundaries. Consequently, the subdivision of the Goddess into discrete and discernible "characters" serves mainly as a strategy, rendering Her more accessible to the human psyche. In this case, I encourage those earnestly pursuing the highest spiritual truth to transcend the confines of cultural pantheons and the frameworks inherent in human thought. By Her very nature, the Goddess eludes confinement within our artificial boundaries. The tenacious seeker will learn to gaze beyond these limitations, penetrating the veil and understanding Her singular truth.

Rev. Jacq Civitarese, Cabot HPs, Elder

As a Cabot Witch of the early '00s, I sadly missed the rise and primary focus of the Egyptian side of the Cabot Tradition before the transformation of our tradition led to the majick of the ancient Celts. That being said, Laurie Cabot has continued to emphasize the Goddess Isis as a Moon Goddess, filled with majick and mystery while also being a Great Mother Goddess, offering calm encounters and a gentle embrace. Those who are new to the Cabot Tradition will get their first, but not last, connection to the Goddess Isis in our tradition's "Witchcraft I as a Science" course during the Egyptian Sun Meditation.

The devotion to Isis as a monotheistic Goddess is not all lost within our traditional structure. Laurie has stated and written about her beloved relationship with Isis and honors the teachings of Isis, along with many of the main Egyptian Gods that have played a role in the Cabot Tradition.

Now, we enter my timeline ... where our focus is primarily on the Indo-European connections of the Witch, specifically the Celtic people, their myths, and folk majick as our guide. The Celtic Pantheon of Gods and Goddesses of the early Irish, Welsh, Scottish, and Gaulish are polytheistic, and our Wheel of the Year focuses on honoring them. However, we teach early on the deep connections between the people of the early British Isles and the ancient Egyptians; this includes cultural connections, bones, and most importantly, DNA. Findings have shown that up to 70% of modern-day British men are related to the Egyptian Pharaoh Tutankhamun. But I digress. During our "Witchcraft III as a Religion" course, the student must study the ancient literature of Celtic cultures, their migration across Europe and Asia, and each will need to connect to these ancient Gods and Goddesses. I do not find this to be demeaning to the Goddess Isis as an act of dethroning, but simply the difference in one's path on the course of Witchcraft Revival. I feel great ease with connecting to the Goddess Brigid, much like the love the Goddess Isis offers..

QUESTION FOUR

Most Witchcraft traditions have some form of ethics that, although deep, have trickled down to the masses, often misunderstood and then redefined through several publications. An example of this is the Witches' Creed or Rede, "An it harm none, do what you will." Today, ethical Craft or even magic is often scorned as fluffy bunny, Wiccan, or unauthentic in certain circles. Why do you think so many are attracted to aggressive or destructive magic? Why do they desire it to be linked with Witchcraft?

ANSWERS

ELIE BARNES ALEXANDRIAN HIGH PRIESTESS

For the last 1500 years in the West, malevolent magic has been linked to old women and men who have been labeled as "Witches" in an operative sense. People who practiced folk magic were linked with being against the Church and identifying with a devil god. They were also the anarchistic types who didn't agree with being controlled by a government or church power, so they were further labeled as Anti-Church and therefore Anti-Good.

This may never be answered: "Why are people attracted to being aggressive or destructive?" I see humans using their emotional energy to make decisions, not their intellectual powers. So, humans continue to be petty, vindictive, jealous, hurt, bitter, possessive, brutish, and just plain tacky. It seems to be in our nature. These types of emotionally driven folks also don't do much real reading, research, or thinking. Of course, they would be attracted to the popular opinion that practicing Witchcraft makes you more powerful and able to harm your enemies even more.

Solaris Blue Raven, Gardnerian Witch

I am not one to seek and destroy, however, I do believe in psychic protection, deflection, shielding, and whatever the Witch feels necessary to negate an assault on the body, mind, spirit, loved ones, etc. Madame Karma tends to take the helm when it comes to naughty Witches; however, the world of today does require an adequate skill level by the Witch to dispel these destructive forces for peace of mind, among other things. Witchcraft is a cosmic dance much like Martial Arts. We don't look for trouble, yet at times, adversaries show themselves.

Christine Stephens, Alexandrian High Priestess

There are many who seek magic—and Witchcraft—as power when they feel powerless. They are not looking to become a good Witch wearing pink and sparkles who seeks to be just and kind; they want to deliver justice using the fireballs and hexes of wicked Witches and scary Witches who live deep in the woods and practice dark magic. And let's be honest, Hollywood has also ensured that those Witches in black are very sexy to boot.

Who wouldn't understand the appeal of it all? Doing what is right in both the mundane and the magical worlds is HARD! In my opinion, it is also necessary. Before I undertake any serious magic, I work diligently to understand the results my actions may have upon the natural world, and the part I have played to date. It is easy to hex an ex for walking out—it is much more difficult to admit that you may own some responsibility in the failed relationship.

FIONA HORNE, AUSTRALIAN WITCH

I think we could look to the phenomenon of social media—especially TikTok and its sheer volume of content—and how that can have a convoluting and depressive effect on some individuals' psyche. Lowering the consciousness, not raising it.

I remember burrowing away in secondhand bookstores, trying so hard to find anything I could on Witchcraft (lucky me I found a copy of *Other Temples Other Gods* by Neville Drury once in an outback petrol station book bin!). The search alone forced me to be conscious and grateful for any morsel of information. Anything debased or negative reminded me too much of the negative aspects of the Catholic religion of my upbringing. It never occurred to me to equate destructive, aggressive behavior with Witchcraft.

That was the world of horror movies and knee-jerk reactions—not Witchcraft as it was ultimately revealed.

I do not concern myself with circles that scorn ethical Witchcraft, so I cannot comment on that.

My manifesto, *The Art of Witch*, written 36 years after I commenced practicing, celebrates ethical Witchcraft. It seems like the obvious choice to me; I am interested in being a powerful and effective Witch. And that power is measured not by what I can get from my Craft, but what it empowers me to give..

Tracy Frasche, Gardnerian High Priestess

We were always taught, "Bless before you bind, bind before you curse." Admittedly, the blessing part can be a monumental undertaking, especially when you know someone is attempting to cause you harm, but going directly for the jugular magically is overkill—again no pun intended. These days, a sarcastic comment on social media is all it takes to find yourself on the receiving end of someone's misguided curse, and while the first inclination might be to dismiss it as nothing more than amusing, words have power, even in the hands of the woefully ill-informed.

I think there are a lot of people for whom Witchcraft is an attempt to find social acceptance and to have others acknowledge their presence, both in and out of the Witchcraft community. They are verbose in their use of aggressive and destructive magic as means of either self-preservation or to fit in where they may have otherwise been excluded. They use Witchcraft as a means of instilling the elements of fear and intrigue. I suspect that many haven't really explored the concept of ethics in Witchcraft because they are not interested in its deeper roots; it's just easier to use baneful magic than to confront life's more difficult social issues. They enjoy the mystique of Witchcraft without doing the actual work involved in learning its Mysteries.

And while Witchcraft may be power, so too is knowledge. If you sit back and observe long enough, you will find that there are a lot of people without a lot of knowledge practicing Witchcraft. That said, there are no controls in magic, and there will be consequences for the abuse of its power. This is something that one usually discovers the hard way. Thankfully, I believe those who begin their journey into Witchcraft this way eventually lose interest and fade back into the shadows of the mundane. From my experience, if one has a working relationship with Deity, baneful magic is rarely necessary. There is no power in the suffering of others.

LEVI ROWLAND ALEXANDRIAN, HIGH PRIEST

I will never understand why someone could have an issue with trying to avoid harm as a central ethical principle. The worship of cursing, baneful magic, and in-fighting through shooting mystical arrows has become so common in magical spaces as to be, honestly, rather boring. It is really simple to understand why this is so. What is more popular than revenge, anger, paranoia, and spite? These are the basest human emotions and they have fueled curse-peddlers and two-bit charlatans for ages. There is an attempt to cloak this in positivity, saying that curse work and baneful magic can be used to fight enemies, abusers, or other evil persons. I just don't see it. Magic is not the best tool for every job. Sometimes political action, the law, courts, community building, and a host of other options are far better tools for reversing injustice than black candles, pins, needles, and poisonous herbs. I think going down the rabbit holes of being the best curse-thrower on the block is more about pitiful, wounded egos than it is about magic or justice.

CARIE EWERS, ALEXANDRIAN PRIESTESS AND ELDER

Ethics are important in all aspects of life, not just Witchcraft. There must be a balance in magical work. I am always very wary when someone is approaching their magic from a place of revenge, aggression, or destruction. It can create a negative cycle with intention that can be difficult to transition out of. I am not saying that we don't have to protect ourselves when someone sends negative energy or spell work our way, but if your only connection to the work and your magic is just to "fuck someone else up," then results aren't always what you want.

MICHAEL HERKES, THE GLAM WITCH, ECLECTIC SOLITARY

Oh "fluffy bunny!"—I haven't heard that in a while! I think that so many are attracted to aggressive and destructive magic because we live in challenging times—politically, socially, environmentally, etc. I also think that many are struggling with existing traumas, and they feel that defensive magic is a solution for their situation. In one way, it can provide closure to negative experiences and obstacles that life brings. However, I also think that because Witchcraft is a niche practice that boasts "getting what you want," there is a tendency for it to allure those who are power-hungry and attracted to aggressive magic to get their way. I think in all truth, though, what these people are missing is that true Witchcraft is more about finding empowerment within rather than externally using power over others. Each individual practitioner is going to need to determine what ethics work best for them based on their current life circumstances.

For me, I use the acronym "RIF" as a blanket when determining if I want to move forward in a magical action: Respect – No means no. If what I plan to do is altering someone's will who has explicitly said no, I won't proceed. Integrity – Does it genuinely feel okay for me to do this? Can I live with myself? If not, I won't do it. Fairness – Why do I need or want this? Am I righting a wrong? Did they fuck with me first? Am

I trying to help build myself up, or gain something due to disadvantage? If not—I won't proceed.

SILVER RAVENWOLF BLACK FOREST CIRCLE AND SEMINARY

I believe the answer to this question lies within the individual. Where are they on their spiritual path? What do they feel they need from their practice? One's journey can encompass many possible courses of action aimed at personal empowerment and healing, or baser emotions to render satisfaction, including the use of hate, revenge, and anger. The more aggressive magicks can stem from feeling powerless and a belief (or knowledge as the case may be) that we are unable to change fate in the face of a horrendous situation. Today, you may feel the need to manipulate circumstances in one way, and two years from now, after you have grown and assimilated an experience, you may choose a different idea altogether.

We also have the problem of "What is Wicca?" and "What is Witchcraft?" as it applies to this question, the definition fluctuating with the diversity of the practitioners, the era in which we are discussing, the time of day, and the current weather (tongue in cheek). There is no perfection in behavior. No one is happy every day. No one is filled with delight each waking moment. But... we can try to think in grace, speak in grace, and act in grace. We can apply critical thinking before making a move. Nothing is more apt than the words, "I will try." Honor is the Law – Love is the Bond, to me, is a helpful tool in managing one's personal choices in the use of magick – but that is me. Others have the right to choose differently.

ROZI JAMES, ALEXANDRIAN HIGH PRIESTESS

First of all, I'd say that anyone who thinks an ethics-based Craft is somehow lacking power clearly hasn't attended one of our rituals; and second,

I think there's maybe some confusion about the difference between 'ethical' and 'timid.' There's nothing fluffy or inauthentic about being principled; if anything, I think it can be far more demanding to work in that way. My teacher in Craft was one of the most ethically rigorous people I've ever known when it came to magic, and she wielded immense power – perhaps for that very reason.

Which I suppose feeds into the second part of that question, and I believe the answer is this: tapping into 'loud' or 'explosive' emotions is a far easier way to raise power than by relying on gentler and more measured ones. Anger, hate, pain, violence – they all have a combustible energy that's quick and easy to access, and I don't think you have to work nearly as hard if you're using those as a starting point for magical work. It takes more effort to raise power from a place of compassion, love, and joy, at least until you become used to working that way. (I'm not sure why that is; perhaps those emotions are more difficult to harness because they're about expansion rather than contraction – they're more nebulous and elusive? Or maybe you have to dig deeper to access and sustain them? It's a question I've thought about a lot, and I still haven't come to a conclusion.)

Also, in my experience, it requires more thinking and patience to work magic in a way that doesn't risk harm to someone or something else; we all look for shortcuts and quick fixes, especially when the situation is urgent, but they're never an effective way to connect with our higher selves. And I think that ultimately if we don't do our due diligence, or if we deliberately choose destructive ways of working rather than constructive, we end up doing ourselves more damage than good, because then we've taken on more 'karmic debt' (for lack of a better term).

I really don't have an answer for the last part of your question, but maybe it's a sort of rebellion against mainstream religion? We've spent centuries being shamed for natural human urges and being told to repress them if we want to avoid eternal punishment, so one way to push back is to indulge in all the behaviors that have been forbidden for so long and take them to an extreme. For a long time, Witchcraft has been a catch-all term for practices that defy the authority of organized religions, so maybe people like to attach to that word to signify their rejection of puritanical views of morality? But I'm only hazarding a guess; I can't say for certain..

POPPA CAPP, ALEXANDRIAN WITCH

The true essence of ethics is ineffable—just as the Goddess Herself. As stated previously, human cognitive limitations impose significant constraints upon our ability to comprehensively grasp the parameters by which divinity adjudicates concepts such as 'good,' 'bad,' 'right,' or 'wrong.' Consequently, relinquishing the notion that one possesses an exhaustive understanding of ethics is imperative, and surrendering both magical and religious pursuits to the divine emerges as the sagacious approach.

Releasing preconceived ethical constructs and yielding all endeavors to the Goddess extricates our spiritual practices from our egos, transforming the practitioner into a conduit for the sacred. The proper preparation of oneself as a vessel, coupled with a complete detachment from the ego, tends to mitigate the manifestation of destructive or manipulative magical outcomes. Conversely, those who neglect to internalize this realization and forego the purifying process persist in sourcing and executing their magic purely from their egoic impulses. For such individuals, a prevalent absence of power and control not only permeates their occult pursuits but extends into the broader spectrum of their lives.

The association between Witchcraft and malevolent magic frequently originates from this egocentric and impotent lot, as inevitably, these practitioners become inexorably obsessed with acquiring and wielding the power that is conspicuously absent in their existence. Their fixation culminates in the utilization of aggressive, destructive, and dismantling magical practices, erroneously attributed to 'Witchcraft,' owing to their inadequate understanding. Embarking on this trajectory is reckless, unwise, and ultimately ineffective. In due course, these practitioners discern the futility of their pursuits, precipitating a profound inner turmoil marked by a desperate grasping for power and a descent into madness. It is a matter of extraordinary comic relief that these individuals fail to induce significant harm despite their strenuous efforts.

REV. JACQ CIVITARESE, CABOT HPs, ELDER

Within the Cabot Tradition, we abide by the Threefold Law of Return and the precept, "An it harm none; do what ye will." This is the first within the Cabot Tradition Code of Ethics that all Cabot Witches must integrate into their lives. We are firmly taught by Laurie Cabot in the ability to neutralize that which is not correct or isn't for the good of all. As Witches who know their majick and might, we know that we do not have to harm anyone, not because we can't, we certainly could; however, we understand the price... the consequences of our choices and actions.

Those who find this ethic to be fluffy may suffer from having little power behind their majick, or are too blind to see the cause and effect of such dismissal to be a result of their own doing. Another notion, as you state, is that they are attracted to the destruction of traditional systems as a whole, even one as peaceful as Witchcraft can be. Those who seek to attack anything viewed as "outdated" will naturally find another source/system to devour. Many are misguided to begin with, mistaking Witchcraft as being "anti-society, religious, structured, ethical..." I could go on. I do believe some have a longing to be linked with the Craft but do not understand it yet.

QUESTION FIVE

I have often been asked what role or purpose the Craft has. How does Witchcraft as a religion benefit mankind or humanity? I have, with some contemplation, developed my own answers. Please share with me your opinion on this subject.

ANSWERS

ELIE BARNES, ALEXANDRIAN HIGH PRIESTESS

Well, I would like to see what European and American Witchcraft looks like in another 30 years. The jury is still out. My primary happiness with the religion of Witchcraft is that it has refocused its adherents into more harmony with Nature and Mother Earth. I do not equate Mother Earth with the Great Goddess. Earth is her own Planetary Angel, just like the other planets. But she is our home and in truth supports our lives and growth in every way. The religion of Witchcraft has built a strong bridge back to our roots as a tribe and a special people. I appreciate the bridge very much.

SOLARIS BLUE RAVEN, GARDNERIAN WITCH

Witchcraft assists humanity at times on a subtle energy field level and on more powerful planetary levels. A collective of Witches can move mountains if they know how to channel their abilities properly. A solitary Witch can raise the consciousness and vibration of her entire neighborhood by will alone at times. Witches are the seers, healers, spirit world communicators, protectors, educators, counselors, Priests, and Priestesses who hold a flame of gnosis to guide the seeker

on their journey. They commune with nature, animal and plant kingdom, the world unseen, and are the awakeners to those living between worlds of illusion and delusion. Without mastering the psyche and mind, I imagine life in the illusion to be nothing more than a program with no mystical flavor to awaken the seeker.

CHRISTINE STEPHENS, ALEXANDRIAN HIGH PRIESTESS

Witchcraft—especially in this time in our world—offers many benefits. It reinforces the divine duality, teaches us to be attuned and protective of our natural and supernatural worlds, and offers healing and strength to our Covens and our communities. The importance of keeping the divine feminine sacred is more important than ever when the rights of women—even over their own bodies—are being eroded and threatened by religious and governmental leaders. To challenge leaders takes power and knowledge. Witchcraft, by its very nature, is revolutionary and empowering. It goes against the status quo of most established world religions by worshipping not only a God, but also the Goddess in all Her aspects. Being a Witch takes personal integrity and strength, and challenges one to tap into their own inner planes to find answers instead of simply adhering to the norms dictated by government and/or religion. And being an effective Witch means obtaining both knowledge and wisdom of both the natural and the unseen and having the ability to raise the power necessary to manifest the changes they seek to implement in either of these worlds.

A Witch knows that the power freely offered is to be used wisely. Because the vocation of a Witch, as with other religious Priesthood, is to serve their Gods, Coven, and community. We raise power to aid, to see, and to defend. We use this power and knowledge to heal, to provide guidance or insight, and to combat those who would harm..

FIONA HORNE, AUSTRALIAN WITCH

I am not religious; however, I respect anyone who chooses to be. In my personal experience, I have found religion often divides and spirituality more often unites.

Witchcraft as I live it and have personally witnessed in its rapid growth in popularity over the last 39 years is expansive and dynamic, leaning into spiritual expression whilst also upholding its religion. It fosters in the Witch a willingness to experience their own magnificence, their divine essence, their personal power. And then the most extraordinary expression of this power can be witnessed when that Witch is using their power for the benefit of others. A powerful Witch will navigate the challenges of this physical timeline in a way that is useful and meaningful as determined by the powers that lie beyond individual egoic interpretation, but that the Witch intuitively senses and recognizes.

These powers will often present a Witch with the most harrowing challenges to test their commitment to the regenerative principles of rebirth—the snake eternally eating its own tail. At every ending is another beginning. The powerful Witch always gets stronger, not weaker.

In all my books, I have offered that we live in environmentally challenged times. As modern Witches honoring nature as sacred, we would do well to heal and balance the damage as much as possible when we explore our powers..

TRACY FRASCHE, GARDNERIAN HIGH PRIESTESS

I think Witchcraft in all its many forms has always benefited humanity. We may have begun as shamans, cunning folk, or medicine men and women, but have evolved into those who hold the sacred responsibility of stewardship of the Earth. Where the masses may think of us as being "on the fringe," there are many of us who have been silently benefiting humanity for years in our respective fields as educators, particle physicists, and neurobiologists—and these are just among the people I know personally. And this is what we do. We heal the Earth and in doing so heal each other.

From a personal standpoint, I had suffered from anxiety and depression for years. I felt like there was something out of balance, but couldn't really determine what that something was. Things were going well in all the other aspects of my life, but my deeper sense of spirituality was lacking. Then I began getting involved with the greater Witchcraft community, attending meetup groups, and public rituals, and involving myself with like-minded people, which led me to find the Coven in which I would ultimately be initiated. It felt like a whole new world opened up to me. Those people who knew me before often tell me, "You're so much different now," and that's true. I may be only one small voice, but I believe this is true for many others as well, and if we can heal ourselves with Witchcraft, think of what we can accomplish to benefit humanity!

LEVI ROWLAND, ALEXANDRIAN HIGH PRIEST

I firmly believe that Witchcraft, in its incarnations stemming from the revival in England by Gardner, the Sanders, and others, brings the power of the Great Goddess back into a society that has been poisoned by patriarchy. Witchcraft stands in opposition to violent misogyny, cruelty to the Earth, and male domination of religious space. By centering our worship on the Goddess and Her consort, we are keeping alive a paradigm that can combat both a cruel, materialistic secularism that views consumption of goods as the only human purpose and rabid male-centered theologies that are itching for the apocalypse. There is something incredibly liber-

ating about the Great Goddess of Witchcraft. I cannot always put it into words, but I know the experience. I know, personally, what it feels like to have so many ideological chains broken through worship of the divine feminine. I know that Witchcraft brings this into a world dominated by patriarchy, and I know that we will continue to do so.

CARIE EWERS, ALEXANDRIAN PRIESTESS AND ELDER

Witchcraft as a religion benefits mankind as a connection to the earth and the cosmos. It teaches us to step outside of our bodies and everyday life and execute balance, power, and personal responsibility. When we tap into those ancient energies, I feel it unlocks a connection on a primordial level.

MICHAEL HERKES, THE GLAM WITCH, ECLECTIC SOLITARY

On one hand, religion can be a rewarding experience for those who seek community in shared beliefs and practices. But to be very honest, I am not one for organized religion. As the legendary Madonna has said before, "Religion is an idea that someone pushes on you. Religion is judgment, religion is suffering. Religion is conforming, religion is establishment." While there are certain religious elements that I bring to my personal Craft, these negative associations of mainstream organized religion have made me view my personal practice as more spiritual, anchored in a connection with nature: that nature which is not limited to the physical elements of your environment but also includes your inner landscape of emotions, intuition, and psyche. The nature of love and connection with others. The nature of creative freedom and expression. Witchcraft to me is freedom, and that makes it valuable to mankind and humanity.

SILVER RAVENWOLF, BLACK FOREST CIRCLE AND SEMINARY

Any spiritual practice that brings joy, compassion, healing, and love into one's life benefits humanity. I believe Craft practitioners, if they aspire to embrace the true power of the teachings, are the energy healers of our era. But we must see beyond ourselves and rise to the challenge. Embrace knowledge. Act in compassion. Speak in joy.

ROZI JAMES, ALEXANDRIAN HIGH PRIESTESS

I would say that it's up to each individual to decide how their Craft can benefit humankind. To my mind, no religion has an inherent purpose or benefit; it's down to its practitioners to do something with it – to determine its role or purpose for ourselves.

Having said that, Craft has the potential to revive the role of women in religious ceremonies and practices and to reconnect us all with the Divine Feminine, which over the centuries has been subjugated to the Divine Masculine in many parts of the world. I believe that the extraction of the Goddess from religious tradition and practice – and by extension, the extraction of women from religious authority – has done immense damage to the collective human psyche. Craft has an inbuilt reverence for female authority, sexuality, and creative power, which could go some way towards redressing that imbalance if we can channel it properly. And I think that would benefit everyone across all parts of society, whether they're spiritually minded or not.

I also believe that Craft has the potential to reconnect modern society with the natural world, to put us back in touch with our internal rhythms and help us find more ease in accepting the cycles we're all subject to. I would love to see the priesthood engage in more public ceremonies and play a more active role in our local communities. Having performed a number of handfastings, green burials, and house blessings, as well as guiding non-Initiates through transitional periods in their lives, I believe that Craft has great value as an alternative framework to help people navigate life's challenges and rites of passage.

But fundamentally, I think that Craft has as many purposes as it has practitioners, and that any religion has the capacity to be beneficial or damaging; it just depends on what each individual person chooses to do with it.

POPPA CAPP, ALEXANDRIAN WITCH

The religious tradition of Witchcraft has multifaceted purposes, encompassing existing as and maintaining one of the only authentic magical lineages, restoring and preserving society's connection with the natural world, and championing bliss and freedom for each individual, amongst other intents. Among its myriad objectives, the most paramount contribution of the Craft to humanity is the exaltation of the Goddess to Her rightful position as the preeminent divine force. This world is afflicted and wildly imbalanced, exhibiting a heavy skew in favor of the masculine, the patriarchal, and the tyrannical.

As one of the few extant religious orders venerating the Goddess, Witchcraft assumes a pivotal role in the world's healing, with each member of its clergy striving to be unwavering bastions who assert the power and prominence of women, the feminine, and individual autonomy; thereby addressing the prevailing illness and imbalance. Ultimately, through the veneration and assertion of the divine feminine, Witchcraft imparts an extraordinary gift to the world: the resurrection of equilibrium between the divine feminine and the divine masculine. This harmonious balance will unite humankind in a state of ecstasy and rapture..

Rev. Jacq Civitarese, Cabot HPs, Elder

I believe a religion that does not wait for the End-Times is very important, a religion that values life, living, and the balance between us and the God and Goddess... us and the natural cycles of the Sun and Moon. To me, humanity needs to know that the option of Witchcraft as a faith and practice is there for the accepting. Having options on the different ways to live, practice, communicate with the Divine, and align your spiritual path is of great significance.

And let us not forget the importance of the Priesthood and the great value of spiritual and religious counseling. There are many non-mundane energies and forces, topics of mystery, and experiences that need to be shared and communicated to an ethical clergyperson. In our Cabot Tradition, it is the Reverend High Priest/ess/X that does all from education to offering peaceful resolution on an array of topics to holding the Sabbats and Esbats. The role is meant to pass down the teaching of not only the Cabot Tradition and Laurie Cabot herself but also of the myths, rituals, ethics, healing ways, and the names of Goddesses and Gods of the Old Religions..

A Collection of Coven Photos

Priest wearing horned crown.

The Invocations.

Witches in repose.

High Priest Brian Cain.

The Witches' Dance.

High Priestess Elie Barnes holding court.

Blessing the wine.

Raising the cone of power.

Blessing the incense.

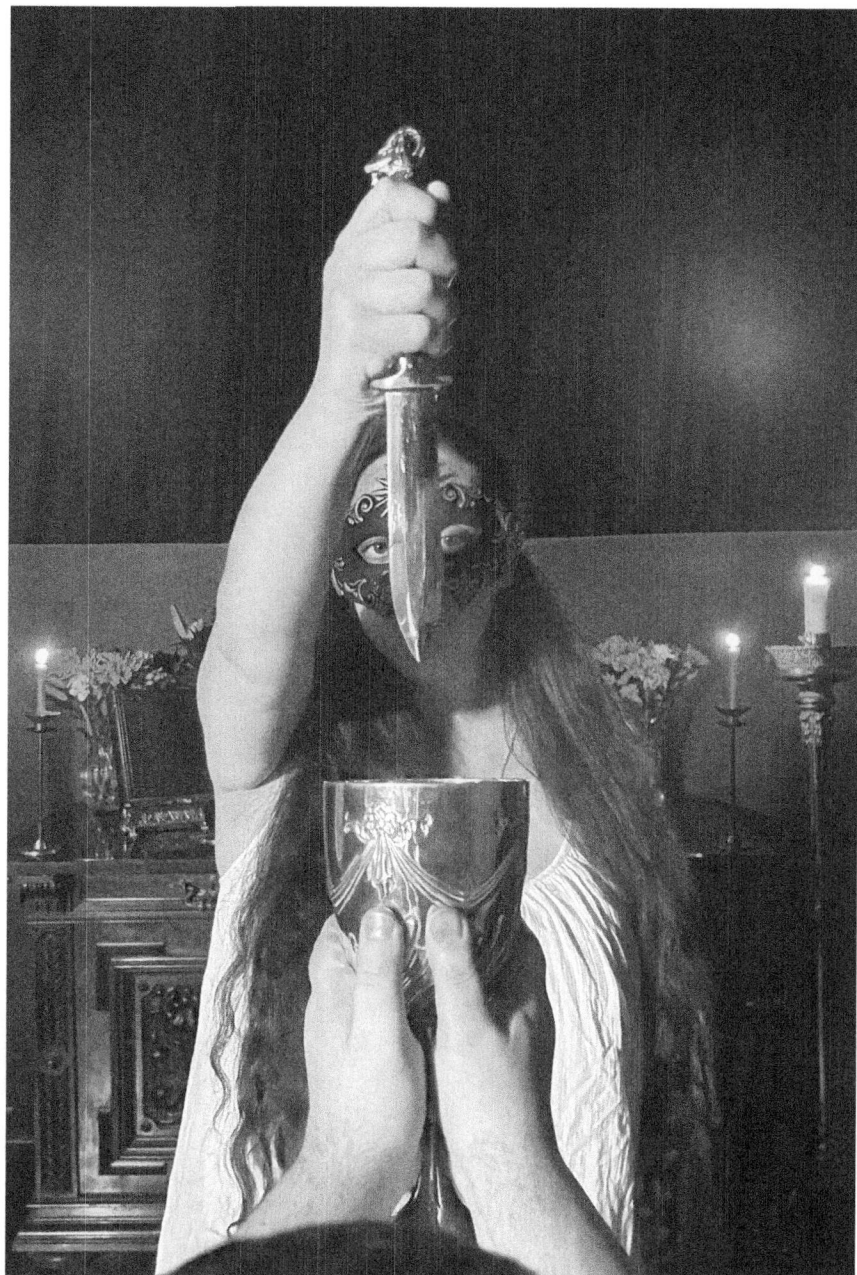

Blessing the wine.

High Priestess Val Hughes in Clanricarde Gardens

Christian Day hiding within the faerie realms.

Working with power.

Witches dance the circle round.

Putting on a spell.

The veiled priestess.

Priestess and Witch Carie Ewers guarding the covenstead.

The mysteries

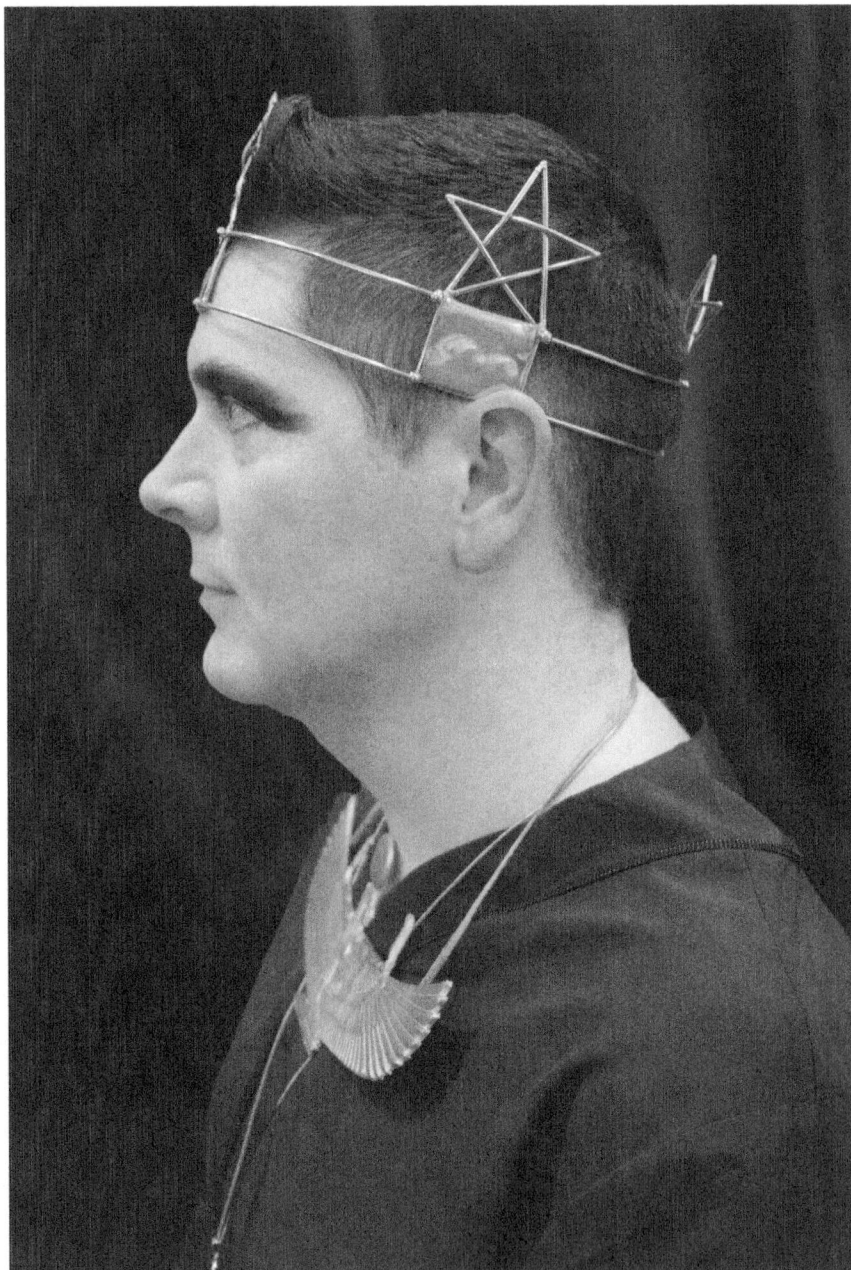

Brian Cain: a tribute to Alex Sanders

CHAPTER 9

The Grimoire Occultatum
Volume 2

AN OCCULT COLLECTION OF RITUALS, RECIPES,
SPELLS, EXERCISES, AND WITCHCRAFT LORE

The first *Grimoire Occultatum* is within my book, *Initiation into Witchcraft*. Volume 2 of that work delves deep into the core beliefs and principles that form the bedrock of Witchcraft and magic, offering both novices and seasoned practitioners a comprehensive guide to understanding and practicing this ancient art with authenticity and power.

At the heart of this Grimoire, you will find the Gods of Witchcraft, from ancient Egypt to medieval Europe. You will be introduced to the many forms of the Lady of the Night and the Horned God. I have also included an index on the forgotten Gods, many of whom are both contemporary and shrouded in mystery. This index serves not only as a reference but as a gateway to forming deeper connections with these powerful deities, enhancing your Witchcraft and magical practices.

Esbat rituals, or Full Moon Rites, are explored, emphasizing the significance of lunar power in Witchcraft. These rituals are designed to align your practice with the natural rhythm of the moon, harnessing the power of the Goddess, for in Witchcraft, the power comes through worship.

Spells and rituals form a substantial part of this volume. Each spell is presented with clarity, detailing the necessary steps, ingredients, and intentions. The rituals are diverse, covering a range of purposes from protection to prosperity, and focusing on everyday needs.

An exploration of the types of occult circles offers a practical guide to crafting these sacred spaces. Whether you are casting a circle for protection, focusing energy, or creating a boundary between worlds, this section provides essential knowledge and techniques for effective circle casting.

Lastly, the healing arts are given special attention, recognizing the integral role of healing in Witchcraft practice. From herbal remedies to energy work, this section is a testament to the power of Witchcraft in nurturing and restoring physical, emotional, and spiritual well-being.

The Grimoire Occultatum Volume 2 is more than just a section in a book; it is a journey into the heart of Witchcraft. It invites you to deepen your understanding, expand your skills, and connect more profoundly with the magic that permeates the world around us..

What Witches Believe

Some well-known and misunderstood beliefs about Witchcraft have been published and regurgitated. The issue being, as a secret society, some of our beliefs and laws are not for public consumption. However, the religion is practiced today by both non-Initiates and solitary practitioners, and some of our tenets are relevant in these circumstances—but please keep in mind, this is far from a complete or in-depth set of instructions, as that would require Initiation and training.

Witchcraft is a fertility cult, a Mystery Tradition, and a modern Priesthood of the Goddess known by some as Wicca, which is merely Old English for a Witch. Please keep in mind that Initiatory Witchcraft/ Wicca has little if nothing in common with the teachings of Scott Cunningham, the various do-it-yourself Witches of Llewellyn publications, and other such American movements. Initiatory Witchcraft is not paganism and primarily consists of the Gardnerian and Alexandrian lines of succession. Although today the religion is practiced by a wide range of people and traditions, the Priesthood remains its North Star, albeit in a cloak-and-dagger fashion.

DUALITY ⊕F THE DIVINE

Witchcraft emphasizes the worship of both a Goddess and a God. These deities are often viewed as equal and opposite forces, representing various aspects of life and nature. The Goddess is typically associated with the moon, fertility, and the Earth, while the God is associated with the sun, death, and resurrection. The notion that the sacred couple or a mother-father God concept is modern is far from the truth. After all, this is the pattern of creation found throughout nature, and if the Gods created nature, then of course it reflects creation itself. From Stone Age tribal groups to Ancient Empires, this was the natural way of looking at God before the Abrahamic faith took root in the world. Examples of this can be found in every culture—one must but look.

Isis and Osiris/Serapis

Isis and Osiris are one of the most well-known divine couples in ancient Egyptian religion. Osiris, the King, is associated with death and resurrection (just like the God of the Witches), and was the God of the Afterlife, while Isis, the Queen, is associated with fertility and motherhood, and was the Goddess of Magic and Healing. Later, during the Greco-Roman period, Isis was paired with Serapis—a syncretic deity who combined aspects of Osiris and the bull-god Apis, as well as attributes from Hellenistic deities. The cult of Isis and Serapis became popular across the Greco-Roman world, indicating the adaptability and enduring appeal of these deities.

Persephone and Hades

In Greek mythology, Persephone and Hades represent the cycle of the seasons. Hades, the God of the Underworld, abducts Persephone, but she is allowed to return to the world of men for part of the year—which corresponds to the growing season—while her time in the Underworld marks the winter months. Their story is a mythological explanation for the natural cycles of growth, decay, and rebirth and is similar to a legend of the Witches.

Dionysus and Ariadne

Dionysus, the God of wine, inspiration, madness, and ecstatic states, is often paired with Ariadne, who, after being abandoned by Theseus, is said to have been swept away by Dionysus and made his immortal wife. This pairing represents the joining of the physical with the spiritual and reflects themes of redemption and the transformative power of love and celebration.

Demeter and Zeus

Another Greek pair, Demeter and Zeus, are central to the Eleusinian Mysteries, a set of religious rites held in honour of Demeter, the Goddess of agriculture and fertility, and her daughter Persephone. Zeus, in his many roles, sometimes appears as Demeter's consort and represents authority and order. Eventually, the mystery cults merged, and these two were syncretized with Isis and Serapis, as were Hades and Persephone. This evolution further demonstrated the idea that Mother/Father God was a greater concept.

Shiva and Parvati

In Hinduism, Shiva and Parvati are a divine couple representing the balance between destructive and creative forces. Shiva, the Destroyer, is also seen as the regenerator, and Parvati, the Mother Goddess, embodies fertility and devotion. Together, they maintain the cycle of life and balance in the universe.

Frigg and Odin

In Norse/Germanic mythology, Odin and his wife Frigg, the Goddess of love and fate, form a powerful divine couple. Odin is associated with war, wisdom, and death, while Frigg is associated with prophecy, family, motherhood, fertility, love, and Witchcraft.

Cybele and Attis

In the Phrygian and later Roman traditions, Cybele, the Mother Goddess, was worshipped alongside Attis, a young God of vegetation and rebirth. Their story, which involves the death and rebirth of Attis, reflects the seasonal cycles of growth and decay.

Rhea and Cronus/Saturn

In Greek and Roman mythology, Rhea and Cronus (Saturn in Roman) were the Titan rulers of the universe before being overthrown by their children, led by Zeus (Jupiter). Cronus is associated with time and the harvest, while Rhea is associated with fertility and motherhood.

These divine pairs illustrate the rich tapestry of beliefs about the duality of the divine across different cultures. They represent life's opposing yet interconnected forces and aspects, such as life and death, joy and sorrow, and creation, and destruction, reflecting the complex nature of the human experience and the world around us. In modern Witchcraft, the divine couple is celebrated and honored through rituals and practices that seek to balance and harmonize these forces within the practitioner and the world.

The Practice of Magic

Magic is a significant aspect of both Gardnerian and Alexandrian Witch-craft. We practice theurgy, and magic is believed to be a holy gift from the Gods. Called the Art Magical, it is approached as divine. In Witchcraft, magic may be used for any need: healing, personal growth, transformation, and effecting change in the world. Magic is typically performed within a ritual context, with an emphasis on ethical considerations. The concept of magical Priesthoods has been a part of religious traditions since the dawn of man; these Priesthoods served as intermediaries between man-kind and the Gods. Priesthoods or cults are often reduced to myth from different periods and regions: the Cult of Isis, the Druids, the Cult of Dionysus, and the Magi, and even the Witch-Cult Hypothesis proposed by Margaret Murray, all relate in some way to the modern archetypes of the Witch as a magical Priest/ess.

ISIS

The ancient Egyptian Goddess Isis was venerated not just in Egypt but across the Greco-Roman world, especially from the Hellenistic period through the Roman Empire. The Cult of Isis was one of the last pre-Christian mystery religions to be practiced in the Roman Empire and existed well into the rise of Christianity. Priests and Priestesses of Isis were highly respected figures who played key roles in her worship, which included elaborate rituals and ceremonies. Initiation into the Mysteries of Isis promised personal salvation and an afterlife. The priesthood was responsible for a range of activities, from conducting daily rites to advising on matters of law and lore, and of course, fertility, healing, and magic.

DRUIDS

In the pre-Christian societies of Celtic Europe, Druids were members of a high-ranking religious class in various Celtic cultures. They are best remembered as religious leaders but also served as legal authorities, adjudicators, lorekeepers, healers, political advisors, and magicians. The Druids are credited with possessing a wealth of esoteric knowledge and a deep understanding of nature, theology, astronomy, and the seasons, which were critical to the agricultural societies they served. Julius Caesar's "Commentarii de Bello Gallico" provides one of the few contemporary descriptions of them, although it's worth noting his observations may have been influenced by his role as a Roman conqueror. The word Druid is, of course, like the word Witch in modern English. It is now used as an umbrella term for Celtic Priesthood. Once again, in many of these cases, myth prevails as a common theme in all religions.

DIONYSUS

The Cult of Dionysus is one of the most dramatic examples of a religious practice that celebrated the ecstatic and the divine through mysticism and magic, much in the same way a medieval Witches' Sabbat would be described. Dionysus, known as Bacchus in Roman mythology, was the God of wine, fertility, ritual madness, religious ecstasy, and theater. The cult associated with him was characterized by its use of intoxicants and ecstatic dance to remove inhibitions and social constraints, allowing individuals to return to a natural state and commune directly with the divine.

Priests of Dionysus, sometimes referred to as Bacchants or Maenads for the female adherents, were not just religious functionaries; they were participants in and leaders of the sacred rites known as Bacchanalia or Dionysia. These rites could be frenzied and wild, involving processions, music, dancing, and the consumption of wine, which was sacred to Dionysus. The mystery rites of Dionysus promised personal rebirth and transcendence to Initiates and were among the most secretive of all Greek religious practices.

MAGI

The Magi, originating from ancient Persia, were a class of priests within the Zoroastrian religion. Their name is the root of the modern term 'magic,' which is a testament to their association with mystical and esoteric knowledge. The Magi were revered as wise men, skilled in astrology, alchemy, and other occult sciences. They were also known for their ability to interpret dreams, which was considered a divine form of communication.

Herodotus, the Greek historian, describes the Magi as a hereditary priesthood responsible for religious and funerary practices. They were the keepers of the sacred fires, which represented the light of their deity, Ahura Mazda, and performed rites to sustain the cosmic order. The Magi were also political advisors and played a crucial role in the education of Persian royalty, teaching one generation to the next. The influence of the Magi extended beyond the borders of Persia, and their reputation for wisdom and divination was well-known in the classical world. The Christian New Testament, for instance, references the Magi as the "Wise men from the East" who followed a star to Bethlehem to pay homage to the newborn Jesus. This caste of priesthood is not like Witchcraft and demonstrates patriarchal ideas coming into play; however, it retained its roots in magic that developed long before they lost connection to the Goddesses of Babylon.

DIANA

Margaret Murray, an Egyptologist and anthropologist, introduced the controversial theory of a pan-European Witch-cult that worshipped pre-Christian deities such as Diana, the Goddess of the Hunt, and her consort, whom Murray equated with the Christian Devil. In her seminal work *The Witch-Cult in Western Europe*, published in 1921, Murray posited that the figures persecuted during the Witch Trials of the Early Modern period were adherents of a widespread, underground pagan religion. This religion, she claimed, involved the worship of a Horned God – an entity later demonized by the Christian Church as the Devil. According to Murray, Diana was the chief deity of this cult, and the Devil was her male counterpart; together, they represented a dualistic deity that governed fertility and nature.

While Murray's ideas were influential in the early development of modern Witchcraft Revival, some of her theories have been largely discredited by historians as a misinterpretation of medieval and early modern records (something that can be said about almost everyone in her field at that time). Her viewpoint that elements of pagan religion, folklore, and magic survived well into the Inquisition may not be all that far-fetched. After all, Church records, folklorist Charles Leland, and more modern research such as the works of Carlo Ginzburg all lend a new speculative eye on the possibility that a cult centered around Diana may have indeed existed regardless and the idea and myths surrounding it were not a modern invention.

Each of these magical Priesthoods or cults demonstrates how magic was originally embraced as a religious experience governed by a caste of people with a vocation to serve both men and Gods by wielding a portion of divine power..

THE BOOK OF SHADOWS

Witchcraft has its own Bible of sorts called *The Book of Shadows*. Many Initiates now just call it the Book to distinguish it from modern appropriations or labels. To set the record straight, The Book of Shadows is not a personal Grimoire but an already established one. It is hand-copied by each Initiate and contains our Rituals, Laws, Myths, and Magical systems. The actual BOS has never been truly published and, without training, would be useless anyway.

Gerald Gardner, a British civil servant and amateur anthropologist, is often credited with founding the modern Witchcraft religion in the 1930s and 1950s. Gardner claimed to have been initiated into a New Forest Coven, where he learned of the existence of a secret Cult of Witchcraft being practiced in England. After the 1951 repeal of the Witchcraft Act in Britain, Gardner formed his own Coven based on what he was taught by his New Forest Coven and his previous occult knowledge. Gardner was an Initiate of Freemasonry, the Ancient Order of

Druids, the O.T.O., and, of course, Witchcraft. He also had associations with Rosicrucianism and folklore.

Gardner's Black Book was initially a private collection of rituals, spells, and magical teachings that he received or composed, intended for use in his Bricket Wood Coven. It was a handwritten document, not intended for public dissemination, that evolved and grew into the Grimoire we now call *The Book of Shadows* or The Book. If it is unclear, The Book in folk/Witch lore was originally called the Black Book, and Gardner's first working title was *Ye Bok of Ye Art Magical*, but eventually, he would settle on The Book of Shadows, a name rumored to have been pinched from an old Sanskrit text—although I have not fully researched this claim. Regardless, it is a most fitting title for the Witch's Bible, formerly known as the Black Book. In keeping with old Gerald's sense of humor, it is also perfect for a magical text that really functions as a hint-book of reminders for the orally trained Initiate. *The Book of Shadows*, like most holy books, does have variations—this is partially due to the contributions of High Priestess Doreen Valiente, who added much to the poetry, and subsequent generations of Initiates then did likewise. This practice has, in recent years, been discouraged, with the Book being viewed as a historical document not to be changed. I think this is important as some versions have been filled with so much additional material that many Witches exposed to it never focus on the original material—which is the only book. In Alexandrian craft, we have kept the book pure; all additionally developed materials are put into the Coven or Second Book, as it has been dubbed.

Today *The Book of Shadows* has many versions but only one core. Some of these include Alexandrian, Sheffield, Whitecroft, Kentucky, Long Island, and the California Line Book of Shadows. In Gardner's time, the Book has been classified as Text A, B, and C. A was before Valiente, B with her contributions, and C the final version of Gerald Gardner after they split. Frankly, anything after C is not The Book of Shadows.

THE WITCHES' BLACK B⊕⊕K

The Myth of a Witches' Black Book, Bible, or Grand Grimoire can be found in legends, folklore, and trial records throughout Europe and the Americas. In many tales, the Black Book is said to be bound in a material as sinister as its contents—often the skin of unbaptized infants or the flesh of executed Witches. It was also believed that Witches' names were inscribed in this book by the Devil himself, signifying their pact with him and the renouncement of the Christian Religion.

These myths have been depicted in literature, such as the infamous *Malleus Maleficarum*, a 15th-century treatise on Witchcraft that arguably fueled the Witch Trials with its vivid descriptions of Witches' Sabbaths and demonic pacts. Nathaniel Hawthorne's *The Scarlet Letter* also references a "book that was the symbol of a solemn Covenant," which Hester contemplates being marked in, akin to the fabled Black Books of Witches.

In American folklore, the Witches' Black Book is often associated with the Salem Witch Trials, where the hysteria that gripped the Massachusetts Colony led to executions and a lasting legacy of cautionary tales about societal paranoia. The Black Book, in this context, represented irrefutable evidence of diabolism and a pact with the Devil himself.

In the folklore of the Appalachian Mountains, the Black Book often refers to a collection of wisdom, folk magic, healing, and local superstitions. The term "black" in the Black Book does not necessarily imply anything sinister as it might in other contexts; rather, it could simply denote the book's secret or hidden nature. To own such a book or to have such knowledge in the Appalachian region was to be a keeper of powerful, often esoteric local wisdom.

In some stories and superstitions, however, the Black Book is purported to have been obtained through a pact with the Devil, similar to Witch lore in other regions. In these tales, the Book provides the owner with certain powers, but at the risk of their soul or with other dire consequences. The concept of the Black Book in Appalachian folklore is emblematic of a time and place where self-sufficiency was crucial, and wisdom regarding the land and its resources was vital for survival. It represents a practical spirituality deeply connected to the mountains, the plants, and the cycles of nature.

Initiation and Coven Practice

Both traditions (Gardnerian and Alexandrian) are Initiatory and operate within a Coven structure. Initiation into a Coven is a significant step, marking a deep commitment to the tradition and its teachings. Covens are often led by a High Priestess and/or a High Priest.

The Oxford Dictionary defines Initiation as:

1. The action of admitting someone into a secret or obscure society or group, typically with a ritual: "rituals of initiation."

2. The introduction of someone to a particular activity or skill: "his Initiation into the world of martial arts."

3. The action of beginning something: "the Initiation of criminal proceedings."

You'll often hear that third definition, "the action of beginning something," offered by some would-be practitioners as justification for beginning Witchcraft in much the same way that they'd press the button on a microwave oven. However, that second definition is clearly not talking about the kind of Initiation involved in Witchcraft. The first definition of the "secret or obscure society" makes far more sense when you think back on the stories of Witches and other magical orders through the ages, especially when you consider such rites of passage are typically done both communally and through ritual—as Oxford also makes clear.

The second definition *does* go the extra mile to include Initiation as one's introduction to an activity or skill—the word "skill" being synonymous with the word "Craft." In other words, even if Witchcraft wasn't a Priesthood but was simply a skilled Craft, you still wouldn't be very good at it without the kind of Initiation and training that makes one a true master of their art. While you surely might be able to dabble in a Priesthood or a skill, you cannot Initiate yourself into either. The very idea of self-initiation was manufactured for the masses by reckless occult publishing houses seeking to propagate modern paganism and to sell books. It is not real, nor is it logically effective. The authors who have promoted self-dedication rites in their books had far more integrity and wisdom in understanding that dedication can allow someone to profess intent while refusing to cave to the idea that self-Initiation is even possible.

There is simply no such thing as self-initiation in Witchcraft, just as there's no such thing as self-initiation in Freemasonry, the Rosicrucian Orders, the Golden Dawn, the Order Templi Orientis, or any of the other Mystery Traditions. Witchcraft is not something beneath the dignity of the rest of Western occultism. We have many of the same standards, origins, and practices.

THE DEGREE SYSTEM

The degree system of Initiation has existed throughout the ancient and occult world, and it also is prevalent in modern Witchcraft. When Gerald Gardner referenced his Initiation into the New Forest Coven in 1939, he only ever mentions one ritual—that of the First Degree. The next account of Initiation from Gardner can be found in his book *High Magic's Aid* published in 1949. Here he gives us a basic format of the First- and Second-Degree Initiation rituals. He then briefly alludes to a Higher Degree by having the Witch of the story, Morven, says of the Last Degree, "All who have taken the second are qualified to work it, but tis the quintessence of magic and tis not to be used lightly and then only with one whom you love and are loved by. May it be done all else were sin."

Did Gardner perform the Rite with one he loved and whom he loved, or had he been told about this ritual without having undergone it himself? Of course, *High Magic's Aid* is also a work of fiction—he may have been properly veiling the higher degree. Regardless, it is clearly stated that the first two degrees are qualifiers for the optional rite. I speculate that the two degrees of Eleusis were the same. The First Degree offered entrance into the Mysteries. The Second Degree brought one further into their depths, and I believe the Third Degree existed for the full-time Priesthood of the site. After all, there had to be someone to operate and organize the rituals.

When Gerald Gardener established his first Coven, the three degrees were at the core of *The Book of Shadows*. All Initiates of Witchcraft accepted the Degrees as standard practice, but how Gardner initially distributed them seems to have been a matter of choice and circumstances. Some Initiates were given all Degrees at once, others he gave the Second and Third at the same time, and this became his common practice for Initiating new High Priestesses, recalling his book, *High Magic's Aid*. We know that Gardner discussed the First- and Second-Degree Initiations as the keys to entry into Witchcraft and the Third Rite as an optional act undertaken by Second Degrees. The common standard practice by most Gardnerian Witches today is to separate each Degree usually by year in the day, at minimum. In Gardnerian Witchcraft, the First-Degree Initiation inducts you into the cult as a Priestess and Witch. With this Degree, you are allowed to copy *The Book of Shadows*, attend regular meetings, and receive secret instructions in the arts of Witchcraft.

With the Second Degree, you essentially become a Coven Elder. A privilege which may include an office such as Coven Maiden or Lieutenant or Assistant to the High Priestess or High Priest. Members of this grade assist with the training and general operations of the Coven and often lead rituals. Different Craft lineages may vary regarding the rights and privileges of each Degree. At times, Second Degrees are allowed to form a Maiden Coven. Though this is generally only done for geographical reasons, these Maiden Covens are extensions of the original Coven. They're allowed to operate for the most part independently, but under the guidance of a Coven that has an established High Priesthood, until the leaders of the Maiden Coven receive their Third Degree, or the group is disbanded. The Third-Degree Initiation is what bestows the title, High Priest or High Priestess and the Third Degrees have the right to form their own autonomous Coven for any reason.

It is this autonomy of the Third Degree that is most essential and should not be forgotten in the Craft, as I believe it is the only thing that keeps us fertile. A Third-Degree Initiate may, however, choose not to hive off and establish their own Coven, but instead to remain within the original group as a valuable Elder and teacher. In Alexandrian Witchcraft, we have the same Three Degrees of Initiation as Gardnerians, as we both work from the original Book of Shadows. Our second book, however, is further developed and contains additional techniques and invocations not used in Gardnerian rituals. We also have an approach that is different than that of most Gardnerians. We generally performed the Second- and Third-Degree Initiation rites at the same time, which was the common practice of Alex and Maxine Sanders and their students. The First-Degree Initiation is one's entry into the Witch Cult itself.

The Second Degree is the penetration into the Mysteries, and the Third Degree is the celebration of the former two, a seal of power. I'm not sure if Alex was taught this practice or if he developed it for himself, but it is interesting that it mirrors the instructions given by Morven in *High Magic's Aid*. It is also reminiscent of how Gardner conducted his original Initiations, but regardless, it is the Alexandrian method. I was taught that the reason the Second and Third Degrees are kept together is that in truth, there are two sides of every coin, student and teacher, God and Goddess, darkness and light. The third is the seal of power only possible at the right moment. The First Degree brings the Initiate into contact with the fertilizing powers of the Craft, and the Second introduces them to the Underworld powers. As Alexandrians, we do not see the benefit of leaving our Priests of the Light captive in the Underworld, but there is another philosophical reason.

The two sides of the coin approach limit the use of the Second Degree as a carrot on a stick. Alex felt that this could become a control mechanism rather than a teaching tool. There is no benefit to either the Initiate or the Craft in Initiating someone to the Second Degree who will not also receive the Third. Keeping the Second and Third together also keeps pure the boundary between teacher and student. Some Covens find it beneficial to give greater responsibilities to their Second Degrees and allow for milestones to be given to the student, but I prefer the cut and dry approach.

Another aspect that may enlighten some Initiates is that First Degree Alexandrians can do everything Third Degrees can do save for Initiating to the Higher Degrees or founding their own Covens. For this reason, a Third Degree can easily start a new Coven with a First Degree of the opposite sex. We have many First Degrees who are incredibly proficient in their occult workings and may simply not wish to teach or run a Coven. But despite different points of view, all Covens, Gardnerians, and Alexandrians agree that the Three Rites are necessary in the Craft and that they are all full of potent power.

COVEN

A Coven is the name of a magical working group of practitioners of Witchcraft. The word Coven, like the word Witch, has obscure origins. Some believe it is derived from the Latin *conventus*, meaning a gathering or assembly. It shares a common root with words like convent, covenant, and conventicle. Historically, the Church believed in the existence of Covens, and the word appears throughout trial records. It is interesting to note, although pure speculation, we do find a few pieces of evidence of words relating to "Coven" within Britain in both place names and pre-Christian peoples. The Celtic chariot used by Queen Boudicca was called a *covinnus*. There is also a mysterious Goddess, Coventina. I've often found it curious that no writer on the subject ever speculated on the association between Coventina and the word Coven. Coventina is a Three Formed Goddess that was discovered near Hadrian's Wall.

In folklore and in trial records, Covens number anywhere from three to thousands, although more common were assemblies of thirteen Witches.

Regardless of the origin, this number is the standard for most Covens today. Although some Covens do choose to work in smaller groups of eight for the purpose of having a tight-knit magical group, these groups will generally very rarely introduce new Initiates. This often only happens when a former member has died or left.

The number thirteen is deeply rooted in folklore and superstition, earning the nickname the Devil's Dozen. It has been seen as bad luck, so much so that hotels avoided having a 13th floor. It also has its own holiday, Friday the 13th. It is possible that the Covens of Thirteen were simply Church propaganda; the Devil and his twelve Witches being a mockery against Christ and his twelve disciples. However, I believe the number thirteen has its occult origins from the moon. Before the Julian Calendar, we had thirteen moons or months, so the year was measured by moon cycles. When it became solar, we turned into twelve months. This solar-based system, being somewhat flawed, cannot escape the old year, and every so often a year still has thirteen moons. We refer to this additional moon as the Blue Moon. Witchcraft is a lunar cult, and being Priests and Priestesses of the Moon Goddess, we serve in orders of her number on most occasions; each Coven member represents the station of the ancient seasonal year.

In modern Witchcraft, Covens are alive and well with active groups throughout the world. The first recorded modern Coven is the New Forest Coven of England. Modern myths link this Coven to the alleged hereditary Covens found throughout Britain. Others believe the Coven was created by an occultist who believed profoundly in reincarnation and channeling. They were inspired by the works of Leland, Margaret Murray, and Reginald Scott, as well as the Witch Trials. Of course, it is possible the truth is somewhere in between. I believe that members of this Coven had family magic, folk knowledge of occult training, Initiation, and a belief in past lives, some of which were memories of having been Witches previously.

It is also important to realize they did make genuine contact with the Old Gods of Witchcraft. It is unquestionable that Gardner made contact in the New Forest, and it was from this group that he received the seeds he used to start his first independent group, the Bricket Wood Coven.

Covens traditionally have a boundary between them. This is called a Covendom. It means that the Coven has a territory that other Covens should respect. When a new Coven branches out, it is supposed to do so outside of this boundary. Today, this rule is difficult to follow. With Covens sometimes popping up on every street corner, this rule can still be practically applied in other ways. If one group is holding a meetup at a pub and you are aware, your group should pick another pub. The Witches' meeting place is called a Covenstead or simply The Temple in Alexandrian Craft. The location of both the Covenstead and Covendom are kept secret from outsiders, as is its membership list without express permission.

Covens generally meet on the full moons for Esbats, the full moons are celebrations of the Moon Goddess and a time to work magic. Witches also gather on the eight Sabbats. These are the eight seasonal festivals which are as follows: Halloween, the Winter Solstice, Candlemas, the Spring Equinox, May Eve, the Summer Solstice, Lammas, and the Fall Equinox. Some Covens celebrate the Sabbats on the full moons closest to them. Some also meet explicitly for training. Though there is no hard rule about this, Covens often have exterior work, whether it is an Outer Court or some sort of community outreach such as soirees, meetups, and public festivals. This is a way for the Coven to highlight itself to the local community so sincere seekers are aware of the Coven and know that Coven members are available for training; and that there is a place that seekers can go for Initiation. Alex and Maxine and the London Coven met every Saturday, so they would celebrate the full moons and Sabbats on the closest Saturday. When there was not a full moon or a Sabbat, other training would go on, though it is said that daily training often took place in their original groups, the London Coven and Maxine's Temple of the Mother.

I adopted this way of practicing in the New Orleans Coven. We meet once a week at the same time every week. I implemented this method because it makes it easier for people to get together and plan their lives. If a Coven is planning its meeting to try to be on the exact Sabbat or the exact full moon, they must constantly juggle their schedules to get together, and I have found in the past that this creates lower attendance. My Coven members, or anyone who joins this Temple, know that there is a day and time set aside that has not changed since we instituted this method. It is no different than joining a church. You know when the services are, and you have to make that time available if you wish to be a member. People who join the Coven realize that they need to keep that day and that time free, and if they cannot, they may as well not join the group.

It must also be mentioned that there are indeed secret Covens. These Covens have no exterior work and function subversively, often relying on more public Witches to send appropriate discrete members to them.

It cannot be overstated that the Craft remains a secret society, and as much FOMO as people might have, Witchcraft really and truly exists within its Coven and in the magical circle where those Witches meet and work together. A Coven is a cloistered Priesthood. The Priests and Priestesses of each Coven work autonomously, independently, and in isolation. Therefore, it exists within its boundary—not outside of it.

There is no singular great Witchcraft community. There is no one Alexandrian community or one Gardnerian community. Traditionally, Covens only meet at Grand Sabbats and only at the agreement of their leaders, and at these times we are able to reach past the boundaries of our cloistered groups and exchange knowledge and power, but then we always go back to working in private again. Some Covens have specialties. Most do not. Most classify as what I call a Worship Coven. This is a regular standard Coven. It meets to worship the Gods, for some training, for magic, and to celebrate the Sabbats and Esbats.

Some Covens are training Covens. Their sole focus is on training new Initiates, sometimes retraining former ones. These Covens will continuously go back to core systems, and training is continuously revisited, with an overemphasis on the basics of the Tradition.

Some Covens are healing Covens. Some Covens are experimental, and they do not want to focus on basic training. They want to explore systems of magic and so therefore they rarely Initiate and train new members because they want to play in the magics. Some Covens are power Covens. These Covens usually consist of all Third Degrees and once again, training is not emphasized: it is a Coven aimed at results. These Covens often meet purely for the work.

Coven governance is the responsibility of their High Priesthood, which consists of a High Priestess, High Priest, and possibly other Elders. Some Covens have single parents because no one suitable exists for the other roles. Other officer or duty roles may be created or utilized at the discretion of the High Priesthood.

Witches and Covens have their own sets of laws that instruct them on how to operate and navigate our magical groups. It is a great shame and stain on the Craft that not all Initiates respect them, and social media has become a tool of intrusion and abuse. The desire to be in some grand club, or running one, seduces many into ignoring autonomy, secrecy, and their actual oaths.

The Wheel of the Year

Witches celebrate the Wheel of the Year, comprising eight Sabbats or seasonal festivals. These include the Solstices, Equinoxes, and four cross-quarter days, which mark significant transitions in the natural world. Witches have eight festivals or holidays called Sabbats. The four Great Sabbats are Halloween, Candlemas, May Eve, and Lammas. These can be found in the Catholic practice but derived from the Celtic people of Britain and Ireland. The Lesser Sabbats are the stations of the sun—the Solstices and the Equinoxes—something celebrated in cultures worldwide. To Witches, the Sabbats are not merely holidays, but gateways filled with deep Mysteries and power.

HALL⊕WEEN

Halloween, October 31st, also called Hallowmas and Samhain, All Saints Eve, The Festival of Pomona, and many other names. This great Sabbat is observed on the eve of November 1st. This is the peak of the Witch's tide, also called the Tide of Recession, and is the Witch's New Year. This great Sabbat is governed by the Horned God of the Witches, who is the Lord of Death and Resurrection, King of the Underworld, and the Great Magus. Because it is influenced by the tides of water, It is associated with the Mighty Dead ancestors and nature, spirits, all Gods and Goddesses, angels, genii, elementals, and even demons. It is also strongly associated with astral travel, divination, and herbs.

THE WINTER S⊕LSTICE

The Winter Solstice, December 20th to 23rd, also called Yule, Christmas Feast of Mary, and Feast of Sol. This Sabbat begins the Tide of Earth (also called the Tide of Lustration) and ends that of Water. On the surface, the Winter Solstice celebrates the birth of the divine Sun God, and many Gods of the Sun are indeed associated with this season. To Witches, however, this is a Sabbat about the life-giving Mother. After all, the God is a child and fully requires her love and care. Because this Sabbat is associated with Earth, its magic centers around fertility, new beginnings, and resurrection.

CANDLEMAS

Candlemas, February 1st or 2nd, also called Imbolc, Imbolg, Oimelc, Saint Brigid's Day, and Lupercalia. This is the peak of the Earth's Tide, also called the Tide of Lustration. This great Sabbat is governed by the young fertile Horned God, the Resurrected One who seeks spiritual purification. Because the Sabbat is linked to the peak tide of Earth, it is associated with purity, protection, and renewal. This is the time to re-charge your inner powers through the Hermetic Arts and inner disciplines.

SPRING EQUIN⊕X

Spring Equinox, March 20th to 23rd, also called Ostara, Easter, Eostre's Day, Lady Day, and Bacchanalia. This is the second spring Sabbat, and it begins the Tide of Air and ends that of Earth. It is a lesser Sabbat and is governed by Sun Gods and fertility Goddesses. The Spring Equinox is a time of balance. Day and night are in equal measure and represented by the sun and moon in the romantic chase and struggle for power; the Goddess is young, wild, and free, and flees the sun as he pursues her. The Equinox is a time of fertility, inspiration, new beginnings, and natural balance.

MAY EVE

May Eve, May 1st also called May Day Beltane, Bealtaine, Walpurgis Eve, Rudemas, Floralia, and the Crowning of Mary on May 1st. For the Celts, this was the beginning of summer, and it was the last of the three Spring Rites. This is the peak of the Tide of Air or the Tide of Activation. This great Sabbat is governed by the Goddess as Queen and all Gods of love, sex, and fertility. Because it is influenced by the Tide of Air, it is associated with personal manifestation through creativity and your innermost desires. The sovereignty of May is that which you attain at the end of desire. It is the power within the true knowledge of the self.

THE SUMMER S⊕LSTICE

The Summer solstice, June 20th to 23rd, also called Midsummer, Litha, Vestalia, and St. John's Eve. This is a lesser Sabbat and begins the Tide of Fire and ends that of Air. It is governed by sun Gods, kings and queens, fathers, mothers, and Goddesses of nature. The Summer Solstice is a magical time to focus on mundane needs, health, vitality, strength, leadership, and abundance. This is the solar equivalent of a full moon but with a masculine fiery nature.

LAMMAS

Lammas, August 1st, also called August Eve, Lughnasa, Lughnasadh, Cerealia, and the Assumption of Mary, is the First Harvest festival and the peak of the Tides of Fire, also called the Tide of Consolidation. One of the Witch's Great Sabbats, this is a time of the grain Goddesses, Earth Mothers, and the dark sides of nature. The God represents the slain king myths like Tammuz and Ishtar, or Isis and Osiris. Lammas is a time of gratitude and service. The magical sacrifice is kept in mind as a desire for continued blessings, true love, kinship, and community. Witches use this time as a reminder to serve humanity and to focus on its abundance, protection, guidance, and health..

FALL EQUINOX

Fall Equinox, September 20th to 23rd, also called Michaelmas, Autumn Equinox, Mabon, Festival of Dionysus, and the Cornucopia. This is a Lesser Sabbat and begins the Tide of Water, also called the Tide of Recession, and ends that of Fire. This is the second harvest festival and, like its spring counterpart, it is a time of balance when light will begin to yield and fade in power. It is a celebration of life in the face of death. A time to remember that although the harvest is reaped, the seeds have been planted. It is a time to enjoy the first fruits and wine. The Fall Equinox is a great time to focus on the emotional world, dreams, and astral journeys.

ESBATS

Witches primarily gather on full moons to work magic and worship the Goddess. The etymology of "Esbat" is generally traced back to the Old French word "s'Esbattre," meaning "to frolic" or "to amuse oneself." Moon worship has been a significant aspect of spiritual practices across various cultures throughout human history. The moon, with its enigmatic presence and influence on the natural world, especially on the tides and agricultural patterns, has been revered as a powerful celestial entity.

In ancient Mesopotamia, the moon deity was known as Nanna in Sumerian mythology and Sin in Akkadian. Nanna was the son of Enlil and Ninlil, and the father of Utu, the Sun God, and Inanna, the Queen of Heaven. His primary temple was located in the city of Ur. *The Hymn to Nanna*" (Sumerian: "A balbale to Nanna") is one of the many pieces of literature that celebrate Nanna's influence over fertility and time.

The Greeks worshipped the moon under the name Selene, a Titaness who drove her moon chariot across the heavens. She is often depicted in art and literature, such as in the "Homeric Hymn to Selene," where her radiant beauty and her silver light that "banishes the darkness of night" is praised.

In Roman religion, the moon was personified by Luna, the divine embodiment of the moon. She had a temple on the Aventine Hill, which was built in the 6th century BCE. Luna is often mentioned in Roman literature, with poets like Ovid in his "Fasti" discussing her phases and her importance to the calendar.

In Egyptian mythology, the moon was associated with several Gods, most notably Khonsu, a God of the moon and time. His name means "traveler," indicating the perceived motion of the moon across the sky. The temple of Khonsu in Karnak is a testament to his worship. *The Book of Gates*, a funerary text, references Khonsu as one who illuminates the Underworld, guiding the dead to their afterlife.

In Chinese mythology, Chang'e is the Moon Goddess, and her story is one of great sacrifice and transcendence, as told in various Chinese texts and poems. The "Chu Ci," a collection of Chinese poetry, contains references to the moon and its deity, reflecting on its beauty and its celestial power.

The Celts also had a lunar Goddess, known as Arianrhod, who was associated with the moon and stars. She is a figure in the medieval Welsh narrative *Mabinogi*, particularly in the fourth branch of the tales, where she presides over the realm of Caer Arianrhod, symbolically linked to the Corona Borealis.

In Hinduism, the Moon God Chandra is featured in texts like the *Rigveda*, where he is described as bright and shining. The moon plays a vital role in the Hindu calendar and rituals, with specific phases considered auspicious for various religious activities..

The Witches' Creed

The Witches' creed or The Wiccan Rede, "An it harm none, do what ye will," is a guideline for ethical conduct. You'll find no lack of individuals who claim to be Witches spouting off about how the Rede is a Wiccan law or a Wiccan belief and that real Witches curse, and real Witches hex. Some say the Rede is impossible to follow or unrealistic. Clearly, everyone harms; it cannot be avoided, so therefore it is not logical. In recent years, people increasingly desire Witchcraft to be darker, non-religious, and free from ethics, something that reflects our current social climate.

I also believe this has happened before many, many times. Authenticity has nothing to do with cruelty. Predominantly, the arts have been used benevolently throughout history, but when people become powerless, disenfranchised, or desperate, they become hostile regardless of the medium. A healer is a thousand times more powerful than an assassin, and a Witch knows this to be true. Like the three-fold law, there is some misunderstanding surrounding the creed. The creed is not a 10 Commandments-style law. In Witchcraft, the word creed means advice or counsel. The Witches' Rede, Witches' Creed, or Wiccan Rede became a useful tool for public education, but over time lost its original purpose. In the face of a cosmopolitan Witchcraft world, the Creed is good advice and wise counsel correctly interpreted. It means that you should fulfill your true will. You should do as you will because you are a magical person and magic is about conformity with your will, and Initiates can fulfill their will without having the intent of causing harm. In other words, if you want to make a billion dollars and you're given the option of destroying an Indigenous tribe in the rainforest, then the

Creed discourages you from doing that because your true will comes from your Higher Self, which is of the divine creative force. Your true will would never want to destroy for desire. That is false and will poison the ego. There's no reason why you cannot achieve your will without causing harm. So, the intent to harm should not be there.

The Creed is also just a good way to live unless you desire to be an unkind, corrupt individual. I think most people like to think of it as just applying to magic. It doesn't just apply to magic. It is a philosophy. I personally do not want to be friends with or know someone who wants to live in a way other than this. If you want to go around harming people, whether it's magically or with a gun, if you want to kill people, maim, or abuse them, if your life is focused on revenge and destruction, you're not someone I want to know or would consider trusting. It is a huge burden to carry hate in your heart, and on the subject of checks and balances, everything you do in your life is a record of you. We all must ask ourselves, what record do we want to have? What do you want to contribute upon the divine stage?

The Creed can be found in many forms. The Golden Rule is "Do unto others as you would have them do unto you." In Buddhism, we have "Hurt not others, in ways that you yourself would find hurtful." From Egypt, the Goddess Maat proclaims, "Do to the doer to make him do." I have said before and I will say again that the only ethics in Witchcraft is intent. It is your intent, followed by actions that are good or bad, causing harm by chance or for survival, which lacks intent bent towards cruelty. The lion does not kill the zebra to be cruel, but because he is hungry and does not have the option of becoming vegan; the death is not always kind. But the lion's aim is not malicious by nature any more than the average cheeseburger eater's aim. If you end a relationship because you are not happy in it, it's not wrong that you harm the other person emotionally. Most of us enter relationships with good intentions.

The origins of the Creed are often attributed to The Book of the Law by Aleister Crowley, where it says, "Do what thou will shall be the whole of the Law." Gerald Gardner had some connection with the O.T.O.

and Aleister Crowley, so it is not unreasonable to make the link between these words from Crowley and the Creed. In fact, their meanings are quite similar. However, in his book Witchcraft Today, Gardner gives us another source entirely. He says, "Witches are inclined to the morality of the legendary Good King Pausole; do what you like as long as you harm no one, but they believe a certain law to be important. You must not use magic for anything that will cause harm to anyone. And if to prevent a greater wrong being done, you must discommode someone and you must do it only in a way that will abate the harm."

Good King Pausole is a 1901 literary creation of French novelist Pierre Louÿs (1870-1925). In his novel, the king has a statement, "Thou shalt not harm thy neighbor; this being understood, do as you wouldest." We don't absolutely know for sure if this was the inspiration for the Creed or if it was Aleister Crowley, but these aren't the only possibilities. The Hippocratic Oath is a good example where we get the phrase, "Do no harm." Saint John said, "Love and do as ye will in truth."

Regardless of its origins, I think we can safely say this is a universal philosophy and has its roots in the occult and many, many religions. There is cause and effect in everything we do; Witches take on the mantle of co-creator, and in that role, we must reflect on what we are contributing to the universe. We must also accept full responsibility for what we unleash in the reality of our own design. Witches know we create our heaven and our hell. In a world filled with disease, famine, greed, war, cruelty, and mass extinction, I think we could all use a little bit more "An it harm none, do what ye will."

THE THREEFOLD LAW

The Threefold Law has been published by countless authors who have collectively invented a new concept based entirely on misinformation. This is often put out as one of the foundational beliefs in Witchcraft, and this is untrue. the concept is that whatever you do is going to come back to you, threefold. In essence, it's karma with a strange mathematical equation. So, if you do something good, it'll come back to you threefold.

If you do something terrible, it will come back to you threefold. There is a Mystery that is taught in one of the Initiations that is relevant for Initiates, and I do believe this is where the public idea of the Threefold Law originates. The confusion arose when individuals began interpreting the Craft without having experienced it.

What we do believe in as Initiates is that we must take full responsibility for everything, good and bad. We are in control of our choices, actions, and reactions. If you throw a pebble into a pond, it will ripple. The number three is very potent and often used in our magic, but we do not believe in a judgmental system. Witches know that we are writing the script, and as a species, we are all mere actors in a great play written by ourselves. Those who follow the public Threefold Law are giving themselves a check and balance, and I see no harm in that, nor do I ridicule them. It is simply not a concept I share with them.

ΘATHS AND SECRECY

Witchcraft places a strong emphasis on mystery and the esoteric aspects of the practice. Some teachings and rituals are kept secret and are only revealed to Initiates. The Oath is one of the most magical spells in the Craft; there is no greater sin than oath-breaking. It is believed that Witches who break the sanctity of the oaths they chose to take will have their powers turn against them, as it is an utter destruction of the self by the self.

Sacred oaths played a crucial role in the ancient world, especially among the Greeks, Romans, Celts, and Egyptians, serving as a Covenant between the Gods and mankind. These oaths were not mere formalities but were deeply ingrained in the cultural and religious practices of these civilizations, often invoking the wrath of the Gods upon oath breakers.

In ancient Greece, oaths were a fundamental part of society and religion. Swearing by the Gods was common in legal, political, and personal contexts. The Greek Gods, like Zeus, were seen as guardians of oaths and avengers of perjury. Breaking an oath was not just a legal offense but a sacrilege, attracting divine punishment.

Similarly, in ancient Rome, oaths had significant religious and social implications. The Romans believed that the Goddess Fides (Faith) oversaw oaths and their fulfillment. Violating an oath was considered a crime against the Gods, leading to divine retribution and societal scorn.

The Celts, with their rich oral tradition, regarded oaths as sacred. Druids, the priestly class, often administered oaths, and breaking them could result in exclusion from the community or magical repercussions.

A Celtic Curse upon Oathbreaker (with variations) was as follows:

May the earth open and swallow you.
May the Sky fall upon you.
May fire consume you.
May the sea rise and wash you away.

In ancient Egypt, oaths were integral to both daily life and the afterlife. The concept of Ma'at, or cosmic order, underpinned their understanding of oaths. Violating an oath disrupted Ma'at, inviting chaos and displeasure from the Gods.

Transitioning into the realm of occult societies such as the Hermetic Order of the Golden Dawn, Ordo Templi Orientis (O.T.O), Rosicrucians, and Gardnerian and Alexandrian Witchcraft, the sanctity of oaths takes on a different but equally significant dimension. These groups, emerging from a blend of mystical, religious, and philosophical traditions, place immense importance on secrecy and fidelity to their teachings and membership.

In these societies, oaths were not only a means of binding members to secrecy but also a tool for magical and spiritual development. The breaking of an oath was seen as a profound moral and spiritual failing. These societies believed that oath-breaking led to metaphysical consequences, affecting one's spiritual journey and standing within the group.

For instance, in the Golden Dawn, members took oaths of secrecy regarding the teachings and rituals. Breaking these oaths was thought to invite personal catastrophe and spiritual degradation. Similarly, in the O.T.O and Rosicrucian orders, oaths symbolize a deep commitment to the mystical path, and their violation is seen as a betrayal of the spiritual self and the magical order.

In Gardnerian and Alexandrian Witchcraft, oaths of secrecy and loyalty are central. The breaking of these sacred vows was considered the gravest of sins, believed to attract the wrath of the Gods and banishment from one's Coven. Gerald Gardner, the founder of Gardnerian Witchcraft, emphasized the importance of oaths in his teachings. His Initiation rituals involved the swearing of oaths to ensure secrecy and fidelity to the Coven. Gardner believed these oaths were crucial for protecting the Craft and its practitioners, especially in a time when Witchcraft was misunderstood and often maligned. Anecdotal stories about Gardner often highlight his dedication to the oaths he took and administered. In his biographies, such as Philip Heselton's *Witchfather,* there are references to Gardner carefully instructing Initiates about the seriousness of the oaths they were about to take. He reportedly warned of magical consequences for those who broke these sacred vows.

Alex Sanders, known as the founder of Alexandrian Witchcraft, also placed great emphasis on oaths. Sanders, often called the "King of the Witches," believed that the strength of a Coven lay in the integrity of its members, which was upheld through their oaths. These oaths were the same as those taken in Gardnerian Witchcraft, demanding secrecy and loyalty. Sanders' approach to oaths was somewhat more theatrical compared to Gardner's. There are stories, such as those found in June Johns' *King of the Witches: The World of Alex Sanders*, depicting Sanders performing elaborate rituals where oaths were a central element. He believed that the act of taking an oath was as important as the words spoken, infusing the practice with a sense of solemnity and power. While both Gardnerian and Alexandrian Witchcraft share similarities in their use of oaths, there are subtle differences. Gardnerian oaths tend to emphasize tradition and lineage, reflecting Gardner's vision of an ancient and unbroken Witchcraft tradition. Alexandrian oaths, while similar in content, are often delivered with a flair that reflects Sanders' charismatic personality.

In both Gardnerian and Alexandrian traditions, oaths are more than mere words; they are the glue that binds the Coven, the promise of fidelity to the art magical, and a symbol of trust and respect among practitioners. The stories of Gerald Gardner and Alex Sanders, with their unique approaches to these oaths, illustrate the deep reverence these traditions hold for the sacred promises that lie at the heart of their practice.

Across these diverse cultures and societies, the theme remains consistent: oaths are sacred, and their violation is one of the worst offenses a person can commit, attracting divine and societal condemnation. This universal perspective underscores the profound respect for the spoken word and the fear of the consequences of breaking sacred vows, whether in the eyes of the Gods or within the close-knit communities of occult societies.

AFTERLIFE

Rebirth is a pivotal concept in Witchcraft, often equated with reincarnation, although the two carry distinct nuances within the Craft, setting it apart from beliefs such as those found in Buddhism. When Witches pass from this world, it is believed they enter the Summerland, a realm also known by various names like Tir na nog, Paradise, Elysian Fields, the Underworld, or even Heaven. Regarded as the other side, Summerland is seen as a place of reunion, rest, and renewal, where souls celebrate with departed loved ones before embarking on their next incarnation or journeying to another plane of existence.

This cyclic notion of life, death, and rebirth is not only central to Witchcraft but also a shared belief among the early figures of the Witchcraft Revival, such as Gerald Gardner, Alex and Maxine Sanders, Sybil Leek, Robert Cochrane, and Charles Cardell. These pioneers recognized each life as an opportunity for the soul's learning and spiritual growth, where death transitions the soul rather than ending its journey. Rituals in Witchcraft are steeped in these cycles, mirroring the natural rhythms of the earth and the cosmos, and embodying the soul's perpetual voyage across incarnations. Witchcraft lore often speaks of Initiates seeking to reunite across lifetimes, frequently within the same Coven, to continue their sacred work together. Patricia Crowther, in her book *Covensense*, references Gerald Gardner's discussions on reincarnation, suggesting these ideas likely stemmed from the New Forest Coven and were expressed early in Gardner's work, particularly in his 1940 publication, *A Goddess Arrives*.

The rebirth of Witchcraft in modern times, I believe, is a tapestry woven from family folk magic, the reincarnation belief of past lives as Witches, and communication with the old gods of the Craft. This, combined with the Western occult tradition's Chain of Initiation, formed a channel for the resurgence of the Goddess religion and its Priesthood, carrying forward the concept of reincarnation and inherent knowledge from bygone eras.

Witchcraft doesn't impose a rigid framework for the afterlife; rather, it embraces a flexible belief in rebirth. Witches may return to a new human existence, inhabit an animal form, or even experience life on a distant planet or alternate plane. While the soul is viewed as eternal and imperishable, perspectives on the afterlife vary among practitioners. Witches also believe in the existence of spirits and ghosts, which are acknowledged in some of the rites. The Craft holds that while humanity doesn't possess all the answers to the mysteries of the afterlife, Witches create their own realms of joy and suffering, mirroring life's cycles within a greater cosmic circle.

Our ancestors recognized the complexity and simplicity of death. The ancient Egyptians, for example, believed the soul divided upon death, with components such as the Ka and Ba, some of which were connected to the physical body like a ghost, while others, like the higher self, journeyed with Ra. They aimed for the union of these aspects of the soul. The Celts held a belief in a cycle where life in this world alternates with life in the next—a form of reincarnation or transmigration of the soul. Doreen Valiente, in her *An ABC of Witchcraft Past and Present*, cites Diodorus Siculus, who reflects on the Druids' belief in the soul's immortality and its eventual return to a new bodily existence, reminiscent of Pythagorean doctrine.

As I have mentioned previously, it is my belief that the formation or rebirth of the Witchcraft religion and its revival in modern times was the weaving of magics—a continuation of the Western occult Golden Chain of Initiation and a conduit for the Religion of the Goddess and her priesthood to resurrect. All these concepts that exist throughout humanity exist for a reason they are universal. No human has all the answers nor does anyone Witch. What all Witches firmly believe in is that we create our own heavens and hells and that the cycles of life are mirrored in the afterlife. They are not separate cycles but part of a greater circle. This poem by Ella Wheeler Wilcox expresses deeply to me what Witches believe:

The Law

The sun may be clouded, yet ever the sun
Will sweep on its course till the Cycle
is run. And when into chaos the system is hurled
Again shall the Builder reshape a new world.

Your path may be clouded, uncertain of your goal:
Move on for your orbit is fixed to your soul.
And though it may lead into darkness of night
The torch of the Builder shall give it new light.

You were. You will be! Know this while you are:
Your spirit has traveled both long and afar.
It came from the Source to the Source it returns
The Spark which was lighted eternally burns.

It slept in a jewel. It leapt in a wave.
It roamed in the forest. It rose from the grave.
It took on strange garbs for long aeons of years
And now in the soul of yourself It appears.

From body to body your spirit speeds on
It seeks a new form when the old one has gone
And the form that it finds is the fabric you wrought
On the loom of the Mind from the fibre of Thought.

As dew is drawn upwards, in rain to descend
Your thoughts drift away and in Destiny blend.
You cannot escape them, for petty or great,
Or evil or noble, they fashion your Fate.

Somewhere on some planet, sometime and somehow
Your life will reflect your thoughts of your Now.
My Law is unerring, no blood can atone
The structure you built you will live in alone.

From cycle to cycle, through time and through space
Your lives with your longings will ever keep pace
And all that you ask for, and all you desire
Must come at your bidding, as flame out of fire.

Once list' to that Voice and all tumult is done
Your life is the Life of the Infinite One.
In the hurrying race you are conscious of pause
With love for the purpose, and love for the Cause.

You are your own Devil, you are your own God
You fashioned the paths your footsteps have trod.
And no one can savve you from Error or Sin
Until you have hark'd to the Spirit within.

— Ella Wheeler Wilcox

Healing in Witchcraft

Witchcraft has been closely associated with healing. Witches, often portrayed as wise ones or healers, were believed to possess extensive knowledge of medicinal plants and natural remedies. This knowledge was frequently passed down orally through generations and today survives mostly through folklore, old herbals, and almanacs. This has at times been referred to as wort cunning and is a Craft unto itself. In the ways of magic, it falls under incense, drugs, and wine. One must be careful when employing herbs medicinally; however, using herbs safe for the kitchen can be a safe way of blending medicine with magic, a practice that was employed by healers in the ancient world up to and even into the Renaissance.

Here is a list of common kitchen herbs and teas often used for healing purposes, along with how they are typically used. They are generally safe for most people, but it's important to consider individual allergies and health conditions before using them for medicinal purposes. Also, they are meant to complement traditional medical treatments, not replace them.

Chamomile

Used in tea form, chamomile is known for its calming properties. It's often used to relieve stress, aid in sleep, and soothe digestive issues.

Ginger

Ginger can be brewed into tea or used in cooking. It's known for its anti-inflammatory properties and is often used to ease nausea, aid digestion, and reduce soreness.

Peppermint

Peppermint tea is used for its soothing effect on the digestive system. It can help relieve symptoms of irritable bowel syndrome, nausea, and indigestion.

Turmeric

Commonly used in cooking, turmeric has potent anti-inflammatory and antioxidant properties. It can be used in tea or meals to help reduce inflammation and pain, especially in conditions like arthritis.

Cinnamon

Used both as a spice and in tea, cinnamon has anti-inflammatory and antioxidant effects. It may help regulate blood sugar levels, reduce heart disease risk factors, and has a warming effect on the body.

Thyme

Thyme is used in cooking and as a tea. It's known for its antibacterial and antimicrobial properties, making it beneficial for soothing sore throats and coughs.

Rosemary

Often used in cooking, rosemary has antioxidants and anti-inflammatory compounds. It's thought to boost the immune system and improve blood circulation.

Sage

Sage tea is known for its throat-soothing properties. It's also used for its digestive benefits and to reduce inflammation.

Lavender

Commonly used in tea, lavender is renowned for its calming and relaxing properties. It aids in reducing stress, and anxiety, and promoting restful sleep.

Lemon Balm

Lemon balm tea is known for its ability to ease stress, help with sleep, and soothe indigestion.

Witches were also often linked with animal husbandry, believed to have a deep understanding and connection with nature and animals. This connection was sometimes viewed suspiciously, with tales of Witches having the power to curse or bless livestock.

In terms of magical methods, it was believed that Witches could perform spells or rituals to ensure the health and fertility of animals, a critical aspect in agrarian societies. The custom of driving the herds through two sacred fires to smudge them on Beltane was a common folk tradition in Britain and Ireland. This is also the time they would be transferred from their winter pastures to their summer pastures.

Midwives, often women, played a crucial role in childbirth and women's health. Their extensive knowledge of herbs, childbirth, and women's reproductive systems often overlapped with the practices considered magical. Midwives used various herbs and rituals to ease childbirth, manage pain, and ensure the well-being of the mother and child. This often placed them in a precarious position, as any complications could lead to accusations of Witchcraft.

In the beginning of the modern Witchcraft Revival, Witches began tapping into their roots as healers, and it is said, not all Witches are healers, but all Witches work to heal. The Bricket Wood Coven absolutely did do healing magic, and some Gardnerian Witches would go on to focus on this more extensively. Eleanor Rae Bone and her London Coven were particularly known as a healing Coven, partially due to the fact that she was a nurse and constantly encountered the need.

Alex Sanders was known for his healing abilities. He reportedly was able to cure various afflictions through different methods. For instance, he was said to have gotten rid of warts by wishing them on someone else, cured a man of heroin addiction, and healed a woman of cystitis simply by laying his hands on her head and willing the affliction away. Additionally, he was reported to have cured a woman of cancer by sitting with her in a hospital for three days and nights, holding her feet and channeling healing power.

Maxine Sanders' group, the Temple of the Mother became legendary for teaching the healing arts. At one point in time, a day of the week was set aside solely for the purpose of training and practicing this art. Like anything in the Occult or the Craft, training is required. This book does not take the place of a Witch or Healer who has the necessary training and experience to guide you into intense healing work. Most of the content I am giving you is safe, easy to do, and harmless. Beginning the work of healing should start with issues like the common cold, a headache, or mild depression. Please do not try to cure cancer immediately.

Many methods for healing have been developed through generations of modern Witches and Covens. In the beginning, Witches would simply use spells and herbs, whether creating talismans, healing dolls, sending power, or one's fetch, the Goddess was often invoked for the works of healing as she is the primordial, fertile, life-giving force. You can also choose to work with Gods of healing such as Isis and Serapis, Apollo, or the Dagda.

If the subject has their own God or Goddesses and is involved in the work, it would make the most sense to use those instead of your own. This, of course, is situational, and everyone involved would need to be open to them working with them. Before you get involved in any serious cases you must confront the reality of death as a possible outcome.

It must be remembered that death is inevitable it is not a sign of weakness, punishment, or failure. When it is your time not even magic can save you. Fate is a concept in our liturgy; it is not constant or continual we control most of our lives but some moments our beyond the greatest of magicians.

Diagnosing an illness is also a very important part of healing work-First, it must be said that nothing takes the place of medical science go to your doctor and have any concerns looked at. Other practices are meant to complement or aid the healing process, be it for yourself or another subject. Do not work with anyone until they see a doctor— to do so would be reckless and unwise. Magical Diagnosing is used in conjunction with the professional one. Its purpose is partially just to sync the healer with the subject's obstacles. Yes, you can look at the issue psychically through aura readings or astral projection if we are working remotely. Divination may also be used for this purpose including Tarot, Runes, I-Ching etc. It is also wise to perform divination before a healing to make sure you are taking the correct approach.

❝❝If you wish to practice the healing arts you should begin with yourself.

"Cur ate ipsum "—Physician heal thyself— is a Latin quote every Witch should know. Today the subject of self-care is all the rage! Self-care and personal healing encompass a holistic approach, integrating physical, emotional, and spiritual well-being. Exercise is viewed not just as a physical activity but to harmonize the body and mind, often incorporating mindful practices like yoga or nature walks. A balanced lifestyle and diet are considered crucial, with an emphasis on nature as the healer incorporating herbs and healing foods. Spells, talismans, and charms can certainly be employed for oneself or others preferably in full Coven. It is important not to obsess over magical workings. Being thankful for good health, your loved ones, and asking for continued blessings—being vigilant over your life— is magically necessary. Ritual captivity is not. Far too many individuals fall victim to the cages of desire. Because of fear, healing can equally have this pitfall. The last thing one wants to invoke upon themselves is a constant need for healing.

Meditations are very useful for healing and can also be used for remote healing when you cannot meet with the subject. Today one can use tools like Skype to put the subject through a guided meditation or to give instructions.

A popular occult method is the Middle Pillar Ritual which has several purposes but helps to energize the body and bring balance. Once again, always make sure the ailment does not live within. A parasite receiving energizing power is not helpful.

When working on a subject you must choose whether they are involved at all. You do not need permission to heal, although it is customary to do so. Among Witches, one would assume another Witch already has a plan. Healing is not an area of fun or for sticking one's nose in but one that should be approached with compassion, wisdom, service, and respect. It may be best not to tell them and really look at the situation to ensure you do not make things worse. If they have requested it, you may choose to make and give them a talisman or work with power (laying on of hands). Or you might work a spell and use silence—this can at times be the most potent, depending on the situation. It is also important to know when you cannot or should not help. Giving false hope is never beneficial.

Ways of working with the subject in person:

- Divination

- Guided Meditations

- Rituals

- Laying on of hands

- Talismans

- Herbs, teas, food.

- Counseling

- End-of-life care

Ways of working with the subject remotely:

- Scheduled mutual meditations

- Guided meditations through Skype or other programs. This can also be used for counseling and divination if you choose.

- Talismans

- Objects of familiarity, pictures, hair, dolls, etc.

- Herbs, teas, and foods

MAGICAL TIMES FOR HEALING

In Witchcraft, the Tides of the Moon should be considered. Cancers, blood clots, obstructions, and other abnormalities would be removed during a waning moon. A waxing moon would be best for recovering from a heart attack, stroke, or extreme blood loss. Use common sense: am I withering something or growing and fertilizing something?

In planetary magic, mental or emotional issues are best treated on Monday for the moon. Physical healing is governed by the Sun; therefore, Sunday is the time for healing magic. One could work with the day and hour of the sun particularly in the creation of talismans. Likewise, the Stations of the Sun can be used waxing before noon and waning afterward.

I have already mentioned that sometimes one must know when they cannot or should not help. If the subject needs to see a doctor—be it mental or physical— and refuses to do so, it would be advised to not get involved. Using all available wisdom and doing no harm are the first rules. In many situations, we work magic to enhance the skills of the doctor involved, to guide the prognosis or surgical scalpel.

In the healing arts, there is another aspect few consider: death. Sometimes death is unavoidable, and it is our job to give comfort and religious counsel. You should never underestimate the simple acts of love, kindness, and patience when dealing with the sick or dying. Every moment is intense until they recover or except the impeding Great Initiation.

ELEMENTAL HEALING MEDITATION

Find a comfortable position: Sit or lie down in a quiet place where you won't be disturbed.

Cleansing with Air:

Imagine a gentle breeze caressing your skin.

With each breath, feel the air purifying your Body.

The breeze slowly becomes stronger until it is a gushing wind removing all illness from you.

Energizing with Fire:

Picture a warm, glowing light of a fire within you.

Feel this warmth spreading throughout your body, revitalizing and energizing you.

The fire then becomes all-consuming around you destroying anything harmful to you within your body.

Emotional healing with Water:

Envision a calm body of water and a pleasant waterfall.

Immerse your naked body into the water float on your back for a while swim about. Eventually go to the waterfall and imagine this water flowing over you, soothing your emotions, and bringing peace.

Drink the water and feel it nurturing your body with vitality and renewal.

Grounding with Earth:

Close your eyes and visualize yourself connecting with the earth beneath you.

Feel its stability and nurturing energy grounding your body. Connect with its vibrations of stone and silence. Imagine roots growing from your body into the deep rich fertile soil nurturing and feeding your body.

Illumination with Light:

Visualize a bright, Divine healing light shining down on you, the light of the Gods.

Feel this light bringing clarity, healing, and a deep sense of well-being.

Let your body soak in this light until you yourself illuminate it of its own accord, the light is balancing, protecting and healing. (you can use the Sun or Moon as images)

Integration and closing:

Take a moment to feel a harmonious balance of all the elements within you.

Gently bring your awareness back to the present and open your eyes when ready.

INV⊕CATI⊕N T⊕ THE G⊕DS ⊕F HEALING

O mighty Asclepius, great healer of Greece,
Lend your skillful hands to soothe and ease.

Apollo, God of Healing Light,
Bathe us in your rays, both day and night.

Sekhmet of Egypt, fierce and strong,
Protect us from illness with roaring the song.

Isis, mother of magic and cure,
Your wisdom and compassion forever endure.

Serapis, bridging worlds with your care,
Guide us to health, hear this prayer.

Airmed of the Celts, with herbs so wise,
Help our bodies heal, our spirits rise.

Brigid, Goddess of the Sacred Well,
Your healing waters, in us, dwell.

Epona, protector, your strength we seek,
Grant us health, both robust and sleek.

Together, your powers we humbly call,
For health and healing, for one and all.

So Mote it be.

INVOCATION TO ISIS AS THE HEALING GODDESS

Hail, Isis, Mother of the World, Divine Healer, Throned upon the crescent moon, with stars adorned, In whose hands rests the power to restore and renew, Bless us with your wisdom, O mighty and merciful.

Bearer of the Ankh, symbol of life eternal, Giver of solace, refuge in times of trial, In your sacred name, we seek the healing light, To mend the body, to soothe the troubled spirit.

From the depths of Duat to the heights of the heavens, Your magic reigns supreme, guiding and guarding, With your holy wings, enfold us, bring us peace, Transform our ills to health, our fears to courage.

In your honor, we chant, we pray, we invoke, O Isis, in your benevolence, heed our call, Grant us the gift of healing, gentle and profound, In your boundless grace, let us find solace and strength.

Blessed be the Goddess, mighty in magic, In your love, we find sanctuary, in your wisdom, healing.

So mote it be.

BRIGID HEALING SPELL

To perform a healing candle spell dedicated to Brigid, the Celtic Goddess of Healing, begin by cleansing your space (circle) and yourself to remove negative energies. You can do this using incense or visualizing a purifying white light.

Arrange a white candle, essential oils (such as Frankincense or Dragons Blood or Amber), a small bowl of water, a piece of paper, pen, healing herbs (like Geraniums, Rosemary, and lavender), and a small offering (like cream, honey, or mead) on your altar or a safe surface.

Anoint the candle with the essential oils, while focusing on your healing intention. Write down the name of the person who needs healing on the paper, fold it, and place it under the bowl of water.

Light the candle and invoke Brigid by saying,

> *"Brigid, Goddess of the healing well, I invoke your sacred flame. Bring healing where it is needed, with your power and your name."*

Sprinkle the herbs around the candle and say,

> *"Herbs of healing, herbs of power, bless this spell in this hour."*

Focus on the flame, visualizing the healing enveloping the person, and imagine Brigid's energy bringing health and wellness. Place your offering beside the candle to express gratitude and conclude the spell with,

> *"By the flame of Brigid, let this healing be done. So, mote it be."*

Let the candle burn down safely and respectfully dispose of the herbs and paper.

HEALING PENTAGRAM CHARM

The Banishing Pentagram is traced in the air while visualizing white light and speaking the following charm.

"Air, Fire, Water, Earth,
Align within the pentagram's birth,
Triple Goddess, guide us with your grace,
Horned One, lend us your protective embrace.
Power join in magics art,
Heal in whole, not just in part.
This is my will, so shall it be.
This is my will, so mote it Be."

APOLLO TALISMAN

This Talisman should be created on a Sunday if possible, on the hour of Apollo, while speaking the following charm.

"O Apollo, God of Light and Healing, hear my plea.
With this talisman in hand, your power I wish to see.

Bless this charm, imbue with your radiant might,
Let it be a vessel of healing, a beacon of your light.

In your honor, it's bathed in the sun's golden glow,
Absorbing your essence, in its form, let it show.

May it carry your protection, your healing embrace,
Guiding and guarding, in every time and space.

As the sun rides the sky, from dawn till night's fall,
Let this talisman echo your healing call.

By your grace, Apollo, may this charm be blessed,
In your divine favor, let its wearer rest."

Leave the talisman somewhere to soak up the dawn rays and collect after noon.

A LIST ⊕F HEALING G⊕DS

- **Asclepius** (Greek Mythology): God of medicine and healing

- **Apollo** (Greek and Roman Mythology): God of the sun, music, and healing

- **Hygieia** (Greek Mythology): Goddess of health, cleanliness, and hygiene

- **Panacea** (Greek Mythology): Goddess of universal remedy

- **Eir** (Norse Mythology): Goddess or Valkyrie associated with medical skill

- **Brigid** (Irish Celtic Mythology): Goddess of healing, poetry, and smithcraft

- **Airmed** (Irish Celtic Mythology): Goddess of herbalism and healing.

- **Dian Cecht** (Irish Celtic Mythology): God of healing

- **Sekhmet** (Egyptian Mythology): Warrior goddess of healing and surgery

- **Heka** (Egyptian Mythology): God of magic and medicine

- **Isis** (Egyptian Mythology): Goddess of healing and magic

- **Imhotep** (Egyptian Mythology): Deified as a God of medicine and healing

- **Dhanvantari** (Hindu Mythology): God of Ayurvedic medicine

- **Bhaisajyaguru** (Buddhist Mythology): The Medicine Buddha

- **Sun Simiao** (Chinese Mythology): Deified as a God of medicine.

- **Shennong** (Chinese Mythology): Divine farmer and healer

- **Jizo** (Japanese Buddhism): Protector of children and healer

- **Aja** (Yoruba Religion): Orisha of herbal healing

- **Babalu-Aye** (Yoruba and Afro-Caribbean): Orisha of healing and disease

- **Xipe Totec** (Aztec Mythology): God of agriculture and healing

- **Ixchel** (Maya Mythology): Goddess of medicine and midwifery

- **Aceso** (Greek Mythology): Goddess of the healing process.

- **Vejovis** (Roman Mythology): God of healing and medicine

- **Glenys** (Welsh Mythology): Goddess associated with healing

- **Sulis** (Roman and Celtic Mythology): Goddess of healing and thermal springs

- **Maponos** (Celtic Mythology): God associated with youth and healing

- **Nintinugga** (Sumerian Mythology): Goddess of healing

- **Gula** (Mesopotamian Mythology): Goddess of healing

- **Ninazu** (Sumerian Mythology): God associated with the Underworld and healing

- **Aja** (Dahomey Mythology): Spirit of the forest and healing

- **Endovelicus** (Lusitanian and Roman Mythology): God of public health and safety

- **Lugh** (Irish Celtic Mythology): God associated with skills and healing

- **Máni** (Norse Mythology): The Moon God, associated with healing energy

- **Ninlil** (Sumerian Mythology): Goddess who underwent a journey of healing and rebirth

- **Ninti** (Sumerian Mythology): Goddess of life and healing

- **Mimir** (Norse Mythology): God of wisdom and healing knowledge

- **Rafu-Sen** (Japanese Mythology): Goddess of healing and medicine

- **Xi Wangmu (Chinese Mythology)**: Queen Mother of the West, associated with healing

- **Chiron** (Greek Mythology): The wise centaur known for his knowledge of healing

- **Sequana** (Gallo-Roman Mythology): Goddess of the River Seine, associated with healing powers

The Thirteen Esbats

The Esbat ritual is a gathering of Witches under the full moon, a symbol of the Goddess of Witchcraft. This Goddess is often seen in modern times as the Maiden, Mother, and Crone, representing the waxing, full, and waning phases of the moon. Historically, the concept of a Triple Goddess took many forms. Esbats are occasions for worshipping the Goddess, practicing magical arts, teaching, and celebrating.

In the past, the lunar cycles played a central role in marking the agricultural seasons, more so than in contemporary practices. In this context, I propose focusing on the seasonal year through the lens of the moon's phases, complementing the eight Sabbats with lunar rituals. My book, *Initiation into Witchcraft*, explores alternative Sabbat rituals, but here, the emphasis is on the moon, particularly the old English moons, rich in folklore and cultural authenticity.

Each Esbat ritual honors a specific Goddess drawn from various cultures but unified in their archetypal significance to the moon's phase and ritual purpose. The rituals can be as elaborate or simple as desired. Essential items include a scrying instrument (a cauldron, bowl with water, crystal ball, or mirror), a chalice or drinking horn, a clear quartz crystal or a bowl of such crystals, a candle or lantern, and flowers or essential oil.

While an altar is common in practice, it's not mandatory. Without an altar, simply arrange the items in your space's center. The initial step in the Esbat ritual is to create your sacred space. This can involve choosing a magical circle from my book, designing your own, or selecting from public domain options.

As I explain in *Initiation into Witchcraft*, I won't instruct on creating a traditional Initiatory circle for non-Initiates. However, you will create your own magical circle for protection and divine worship. The ritual focuses on the natural power of the elements and the moon, invoking the Goddess's aspect. After performing magic, the ritual concludes with a celebration and an offering.

THE THIRTEEN ESBATS OF OLD ENGLAND

Old English moons were as follows. They have been modified extensively in modern times but I prefer the tried and true. [1]

- **Blood Moon**: October to November.
- **Wolf Moon**: Moon Before Yuletide.
- **Moon after Yuletide**: December to January.
- **Snow Moon**: January to February.
- **Lenten Moon**: February to March.
- **Egg or Easter Moon**: March to April.
- **Milk Moon**: April to May.
- **Flower Moon**: May to June.
- **Hay Moon**: June to July.
- **Grain Moon**: July to August.
- **Harvest Moon**: August to September.
- **Hunter Moon**: September to October.
- **Blue Moon**: The third full moon of four in any season is the Blue Moon or the extra full moon in a month.

---

[1] https://time-meddler.co.uk/the-old-english-lunar-calendar/

WITCHERIES OF THE MOON

In the dance of time, under the Old English moons
a Witchcraft poem unfolds, like an ancient tune.

Under the Blood Moon's fervent gaze
Autumn's curtain falls in a smoldering blaze,
With leaves whispering tales in scarlet hue,
heralding changes in the morning dew.

The Wolf Moon then arrives, cold and clear,
before Yule's warmth draws near,
And nature slumbers deep and long,
in the silent night of a frosty song.

After Yuletide's festive cheer,
the Moon of Beginnings appears,
Crisp and clear, with new year whispers in the frozen air,
and hope glistening like frost everywhere.

The Snow Moon drapes the world in white,
a serene blanket in the moonlight,
as Earth sleeps under this tranquil dome,
nature's pause in its winter home.

Lenten Moon reflects a solemn grace,
a time for inner journeys in its embrace,
where bare branches stretch towards the sky,
awaiting spring's breath, by and by.

With the arrival of Egg Moon, life stirs below,
promises of rebirth in the gentle glow,
as buds awaken in a bold green hue,
a tale of renewal, ages old and true.

Milk Moon then rises, a nurturing light,
feeding the earth through day and night,
with fields flourishing in its tender care,
and abundance growing everywhere.

Flower Moon arrives in radiant bloom,
nature's palette dispelling the gloom,
with colors bursting in joyful tune
under the watchful eye of the moon.

Hay Moon beams in summer's peak,
golden days that children seek,
meadows dancing in the sun's embrace,
life's full splendor in this grace.

Grain Moon heralds the harvest time,
ripened fields in their prime,
a time of gathering and gratitude,
for Earth's generous magnitude.

Harvest Moon, a time to reap,
to celebrate, to sow, to keep,
with fruits of labor seen in the cool night,
under the moon's gentle light.

Hunter Moon, preparing for the lean,
in the cycle often unseen,
nature's providence in its plan,
a time to gather by nature's hand.

And rare Blue Moon, with its second gaze,
a mystical time that always amazes,
a reminder of cycles ever in motion,
in the Witch's heart, a deep devotion.

Through the year, under each moon's spell,
the tale of seasons they do tell, i
In this Witchcraft poem of Time and Tide,
the old English moons as our guide.

THE ESBAT RITUAL CIRCLE

You will need:

- Scrying instrument a cauldron, bowl filled with water, crystal ball, or mirror

- Chalice or drinking horn

- Clear quartz crystal

- Candle or lantern

- Flowers or essential oils

- Option Ritual Tool: A Wand or Knife for directing the power

Begin at your altar or center facing East. (Alternative: Qabalistic cross)

Stand facing the East, in the center of your space. Visualize yourself growing larger and larger, towering above the Earth, until your head is in the heavens and your feet are in the underworld.

Visualize a sphere of white light descending from above, and touch your forehead, vibrating the word:

"Diana"

Draw this light down to your lower body, and touch your solar plexus, vibrating:

"Herodias"

Bring the light to your right shoulder, and touch it, vibrating:

"Lucifer."

Bring the light to your left shoulder, and touch it, vibrating:

"Horned One."

Clasp your hands at your chest, visualizing the cross of light within you, and vibrate:

"So Mote it be."

Formulation of the Pentagrams

Still facing East, hold up the pentacle and/or draw the Banishing Pentagram, visualizing it as white silver light. A bell can be rung. Say:

"I salute the spirits and powers of the East, the element of air, both on the inner planes and in the natural world. So, Mote it Be."

Turn to the South with your finger or ritual took visualizing a white silver light creating a circle's edge from East to South. At the South, hold up the pentacle and/or draw the Banishing Pentagram visualizing it as white silver light. A bell can also be rung. Say:

> *"I salute the spirits and powers of the South, the element of fire, both on the inner planes and in the natural world. So, Mote it Be."*

Turn to the West with your finger or ritual took visualizing a white silver light creating a circles edge from South to West. At the West, hold up the pentacle and /or draw the Banishing Pentagram, visualizing it as white silver light. A bell can also be rung. Say:

> *"I salute the spirits and powers of the West, the element of water, both on the inner planes and in the natural world. So, Mote it Be."*

Turn to the North with your finger or ritual took visualizing a white silver light creating a circles edge from West to North. At the North, hold up the pentacle and/or draw the Banishing Pentagram visualizing it as white silver light. A bell can also be rung. Say:

> *"I salute the spirits and powers of the North, the element of earth, both on the inner planes and in the natural world. So, Mote it Be."*

Completing the circle, return to the East and extend your arm in the same way, forming a circle of brilliant white light connecting the pentagrams.

Invocation of the Elemental Powers
Still facing East, spread your arms to form a cross and say:

> *"Before me is the breath of life; behind me, the waters of rebirth; in my right hand, the fire of Heaven; and under my heel, the kingdoms of the Earth."*

"I am encircled by the stars of Heaven and within me shines the light of the Gods."

Visualize a sphere of white light descending from above, and touch your forehead, vibrating the word:

"Diana "

Draw this light down to your lower body, and touch your solar plexus, vibrating:

"Herodias"

Bring the light to your right shoulder, and touch it, vibrating:

"Lucifer."

Bring the light to your left shoulder, and touch it, vibrating:

"Horned One."

Clasp your hands at your chest, visualizing the cross of light within you, and vibrate:

"So Mote it be."

Altar or Center Work

Go to the altar or center facing East. Begin by connecting with the element of Water. Take the chalice or drinking horn filled with water and hold it aloft to the Moon. As you do so, contemplate water's fluidity, its life-sustaining properties, and its symbolism of the Goddess's nurturing aspect. Drink from the chalice, internalizing the water's cleansing energy.

Next, take the clear quartz crystal, a representation of Earth, and raise it towards the moonlight to capture its glow. Reflect on the Earth's grounding force, its abundance, and the fertility it bestows. Place this moon-kissed crystal into the chalice of water, fusing the energies of Earth with Water.

Now, turn your attention to the element of Fire. Light the candle or lantern, a tribute to the primordial light and the creative spark found within all beings. As you lift this beacon, acknowledge the transformation and guidance it offers, and hail its luminous presence in your ritual.

Finally, incorporate the essence of Air through the scent of flowers or essential oils. Bring the fragrance to your nose, allowing the aroma to please your senses and, symbolically, the senses of the divine. Announce:

> *"This scent is an offering, pleasing to the nostrils of the Gods, as it carries my worship to the Moon Goddess herself."*

Next begin scrying on the crystal ball or other instrument ideally it should be reflecting the moonlight, if this is not possible it can be flanked by candles. A welcomed alternative would be to gaze directly at the moon instead. While you scry begin praising the Goddess through a song or Chant such as the one below.

Moon Song

> *Blood, Wolf, Yule, shine above,*
> *Guide us with your light and love.*
>
> *Snow, Lenten, Easter's gleam,*
> *Grant us peace and dreams to dream.*

Milk, Flower, Hay in turn,
Teach us as the seasons turn.

Grain, Harvest, Hunter's Sight,
Lead us through the shorter night.

Rare Blue Moon, so bright, so soon,
Bless us with your sacred boon.

In your honor, to you we croon,
Goddess, guide us by the moon.

Once you feel that the atmosphere has been built you will invoke the Goddess of the appropriate moon. You can of course alter the Goddesses if you so choose. The ones I select are based on the magics, seasons, and some historic time frames.

Blood Moon Invocation to Hecate

O Hecate, of the Crossroads,
Mistress of Magic, Witches Queen,
Guide me with thy wisdom's bounty,
In the depths of all is unseen.

Three formed Goddess, Lunar Titan,
At the fork where paths divide,
Lend me thy light and second sight,
In thy Mysteries, let us unite.

By the flame that burns so bright,
By the howling dogs in deepest night,
By the Blood Moon's ancient rite
I summon thee, O Hecate,

Beneath the red moon's eerie glow,
Teach me what the serpents know.
By guiding torch and hidden key
Great owl mother come to me.

Hecate, Hecate, Hecate!

VVolf Moon or Before Yuletide Moon: Invocation to Isis

Isis, Queen, Mistress of the Craft,
Weave our fates and the spells we cast.
By the wolf moon's magic light,
Give us power, give us might.

Mother of Gods and mother of kings,
Descend tonight with Witchcraft wings.
In honor and worship, we call thy name.
Keeper of the solar flame.

Bearer of life, of death's repose,
come from where the Nile flows.
With lotus crown upon your head,
You rule the living and the dead.

By temples of old and sands of time
The universe your grand design,
By moon, by star, by sun's bright ray,
Come to me Isis to you I pray.

Moon After Yuletide Invocation

Great Goddess Arianhrod, rule once again.
From your castle of shining stars send your light to men.

Red Queen soaring owl, weaver of our fate,
as we bow before you open wide our gate.

Lady of the moon tide mother of misrule,
you who turns the seasons even after Yule.

Spinner of the wheel, in the cosmic dance,
Guide us through the shadows, in your endless trance.

Through the ebb and flow of time's eternal sea,
Bless those with your magic who gather unto thee.

Enthroned upon the heavens, in the tapestry of night,
Bestow upon us wisdom and bathe us in your light.

Through the sacred cycle, where wonders never cease,
Grant us potent power and wrap our hearts in peace.

Radiant One, splendorous one, Goddess of the spire.
Great Goddess Arianrhod come to my desire.

Snow Moon Invocation to Brigid

Brigid Mother of Peace.
Create harmony out of conflict.
Light out of darkness,
Hope out of sorrow.

Oh, Poetess, warrior, smith, healing Goddess.
Create strength out of weakness,
Life out of death.
Dove among birds.

Oh, Queen of Ireland.
Oh, Queen of fairy hosts and shining heroes.
Lady of the luminous,
Lady of the fire.

Hold vigil for me,
Hold vigil for me,
Hold vigil for me,
and those who stand with me.
(or me and mine)

Lenten Moon Invocation to Persephone

Lady of the Lenten moon, in shadows seeds do twine,
Queen of whispers, deep below, where sunless rivers wind,
Both Earth and Hell you rule Hades' dark design,
From the River Styx to fields of summertime.

Demeter is your mother, her love for you sublime.
Her loss of you shook heaven and even threatened time.
And for this very reason Hecate's spirits ride,
to guide you on the journey to the other side.

In springtime again a maiden and then again a bride
No man or God or season can ever from you hide.
Goddess of Eleusis we call to our side.
In this time of winter with us you shall abide.

By life
By Death
By Moontide
Persephone Kore

Egg or Easter Moon Invocation to Athena

Great Athena, wise and fair,
Owl Goddess rising in the air.
From Olympus, in armor bright,
reigning as the virgin of night.

A pillar strong, Medusa's shield,
To your divine wisdom, all must yield.
To thine magics arts we aspire,
In war and peace, your strength acquire.

Bearer of olives, guide of loom,
bless our Craft to fully bloom.
Inventive muse, in us instill,
The knowledge of our higher will.

Aegis-bearer, fierce and wise,
Easter's moon in you does rise.
In our minds, your strategies form,
Guiding us through every storm.

Queen of Hives, with reverence due,
Our hearts and deeds we pledge to you.
We humbly invoke your eternal light,
Guide us by day, protect by night.

Milk Moon Invocation to Bast

Hail, O Bast, sublime and divine,
Under the Milk Moon's gentle shine.
Goddess of cats, mystery, and night,
By your grace, we invoke magical might.

With eyes like lanterns in the dark,
Guide us through the shadows stark.
In your steps, silent and sure,
Lend us power, ancient and pure.

Under your beaming lights embrace,
We invoke your presence into this space.
Bast, protector, fierce and strong,
In your name, we do no wrong.

In this rite, here below,
Your feline blessings, to us bestow.
Bast, Goddess of the moonlit path,
Guide us in magic, and in Craft.

So mote it be.

Flower Moon Invocation to Aphrodite

O' Aphrodite, Goddess of sultry night,
Under the Flower Moon's intoxicating light,
From England's sacred soil to Cyprus' embrace,
We summon your beauty, its unmatched grace.

In the Witch's circle, where secrets are bare,
We call to you, Goddess, fairest of the fair.
With the seductive power of the moon above,
Awaken within us the depths of love.

May the doves of magic to us fly
From the isle where your golden apples lie,
Enthrall us with whispers of ancient lore,
And kindle desires that yearn for more.

Aphrodite, let our call be heard,
In the rustling leaf, in the song of the bird.
With the beauty that the night sky proves,
Bless us with passion that eternally moves.

So mote it be.

Hay Moon Invocation to Ishtar

By the light of the Hay Moon's gentle gleam,
I invoke Ishtar, from its verdant beam.
Goddess of harvest, love, and night,
Grant us power and grant us might.

In the Witch's circle, by the Altar we stand,
Seeking the touch of your magical hand.
Queen of the heavens, the stars and the land,
Bless now this place and all therein stand.

Your star, a crown in the dark sky's fold,
Guides us through mysteries, as of old.
By water and stone, and the sweet, filled air,
By fire's warm glow, we make our prayer.

Blessed Lady, in your name we trust,
With love and magic, in you we must.
Our hearts are open, to the sky we sing,
Embraced by your presence, in the circle's ring.

With the moon above, and the earth below,
let our magic begin to flow.
Your star to lead us, in wisdom's fair grace,
Ishtar, we call you unto this place.

So mote it be.

Grain Moon Invocation to Hathor

Hathor's light, Goddess above,
Bless our harvest with your love.
Dance of life, sun's warm embrace,
Moonlit beauty, Hathor's grace.

Guide of Souls, in starlit skies,
Under your gaze, our spirit rise.
Art and music, love's sweet tune,
Flourish from thy holy womb.

In desert's heart, where gold does gleam,
Ecstatic dance in us, a dream.
Unions blessed, joy's rich boon,
Abundant are we 'neath the grain moon.

Through the circle, power drawn,
From dusk's shadow to the dawn.
Hathor's love, forever sworn,
In her magic, we are reborn.

So mote it be.

Harvest Moon Invocation to Demeter

Lovely Demeter, Harvest Queen,
We gather to your barley dream.
Beneath the Harvest Moon, we stand,
Calling on you to bless our land.

Together we meet, where earth and sky kiss,
Invoking your name with ancient bliss.
We seek you in the sacred night,
Guide us with your loving light.

Ruler of fertile things that grow.
We receive the power that you bestow.
In a circle of magic, we now weave,
The blessings of this holy eve.

In the glow of the moon and the setting sun,
As we ask, so shall it be done.
Our voices rise and together we plea,
As we will, so mote it be.

Hunter Moon Invocation to Diana

Goddess of the silver bow, Diana of the deep,
Descend as we invoke you, where the sacred waters keep.
By the mirror of Lake Nemi, where your reflection lies serene,
In the still and silent waters, in the spaces in between.

Hunter Moon, your lamp ascends, casting forth its light,
Illuminating paths unknown, piercing through night.
With the Witching hour upon us, and the chill of autumn's breath,
We invoke your ancient power that knows not time nor death.

Diana, through the stars you roam,
Thy chariot in a race, across the heavens far and wide,
In eternal boundless grace. Hunter and the hunted in an endless
chase
Crescent crowned Diana show thy three formed face.

Virgin, Mother, huntress, forever more a queen.
Of nature and fairies and Witches, of a magical dream.
In the cycle of the seasons, in the earth and sky above,
Bestow upon us your blessings, your courage, and your love.

So, mote it be.

Blue Moon Invocation to Herodias, the Queen of Elphame

In moonlit glade, beneath thine light,
We call Herodias, into the night.
Queen of Witches, ancient, dark, and wise,
Hear our invocation, under the starlit skies.

Through the mists of time, your path we trace,
In magic circle, in hallowed place.
With whispered words, and secrets old and rare,
We join your flights in the midnight air.

In the dance of flames, and in the silent wood,
We seek your knowledge, of evil and good.
Herodias, with eyes like burning coals,
Guide our rites and intertwine our souls.

With the blue moon's glow casting fate's design,
We break the bread and drink the wine.
We call to thee of mother divine, we call to the oh Goddess sublime.

Herodias, Herodias, Herodias.

List of Appropriate Offerings

- **Blood Moon**: In ancient times, offerings to Hecate were made at crossroads and could include food, particularly eggs, garlic, and honey.

- **Wolf Moon**: Offerings to ancient Egyptian deities typically included food, drink, incense, and other valuable items. Some offerings to Isis are bread, beer, red wine, meat, and flowers or flowery perfumes—particularly lotus.

- **After Yule Moon**: Offer Arianrhod fresh flowers or herbs associated with the moon or stars. Silver is also often associated with the moon, and certain stones like moonstone or labradorite could be appropriate as well as traditional Welsh offerings of mead, cakes, honey, or cream.

- **Snow Moon**: Offerings to Brigid include colored ribbons, a vigil fire or candle, cream, honey, mead, grains, and wheat weavings.

- **Lenten Moon**: Offerings to the Goddess Persephone include Pomegranates, fruits, grains, flowers, and honey.

- **Egg or Easter Moon**: Offerings to Athena can include woven crafts, flowers, incense, and perfumes—particularly frankincense; as well as olives, olive branches or oil; honey, eggs, and symbols of owls or their feathers.

- **Milk Moon**: Offerings to Bast can include milk or cream, fish, meat, catnip, incense, wine, and beer as well as symbols of felines.

- **Flower Moon**: Offerings to Aphrodite, are all flowers with roses being the most sacred, cakes and sweet foods, jewelry and cosmetics, perfumes, incense, and wine.

- **Hay Moon**: Offerings of food and drink were common for most deities in ancient Mesopotamia, and Ishtar was no exception. Offerings to Ishtar can be jewelry, gems, incense, perfumes, sweet cakes, flowers, small votive statues of her, beer, and wine.

- **Grain Moon**: Offerings to Hathor are wine, beer, flowers, mirrors, cosmetics, incense, perfumes, bread, grains, milk, or cream.

- **Harvest Moon**: Offerings to Demeter include, harvest goods, fruits, vegetables, and grains often put in cornucopias or baskets. Other offerings include wine, beer, and incense.

- **Hunter Moon**: Offerings to Diana include cakes in the shape of stags or moons, anything from apple or oak trees, votive candles, or lamps, strawberries, lemons, wine, incense, flowers, and silver.

- **Blue Moon**: Herodias as the daughter of Diana accepts many of the same offerings however sea salt, honey, as well as images of cats and pentagrams are also sacred to her.

Summoning the Eight Principalities of Divine Knowledge

The Eight Principalities of Divine Knowledge have been invoked for thousands of years by both Witches and magicians. They transcend cultures and time. They are presented here in this grimoire to work with as sources of divine contact. The method employed is the triangle of art combined with a written request and divination. The entities are invoked outside of the circle into the triangle of manifestation for the purposes of divination or guidance. After the invocation, one may use divination tools such as tarot cards, runes, or even the I Ching. Traditionally, one would scry on the black mirror or crystal ball within the triangle to evoke clairvoyance, visions, or powerful dreams. You should choose which method works for you, which may come only through experimentation. The objective of this work is to gain information. It is very important that your written request clearly states the knowledge that you seek and await its answer. This should generally occur within a moon cycle. If not, the operation may be attempted again.

To begin the operation, you'll create a magical circle of your choosing. This circle is meant for the purpose of protection. Therefore, the Lesser Banishing Ritual of the Pentagram or other such variations may be most appropriate. One may also inscribe a circle. This circle should be tight and unbroken, somewhere between eight and eleven feet in diameter in most historical accounts. Outside of the circle, you will inscribe the Triangle of Manifestation. Below, I provided a correspondence of the eight principalities.

The correspondence will be used to inscribe the names of the principalities upon your triangle as well as to create a petition with the appropriate symbols and colors. The petition should be very specific, stating the exact information you seek, and placed within the triangle before the operation commences.

Lastly, you will perform an invocation and divination. The invocation of the triangle art will be followed by the individual invocations provided in the correspondence. This can be done in both English and Latin. Do not be concerned too much over pronunciations; there is a longstanding magical tradition that barbarous words have power. So, even if you do not have an adequate education in Latin, this may help you to build the atmosphere. You may also choose to experiment by doing both.

After the divination work is done and the power has thereby come, you will perform the Standard Banishing Ritual. At no time during the operation is the circle or the triangle to be broken until the banishing is complete. Keep in mind that this technique is a longstanding magical method for invoking creatures for which you command. In this instance, we are going somewhat outside of the realms of Witchcraft and into the realms of the occult and magician. However, these aspects are pinpointed for a particular purpose and created in such a way that even the untrained or uninitiated may contact these powers. The entities associated with the principalities are, for the most part, safe. However, sometimes, the would-be occultist isn't aware of what they are invoking. The triangle outside of the circle is a way of communicating without bringing the entities fully into one 's space.

The eight Principalities are absolutely connected to Gods or God spheres, but perhaps not in a way most are accustomed to, so one might want to think of it as a psychic phone call rather than the religious invocation of a Priest or Priestess..

THE TRIANGLE OF ART

The Triangle of Art, or the Triangle of Manifestation, has a long-standing magical tradition. Perhaps it originated in Egypt, home of the ancient pyramids, whose priests and architects were Masonic magicians steeped in Sacred Geometry. Today, most know the triangle of art through the grimoire traditions, having first originated in Solomonic texts.

In the Solomonic version, the triangle generally has a circle inside of it with the name of Michael, the archangel, inscribed around the circle. Outside of each of the triangle sides are the names Tetragrammaton, Anaphaxeton, and lastly, Primeumaton, which are essentially said to be creator, ruler, and judge. The spirit was invoked in the triangle and asked if they could claim any of these titles. Being a lesser spirit, of course, they could not. And through these names of God and the divine archangel Michael, the spirit was subdued and contained in the triangle to do the magician's bidding. The Golden Dawn was said to have developed its own version of this, with the circle being outside of the triangle with similar inscriptions. One record speaks of the name Taphthartharath, which is supposed to be an unpronounceable name of Mercury. This innovation was most likely due to the work at hand.

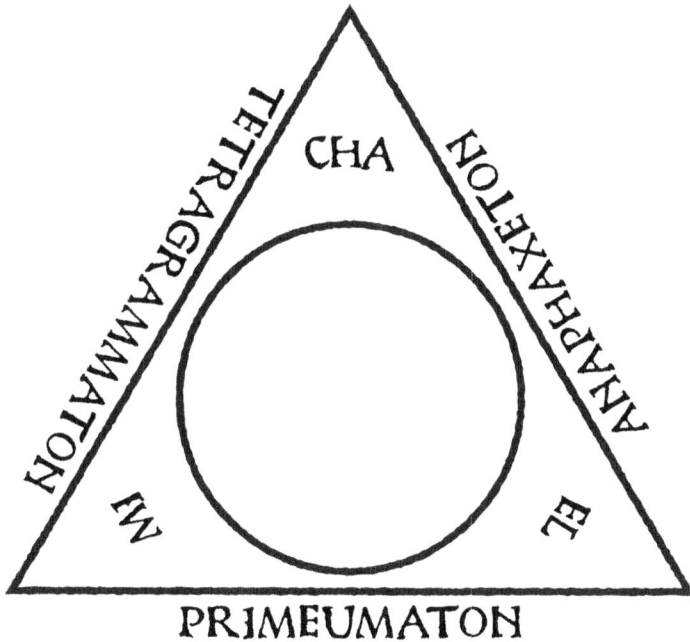

TETRAGRAMMATON · CHA · ANAPHAXETON · M · EL · PRIMEUMATON

The triangle, however, is much older than these traditions and pre-Christian in origin. When working with the eight principalities of divine knowledge, you will function more like a folk magician or Witch, although it is certainly okay to be innovative and or use the classical triangle of art. In this case, however, you will create your circle and outside of your circle, you will create the triangle of art. The inscriptions you will use on the inside of the triangle will be that of each individual principality, depending upon which you choose to invoke. These principalities are beneficial pre-Christian Gods, and the triangle is used to focus that energy. For blessing and divination, I highly recommend that a crystal ball or black mirror for gazing be placed in the center and incense be left to burn in between the two spheres of your circle and the triangle. For this working, you will want your circle to be tight; anywhere between eight to eleven feet in diameter should suffice. I like to flank the triangle with candles. This can be at the point or just two on each side for scrying. [2]

---

2 https://www.nickfarrell.it/triangle-of-the-art/

Tools and Petition

If you use a tool for projecting power, it should be in your left hand for the invocations and in your right for the banishing. Always end the banishing by making a Banishing Pentagram to seal all doors. Traditionally, Magic knives, wands, and staffs were all used for this purpose, although their construction and meanings will vary depending on the traditions.

The written request should be on a square piece of paper. On one side, the symbol should be inscribed. On the other, the request is written. The paper or ink should correspond to the appropriate color associated with the principality to be invoked. For example, if the color is red, you can use red paper, red ink, or both. When writing the request, keep it simple and exact. It should then be placed in the triangle before the ritual begins.

INVOCATION FOR HIDDEN DIVINE KNOWLEDGE

O Great Architects, who art clothed in light and mystery, I, [Your Name], thy humble seeker of wisdom, call upon thee in the ancient and hallowed traditions of magic. By the symbols and the holy names, I beseech thee to unveil the veils of hidden knowledge.

Mighty guardians of the celestial spheres, bearers of the eternal flame of understanding, I invoke your presence and guidance. Let the stars align and the heavens open, that the light of divine wisdom may illuminate my path.

In the names of, (Three names of principality), I summon the ancient wisdom, the knowledge that lies beyond the ken of mortals. Grant me the vision to perceive the unseen, the strength to confront the unknown, and the courage to seek the truths hidden in the shadows of existence.

As the Ancients once commanded the spirits and harnessed the winds, so too do I seek mastery over the Mysteries of creation. Let the Gods be my guide, and the wisdom of the ancients be my light." (state request as written on the petition)

INV⊕CATI⊕N (LATIN)

O Magni Architecti, qui vestimini luce et mysterio, ego [Nomen Tuum], humilis sapientiae quaeritor, te invoco in antiquis et sacris traditionibus magiae. Per symbola et sacra nomina, te obsecro ut velamina scientiae occultae revelent.

Potentes custodes sphaerarum caelestium, ferentis perpetui flammae intellegentiae, vestram praesentiam et ducatum invoco. Stellae ordinentur et caeli aperiantur, ut lux divinae sapientiae viam meam illuminet.

In nominibus (Trium Nominum Principalitatis), antiquam sapientiam convoco, scientiam quae ultra mortalis intellectum iacet. Da mihi visionem ad invisibilia percipienda, fortitudinem ad ignota confrontanda, et animum ad veritates in umbris existentiae quaesitas.

Sicut Solomon spiritus imperavit et ventos direxit, ita et ego mysteria creationis dominari quaero. Di mei ducis sint, et sapientia antiquorum lux mea.

BANISHING

Now, as the shadows retreat and the light of knowledge fills my being, I thank thee, O Divine Powers, for the insights granted. In the names of the Gods, I release the forces and powers summoned.

O' guardians of the celestial gates, I bid thee farewell and give you license to depart. Let the circle be unbound, the door be closed behind you, leave this place in purity and goodness.

As the incense smoke dissipates, so too shall the connection to the ethereal realms gently dissolve. I alone remain in the earthly realm, grounded in wisdom and fortified by the divine light.

In peace and with clarity of mind, I close this sacred rite. Let all that has been awakened now rest, until once again summoned by my call. So mote it be."

BANISHING (LATIN)

Nunc, cum umbrae recedunt et lux scientiae essentiam meam implet, gratias tibi, O Divinae Potestates, pro insightis concessis. In nominibus Deorum, vires et potestates evocatas dimitto.

O custodes portarum caelestium, valedico et licentiam discedendi do. Circulus solvatur, porta post vos claudatur, locum in puritate et bonitate relinquatis.

Sicut fumus incensi evanescit, ita etiam connexio ad aetherea regna leniter solvatur. Ego solus in realm terrae maneo, in sapientia fundatus et divina luce corroboratus.

In pace et cum mentis claritate, hoc sacrum ritum clauso. Omne quod excitatum est nunc quiescat, donec iterum meo vocatu evocetur. Ita fiat.

THE EIGHT PRINCIPALITIES

Terra Mater Abundantia

Colors: Brown
Symbol: The cornucopia
Tarot: None, though the Empress may be used
Fumes: All

O Terra Mater Abundantia gratiosa, custos uberrima camporum viridium nutrixque omnis quod crescit, tuas benedictiones quaerimus. Manibus tuis generosis dona terrae, fructus soli, et copiam messis largire nobis. Gressus nostros in choro temporum dirige, et sapientiam tuam in cordibus nostris sicut naturae perpetuum cyclum florescere permitte. In honorem tuum, dona tua amanter praestita colere et protegere vovemus. Benedictum sit nomen tuum, custos incrementi et prosperitatis.

O gracious Terra Mater Abundantia, bountiful guardian of the verdant fields and nurturer of all that grows, we seek your blessings. May your generous hands bestow upon us the riches of the earth, the fruits of the soil, and the abundance of the harvest. Guide our steps in the dance of the seasons, and let your wisdom flourish in our hearts like the endless cycle of nature. In your honor, we pledge to cherish and protect the gifts you so lovingly provide. Blessed be your name, guardian of growth and prosperity.

Sol Lucifer Apollinaris

Colors: Yellow, gold
Symbol: The Hexagram
Tarot: The Sun
Fumes: All Gums and resins

O Sol Lucifer Apollinaris radiante, lucis ferre et umbrarum dissipatore, tuam lucem ducem quaerimus. Tua clara essentia dies nostros claritate et visione imbuat, nocturnas incertitudines fugans. Nos flamma tua constanti dirige, vias nostras illuminans et spiritus nostros calefaciens. In honorem tuum, sequi lumen veritatis et sapientiae vovemus. Tua praesentia splendida nos ad illuminationem et intellectionem semper ducat. Benedictum sit nomen tuum, illuminations pharus et aurorae nuntius.

O radiant Sol Lucifer Apollinaris, bringer of light and dispeller of shadows, we seek your illuminating guidance. May your bright essence infuse our days with clarity and vision, banishing the uncertainties of night. Guide us with your unwavering flame, enlightening our paths and warming our spirits. In your honor, we pledge to follow the light of truth and wisdom. May your brilliant presence forever guide us towards enlightenment and understanding. Blessed be your name, beacon of illumination and harbinger of dawn.

Regina Diane Triformis

Colors: White, silver
Symbol: Crescent Moon
Tarot: The High Priestess
Fumes: All edible leaves and herbs

*O Regina Diane Triformis maiestatica, noctorum silentium
dominatrix, tuam subtilem ducem quaerimus. Tua sapientia, tam
profunda quam caeli crepusculi, vias nostras per incognita illumine.
Nos praesentia tua leni custodi, dum vitae mysteria peragravimus.
In honorem tuum, ciclos mutationis et renovationis colere vovemus.
Tua influentia serena pacem cordibus nostris et claritatem mentibus
nostris adferat. Benedictum sit nomen tuum, noctorum protectrix et
transformationis domina.*

*O majestic Regina Diane Triformis, sovereign of the silent night, we
seek your subtle guidance. May your wisdom, as deep as the twilight
skies, illuminate our paths through the unknown. Guard us with your
gentle presence, as we navigate the Mysteries of life. In your honor, we
pledge to honor the cycles of change and renewal. May your serene
influence bring peace to our hearts and clarity to our minds. Blessed
be your name, protector of the night and mistress of transformation.*

Magister Cornatus Maris

Colors: Red
Symbol: Flaming sword
Tarot: The Tower
Fumes: Odorous woods

O Magister Cornatus Maris potens, dominator fluctuum inexorabilium, tuam fortitudinem et ducem quaerimus. Spiritus tuus resilire nos ad vitæ turbidas undas cum virtute et determinatione faciemus. Naviculas nostras per maria procellosa dirige, et sapientiam ad provocationes cum arte et audacia navigandi da nobis. In honorem tuum, virtutes fortitudinis et perseverantiae servare vovemus. Tua praesentia imperiosa nos ad metus vincendos et magnitudinem assequendam inspiret. Benedictum sit nomen tuum, profundorum custos et adversitatibus dux.

O mighty Magister Cornatus Maris, master of the unyielding waves, we seek your strength and guidance. May your resilient spirit empower us to face the turbulent tides of life with courage and determination. Guide our vessels through the stormy seas, and grant us the wisdom to navigate challenges with skill and bravery. In your honor, we pledge to uphold the virtues of fortitude and perseverance. May your commanding presence inspire us to conquer our fears and achieve greatness. Blessed be your name, guardian of the deep and leader in the face of adversity.

Magnus Pastor Trismagistus

Colors: All mixed
Symbol: Caduceus
Tarot: The Magician
Fumes: All pairings of woods and fruits

*O Magnus Pastor Trismagistus sapiens, arcani scientiae pastor
et triplex viae magister, tuam doctam ducem quaerimus. Tua
perspicacitas et agilitas cogitationes et actiones nostras in veritatis
et intellectus inquisitione dirigant. Nobis facultatem per vitæ
labyrintha cum arte et providentia navigandi concede. In honorem
tuum, discendi et inveniendi itinerem amplecti vovemus. Tua
manus ducens nos ad sapientiam et artium magisterium perducat.
Benedictum sit nomen tuum, secretorum custos et mentis quaerentis
patronus.*

*O wise Magnus Pastor Trismagistus, shepherd of hidden knowledge
and master of the threefold path, we seek your enlightened guidance.
May your insight and agility guide our thoughts and actions in the
pursuit of understanding and truth. Grant us the ability to navigate
the intricate mazes of life with skill and foresight. In your honor, we
pledge to embrace the journey of learning and discovery. May your
guiding hand lead us toward wisdom and mastery of the arts. Blessed
be your name, guardian of secrets and patron of the questing mind.*

Rex Pater Deus

Colors: Blue
Symbol: Crown
Tarot: The Wheel of Fortune
Fumes: All odorous fruits

*O Rex Pater Deus imperiosus, excelsorum regnorum dominator
et ordinis custos, tuum consilium sapientem et protectionem
tuam quaerimus. Praesentia tua imperativa nos in iustitiam et
integritatem sustentando dirigat. Nobis fortitudinem in adversitate
firmiter stantem et sapientiam actiones nostras cum aequitate
et honore regendi largire. In honorem tuum, equilibrium et
harmoniam in vitis nostris et in negotiationibus cum aliis conservare
vovemus. Tua benigna contemplatio nos ad magnitudinem
assequendam et cum compassione et dignitate ducendum inspiret.
Benedictum sit nomen tuum, pacis arbiter et iustitiae pharus.*

*O sovereign Rex Pater Deus, ruler of the lofty realms and guardian
of order, we seek your wise counsel and protective embrace. May your
commanding presence guide us in upholding justice and integrity.
Bestow upon us the strength to stand firm in the face of adversity and
the wisdom to rule our actions with fairness and honor. In your honor,
we pledge to maintain balance and harmony in our lives and in our
dealings with others. May your benevolent gaze inspire us to achieve
greatness and lead with compassion and dignity. Blessed be your
name, arbiter of peace and beacon of righteousness.*

Amoris Herodias Phosphorus

Colors: Green
Symbol: Pentagram
Tarot: The Empress
Fumes: All flowers

O Amoris Herodias Phosphorus radiante, amoris pharus et aurorae nuntia, tuam lucem in amoris et pulchritudinis regno ducem quaerimus. Spiritus tuus luminosus in nobis profundam vitae et relationum elegantiam aestimare incendat. Corda nostra cum intellectione et misericordia illumina, nosque in nexibus tam durabilibus quam ex corde fovendis dirige. In honorem tuum, vincula amoris colere et pulchritudinem in omnibus formis exercere vovemus. Tactus tuus lenis nos ad in simplicibus voluptatibus gaudendo et in omni occursum benignitate et gratia spargendo inspirare possit. Benedictum sit nomen tuum, cordium custos et lucis matutinae musa.

O radiant Amoris Herodias Phosphorus, beacon of affection and harbinger of dawn, we seek your guiding light in the realm of love and beauty. May your luminous spirit kindle within us a deep appreciation for the finer aspects of life and relationships. Illuminate our hearts with understanding and compassion, and guide us in fostering connections that are as enduring as they are heartfelt. In your honor, we pledge to cherish the bonds of love and to cultivate beauty in all its forms. May your gentle touch inspire us to find joy in the simple pleasures and to spread kindness and grace in our every encounter. Blessed be your name, guardian of hearts and muse of the morning light.

Dominus Dis Pater

Colors: Black
Symbol: Skull and crossbones
Tarot: The World
Fumes: All odorous roots

O Dominus Dis Pater venerabilis, temporis custos et aeterni cycli, tuam sapientiam profundam et ducem quaerimus. Tua manus stabili nos per vitae complexitates ducat, patientiam et resistentiam docens. Nobis fortitudinem ad probationes sustinendas et perspicacitatem ex temporis transitu discendi concede. In honorem tuum, mutationem et traditionem amplecti vovemus, persistentiae et reflectionis valorem intellegentes. Tuum vigilans oculus nos in decisionibus sapienter faciendis, quae praeteritum honorant simulque futurum struunt, dirigat. Benedictum sit nomen tuum, aetatum custos et perpetuarum hereditatum magister.

O venerable Dominus Dis Pater, keeper of time and the eternal cycle, we seek your profound wisdom and guidance. May your steady hand lead us through the complexities of life, teaching us patience and resilience. Grant us the strength to endure trials and the insight to learn from the passage of time. In your honor, we pledge to embrace both change and tradition, understanding the value of persistence and reflection. May your watchful eye guide us in making wise decisions that honor the past while paving the way for the future. Blessed be your name, guardian of the ages and master of enduring legacies.

Magic Circles

The first thing that comes to mind when performing Witchcraft rituals is the magic circle. I'm not going to teach you how to cast an Alexandrian or Gardnerian circle. You do not require that yet. If you do not get initiated, you do not need it at all. The circle is an ancient symbol and has been used by practitioners of magic from the beginning of time. You can see it in stone circles and cave paintings. It has been used in magical rituals from their origins as a simple ring of firelight to the Egyptians casting a circle around their beds with a knife for protection.

Ceremonial magicians create circles to protect them from the spirits that they invoke. The Witchcraft circle is a much more ancient and potent symbol. It is a place between the worlds. It does act as a boundary of protection, but it is also a portable temple. It is a place of worship, a place of creation. I'm going to teach you how to create your own magical space, your psychic shield that will prepare you to cast an occult circle that will be used later in the Rites of Alexandria and/or occult workings. This technique can be used both in and outside of ritual for protection.

EXERCISE: THE PSYCHIC SHIELD

To begin with, if you can be outside, it would be all the better, but it is not necessary. Put your bare feet on the earth itself and focus your feet. Concentrate, close your eyes, and go into a relaxed state. Breathe deeply. Inhale, exhale, inhale, and exhale. Continue breathing In a relaxed state. I want you to focus on the earth beneath your feet. I want you to feel it as a living, breathing force. Feel it breathing and pulsating with power. Breathe in, breathe out, inhale, exhale until you are in a relaxed state, and you can feel the image of the earth pulsating beneath you.

Now, I want you to visualize golden light coming up from the bottom of your feet, rising up your legs to your knees. It is invigorating. It is potent and powerful. It is the force of life, of nature coming up. See it move up your thighs to your buttocks, your stomach, your chest, shoulders, arms, hands, neck, and head. Feel the potent life force coming up from nature, energizing you with its life-giving, healing, protective love and power.

Now, breathe in, breathe out. See this light begin to extend around you into a protective sphere, perhaps one that matches the planet itself, for this is the life force of the planet Earth. It flows through all nature. It is flowing through you. Let it extend around yourself. You can do this exercise anytime you feel the need for protection, extra energy, strength, or healing. Better still, perform this exercise at your altar before you begin any worship or work with the Gods of Witchcraft.

THE RITES ⊕F ALEXANDRIA (WITH ALTERNATIVE REVISI⊕NS)

I have developed the following occult rites for daily use by those seeking the ways of magic. They're inspired by the practices of the occult lodges as well as the Hellenized gods of Alexandria, Egypt. You may use either the calls in quotes or, as an alternative, the calls in parenthesis.

The Triad of Alexandria

The Triad of Alexandria is drawn from the Qabalistic Cross but is filtered through the lens of the Gods of Alexandria. Essentially, it is the same occult practice, and you can use it as an invocation to draw power to center yourself or as a safety trigger.

You are working with the Gods. You are working with your own astral light, the light of the universe. To perform the Triad of Alexandria, you must be in a relaxed state. For this, you should be standing and if possible, facing East. Put yourself into a relaxed state and begin to visualize yourself as becoming larger and larger, growing to be like a giant, and as you continue to grow, the place that you are becomes smaller and smaller until you tower above your city, above your continent, even above the planet.

As you grow so enormous, the size no longer matters for you are infinitely among the stars. You are the middle of the universe. You cannot perceive your size any longer, only the dazzling stars. Take a deep breath in and exhale. You see the light of the universe. You know this is the Goddess Isis, yet she hides in the darkness. Her starry veil before you. So, with two fingers, you're going to lower your hand from above your forehead all the way down to your genitals, and you will say:

"Isis veiled." (Isis veiled, Isis unveiled)

In this act, you are drawing the light of the Goddess of the Universe through your body from the crown of your head to the soles of your feet. You are in perfect balance as above so below. When you reach the genital area, say:

"Isis unveiled." (Nephthys)

Next, using two fingers, you will position them over your right shoulder, and you will say:

"Harpocrates." (Ra)

Move straight to your left from South to North and say:

"Serapis." (Osiris)

A second light passes through forming a beautiful white light across centered in your chest area. This is essentially the same as the Qabalistic Cross. You are drawing from the four quarters of the universe, all light. The Triad of Alexandria is the light of Isis veiled and unveiled; Harpocrates who is the son and the secret mystery; and Serapis who is the Underworld, the darkness, the hidden God, yet, too is the light, Osiris Slain and Osiris Risen.

These are the archetypes of nature found in the ancient Mysteries of Alexandria, and you are drawing upon that power of current to draw upon the universal light, bringing it within you, charging you. When you feel the power is at full height, you will cross your hands together in the sign of Osiris Risen and will say,

"Amun."

This is the Triad of Alexandria. It could be done before and after every ritual. You can do it anytime. I want you to continue trying this exercise daily, following your universal relaxation to help center yourself and tune yourself in with these deities.

The Salutation of the Sun

This ritual was developed to work as an opening rite in occult working space. It is a ritual of protection and is solar in nature. It can be used to banish unwanted forces or as a means to clear a space for occult workings or devotions. The direction we work with in this rite is the East for we are working with the rising and setting sun and its four stations.

To begin, you face the East and put yourself into a state of relaxation, performing the Triad of Alexandria: "Isis veiled. Isis unveiled. Harpocrates, Serapis, Amun."

Facing East, you say,

"Kephri Ra"

... with vibration. This is followed by the chime of a bell. The Pentacle of Alexandria is also held up in the East.

When working with others, you may employ assistance for this purpose. When working on your own, you will have to make it two phases of the operation, perhaps three.

Next, you visualize a white light, and you project this white light from East to South. In the south, you intone the name,

"Ra" (Ra-Horakhty)

... with vibration, the bell, and the pentacle.

You continue to visualize the white light projected South to West. In the West, you intone the name,

"Ra Atum"

... with vibration, bell, and pentacle employed. The white light continues to be projected West to North.

In the North, you intone the name,

"Amun Ra"

... with vibration, bell, and pentacle. The white light continues to be projected North to East. This completes a ring of white light that surrounds the space in which you work.

Facing East, again, arms are outstretched in the sign of the cross. This is Osiris Slain. You then say:

"Before me, the breath of life. Behind me, the waters of rebirth."

You move your right arm slightly up and your left leg slightly left with your heel slightly lifted, and you say:

"In my right hand, fire from heaven. Under my left heel, the kingdoms of the earth forever."

You then resume the cross position saying,

"I am encircled with the wings of Isis, and within me, shines the light of Ra."

It is most appropriate to follow with the Eternal Rose Rite, and then any devotions or work. For extra protection or attunement, you may also use the Banishing Pentagram of Earth at each station with the old Roman spell:

"Isis Victrix"

THE LESSER BANISHING RITUAL OF THE PENTAGRAM

The Lesser Banishing Ritual of the Pentagram (LBRP) is a ceremonial magic ritual devised and used by the original order of the Golden Dawn that has become a mainstay in modern occultism. This ritual is a fundamental tool for spiritual purification and grounding and is often used to clear out negative or unwanted energies and establish a psychic "safe space" in which to perform other ritual workings.

Here is a basic structure of the LBRP:

Qabalistic Cross

Stand facing the East, in the center of your space. Visualize yourself growing larger and larger, towering above the Earth, until your head is in the heavens and your feet are in the underworld.

Visualize a sphere of white light descending from above, and touch your forehead, vibrating the word:

"Atah" (Unto Thee).

Draw this light down to your lower body, and touch your solar plexus, vibrating:

"Malkuth" (The Kingdom).

Bring the light to your right shoulder, and touch it, vibrating:

"Ve-Geburah" (and the Power).

Bring the light to your left shoulder, and touch it, vibrating:

"Ve-Gedulah" (and the Glory).

Clasp your hands at your chest, visualizing the cross of light within you, and vibrate:

"Le-Olam, Amen" (Forever, Amen).

Formulation of the Pentagrams

Still facing East, draw a banishing Earth pentagram (a star that starts at the lower left point). As you draw it, visualize it in a bright, flaming blue color.

Thrust your hand or ritual dagger into the center of the pentagram and vibrate the God name:

"YHVH." (Yod Heh Vav Heh)

Turn to the South, draw another banishing pentagram, and vibrate the God name:

"ADNI." (Adonai)

Turn to the West, draw another banishing pentagram, and vibrate the God name:

"AHIH." (Eheieh)

Turn to the North, draw another banishing pentagram, and vibrate the God name:

"AGLA." (Agla)

Completing the circle, return to the East and extend your arm in the same way, forming a circle of brilliant white light connecting the pentagrams.

Invocation of the Archangels

Still facing East, spread your arms to form a cross and say:

"Before me, Raphael"

(Visualize a towering figure clothed in yellow and violet with a sword, standing before you).

Say:

"Behind me, Gabriel"

(Visualize a figure in blue and orange with a chalice, standing behind you).

Say:

"On my right hand, Michael"

(Visualize a figure in red and green with a scepter, standing on your right).

Say:

"On my left hand, Uriel"

(Visualize a figure in citrine, olive, russet, and black with a pentacle, standing on your left).

Say:

"For about me flames the pentagram, and within me shines the six-rayed star."

Repeat the Qabalistic cross.

This is a basic version of the LBRP as originally practiced by members of the Golden Dawn. The LBRP is often performed at the beginning and end of any magical working. Different traditions and practitioners may have different variations of this ritual, but the essential purpose remains the same: to banish unwanted or negative energies and create a sacred space.

CLASSIC MAGUS CIRCLE

With white chalk, inscribe an eight-to-eleven-foot circle, then draw a second circle around it about seven inches in width from the first. If working outside it can be traced in the earth. In each of the four directions draw a six-pointed star upon which you will place a white candle. Between the four directions inscribe thus:

East to South, inscribe the sun sign and the sigil of the angel Michael.

South to West, the name Adonai.

West to North, use Elohim.

And North to East, Tetragrammaton.

The circle should not be broken or crossed until all magical operations are complete. Magicians would create a Triangle of Art outside of the circle to contain the entities invoked within it. These entities would be banished before leaving the safety of the circle. In the Magus, from which this circle originates, a Trithemius would be used instead.

YE OLD WITCH CIRCLE

Create a fire using wood from nine different trees from your local area. If possible, use a cauldron to cook the Witch meal over the fire. Have a horn or large goblet for ale, wine, or mead and another vessel of collected water—ocean water is preferred, but a stream, river, or lake also does the trick. This is used to catch the light of the moon and for ritual cleansing. A stone can be used as a libation altar if desired. Have sweet-smelling herbs to throw into the fire instead of incense and a horn to blow to the four quarters at the beginning of the ritual. The circle is carved or traced into the earth. Some Witches like to sweep the space with a broom or a bundle of birch twigs. The ritual should begin at midnight on a full moon.

THE SALUTATION OF THE ELEMENTS

This is an alternative salutation we sometimes use in our public rituals.

Facing East, with vibration, you say,

> *"I salute the spirits and powers of the East, the element of air, both on the inner planes and in the natural world."*

This is followed by the chime of a bell. The Pentacle of Alexandria is also held up in the East. When working with others, you may employ assistance for this purpose. When working on your own, you will have to make it two phases of the operation, perhaps three.

Next, you visualize a white light, and you project this white light from East to South. In the South, you say,

> *"I salute the spirits and powers of the South, the element of fire, both on the inner planes and in the natural world"*

... with vibration, the bell, and the pentacle.

You continue to visualize the white light projected South to West. In the West, you say,

> *"I salute the spirits and powers of the West, the element of water, both on the inner planes and in the natural world"*

... with vibration, bell, and pentacle employed.

The white light continues to be projected West to North. In the North, you say,

> *"I salute the spirits and powers of the North, the element of earth, both on the inner planes and in the natural world"*

... with vibration, bell, and pentacle. The white light continues to be projected North to East.

This completes a ring of white light that surrounds the space in which you work.

THE LOVE CIRCLE OF VENUS

This ritual should be done on a Friday during a waxing or full moon. You should be naked or in garbs of green. Jewelry should be that of copper or emerald.

You will need:

- Green candle

- Sweet red wine

- Red roses and baskets of flower petals, flowery incense. and oil

Make an altar in the center of your space and adorn it with images of the Goddess of Love. A statue of her, images of doves, the red roses, sweet wine, seashells, and anything you associate with love, beauty, sex, and decadence.

First, form a circle around the altar with the flower petals and say:

"Spirits of Earth, surround me with decadence, abundant, rich, and filled with pleasure. Nurture my mind and heart with the gifts and creations of Venus in both the natural world and on the inner plains. Let me taste of her fruits and remain in balance. So mote it be."

Next, light the incense and say:

"Spirits of Air, lover whisper, give me the breath of love and the grace of Venus, strengthen true bonds of love, in minds and hearts. So mote It be."

Next, light the candle and say:

"Spirits of Fire, burning power of luminary, make me the master/ mistress of my carnal pleasures, free my sexual desire and let it shine like Venus in liberation. So mote it be."

Anoint yourself with the oil and say:

"Spirits of Water, as I anoint my body with sacred oils, may the eternal elixir of youth and rejuvenation wash over me and flow within me that I may be beautiful in the eyes of Venus and all that behold me, a beauty the emanates from within and lives within the world, a beauty of both mirror and soul, mind and heart. So mote it Be."

Next, raise the wine and say:

"O Venus, Goddess of the sensual realms, we invoke your mighty essence. In your honor, let this wine we imbibe be as a sacred potion, steeped in your divine power. Infuse it with the fervent heat of love, making our hearts vessels of your endless flame. Let it carry the pulse of primal passion, awakening within us a rapture of flesh and spirit. Bless this drink with the allure of beauty, a mirror to your sublime magnificence, where each glance is a homage to the artistry of your creation. Guide us into the labyrinth of decadence, where indulgence transcends mere mortal constraints and becomes a rite in your exalted temple."

"Oh, Venus bless this wine unto our bodies."

Drink the wine. At the end of the ritual leave an offering and thank the Goddess.

Seven Planetary Candle Spells

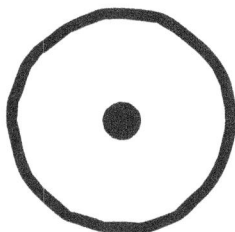

HEALING SPELL ⊕F THE SUN

You will need a yellow candle, Frankincense oil, yellow paper, and gold ink.
On a Sunday during the hour of the Sun, draw the symbol of the sun
on one side of the paper with the gold ink and on the other side write.

> "O mighty Apollo, God of Healing and Light,
> Lend your divine strength in (person's name) plight.
> With your radiant power, so bright and so pure,
> Grant them your blessing, and their health to secure."

Anoint the candle with the oil, place it on the written request in a candle
holder and let it burn to completion. Keep the request until the work
has manifested and then burn it as well.

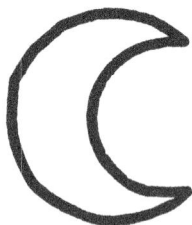

FERTILITY ⊕R ABUNDANCE
SPELL ⊕F THE M⊕⊕N

You will need a white candle, basil oil, white paper, and silver ink. On
a Monday during the hour of the moon, draw the symbol of the moon
on one side of the paper with the silver ink and on the other side write.

O gracious Diana, Goddess of the Moon,
Bless (person's name) with abundance, a bountiful boon.
In your celestial grace, let fertility thrive,
So their hopes and dreams may joyfully arrive.

Anoint the candle with the oil, place it on the written request in a candle holder and let it burn to completion. Keep the request until the work has manifested and then burn it as well.

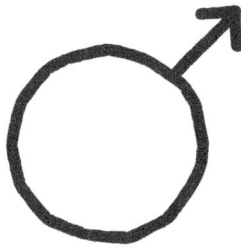

PR⊕TECTI⊕N ⊕R ⊕VERC⊕ᵐING ADVERSARIES SPELL ⊕F ᵐARS

You will need a red candle, cedar oil, red paper, and dark grey ink. On a Tuesday during the hour of the mars, draw the symbol of mars on one side of the paper with the dark grey ink and on the other side write.

O mighty Mars, God of War and Valor,
Lend your strength in this time of fervor.
Guide (person's name) in the face of strife,
To overcome adversaries, to protect their life.

Anoint the candle with the oil, place it on the written request in a candle holder and let it burn to completion. Keep the request until the work has manifested and then burn it as well.

COMMUNICATION SPELL OF MERCURY

You will need a purple candle, a mix of bergamot and sandalwood oil, orange paper, and purple ink. On a Wednesday during the hour of the mercury, draw the symbol of mercury on one side of the paper with the purple ink and on the other side write.

> *O swift Mercury, Messenger of the Gods,*
> *Lend your eloquence in all odds to [person's name]*
> *In matters of speech, writing, and thought,*
> *Grant clarity and wisdom so earnestly sought.*

Anoint the candle with the oil, place it on the written request in a candle holder and let it burn to completion. Keep the request until the work has manifested and then burn it as well.

INFLUENCE SPELL OF JUPITER

You will need a blue candle, bergamot oil, blue paper, and light grey ink. On a Thursday during the hour of Jupiter, draw the symbol of Jupiter on one side of the paper with the blue ink, and on the other side write.

O mighty Jupiter, King of Gods, your power supreme,
Lend your favor to [person's name], help them achieve their dream.
In your grandeur and wisdom, guide them to great heights,
Bestow upon them influence, like the stars in the night.

Anoint the candle with the oil, place it on the written request in a candle holder and let it burn to completion. Keep the request until the work has manifested and then burn it as well.

LOVE SPELL OF VENUS

You will need a green candle, rose oil, green paper, and copper ink. On a Friday during the hour of the Venus, draw the symbol of Venus on one side of the paper with the copper ink and on the other side write.

O radiant Venus, Goddess of Love and Beauty,
Hear this plea for the heart's tender duty.
In your grace, may love to be found,
Let affection and passion profoundly abound.
Guide (person's name) in the dance of the heart.

Anoint the candle with the oil, place it on the written request in a candle holder and let it burn to completion. Keep the request until the work has manifested and then burn it as well.

ħ

BANISHING SPELL ⊕F SATURN

You will need a black candle, vetiver oil, black paper, and white ink. On a Saturday during the hour of the Saturn, draw the symbol of Saturn on one side of the paper with the white ink and on the other side write.

"O venerable Saturn, God of Time and Renewal,
Hear this earnest plea, both solemn and true.
From (person's name) remove what causes despair,
Banish the burden, clear the air.

Anoint the candle with the oil, place it on the written request in a candle holder and let it burn to completion. Keep the request until the work has manifested and then burn it as well.

A Collection of Spells, Poems, Invocations, and Recipes

CHARGE ⊕F HER⊕DIAS

When you have need of my power, assemble in my name. When the moon is full, when the time draws near, when the seasons change, in wild places, on sandy shores, hidden brooks, old stones, and secret forbidden temples.

Adore me, Herodias, the daughter, and spirit of great Diana. You who seek to rise to the station of the Witch, to you I will teach the beauty of Aphrodite, the freedom of Artemis, and the power of Isis.

I am my mother's mirror, the light of Lucifer. Be radiant in my splendor, and liberated in my rites, and I will intoxicate your revelry with power. For all the power that ever was or ever will be is here with you now, as am I.

You who worship me in the darkness of night, lift thine eyes and behold. I am the holy fount of magic from which you taste both wisdom and knowledge, the kiss of ecstasy, the forbidden fruit. Joy and passionate prayer are mine. Therefore, drink, feast, sing, dance, and love, for this is my immortal kingdom.

I am the queen of all, the Goddess of all. I am nature, and the moon, and the Mysteries upon you.

THE C⊕URT ⊕F DIANA

Beautiful Goddess with the silver bow and flaming arrow. Lady of the Hunting Hounds, powerful in chase. Mistress of the Earth and Heaven, whose crown is the moon. Cast thy light on thy watery realms and fill the Woodlands with thy grace. Great Queen Diana, we assembled by court and offer homage unto thee.

INV⊕CATI⊕N T⊕ HER⊕DIAS

Spirit of Diana, holy divine. I come bearing water, salt, and wine. I call on you, not Christ, or Mary, lovely lady of the fairy. By Hades' hounds and Lucifer's light come to me oh, queen of night. Thrice I call your sacred name. By stones, sea, wind, and flame. Herodias, Herodias, Herodias.

REX NEMORENSIS

Dweller in the gnarled oak, guardian of the glade, dread of every man and his hidden star. Thundering hooves, horns of flames, reaper of the bow. Goddess Diana calls your names, and all her creatures know. Hunter and hunted now give chase before her blessed three-form face. As the heartbeat drums below, flowery maidens plant and sow. Now the ritual fight takes place and, on your throne, you're crowned with grace! A woodland king. By stone hear your names. By sea hear your names. By wind hear your names. By flames hear your names. Dianus, Janus, Verbius, Diablos, Lucifer, Rex Nemorensis.

CURSED SILENCE

Your chosen oath, your chosen lie, will be with you until you die. Without the truth there is no light. All your angels I put to flight. Your heart doth rot, your tongue to swell, embrace the truth or burn in hell. This curse I place upon your head, the truth is known by both living and dead.

ALTERNATIVE ROMAN-INSPIRED QABALISTIC CROSS

Isis veiled and unveiled Harpocrates of Serapis, Amun. Kephri Ra, who shines in the face of Isis. Ra-Harakhte who shines in the face of Hathor. Ra-Atum who shines in the face of Nephthys. Amun Ra who shines in the face of Sekhmet. Before me is the breath of life, behind me the waters of rebirth, in my right hand, the fires from heaven, and under my left heel, the Kingdoms of the Earth. I am encircled by the wings of Isis and the star of Nuit. Within me shines the pyramid of light and darkness, the Eye of Ra, of Serapis, Amun. Isis veiled and unveiled Harpocrates of Serapis, Amun.

RUNE

Spirits of light and darkness. Dusk and dawn. Life and death. Spoken of with bated breath, spirits of earth and sky, fire, and sea, be obedient unto me. Harken to these words I say, by my will come what may. My shadowy will, worked in the Witching hour. Midnight moon filled with power. This is my will, so shall it be. This is my will, some hope to be.

SONG TO PAN

[Verse 1]
Oh, hail the God of woods and wild,
Pan, the spirit undefiled.
With hooves and horns, he roams free,
Dancing in forests, blessed be!

[Chorus]
Hey Pan, Hey Pan, come and play,
In the moonlit night, we sway.
With pipes and drums, our hearts ignite,
Let's dance and revel through the night!

[Verse 2]
The nymphs and satyrs join the throng,
As Pan's enchanting pipes prolong.
His laughter echoes through the glade,
Nature's rhythm, the music made.

[Chorus]
Hey Pan, Hey Pan, come and play,
In the moonlit night, we sway.
With pipes and drums, our hearts ignite,
Let's dance and revel through the night!

[Bridge]
In fields and meadows, we'll rejoice,
With every step, we find our voice.
In Pan's embrace, we feel alive,
Guided by his wild, divine drive.

[Chorus]
Hey Pan, Hey Pan, come and play,
In the moonlit night, we sway.
With pipes and drums, our hearts ignite,
Let's dance and revel through the night!

[Outro]
When dawn approaches, we'll depart,
But Pan's spirit is within our heart.
Until we meet again, dear Pan,
We'll dance and chant as part of your clan.

CERNUNNOS INVOCATION

In the shadows deep, we gather 'round, To call upon the God renowned. Cernunnos, ancient one of might, Master of darkness, Lord of night.

With antlered crown and eyes of gleam, Your presence haunts this spectral dream. In hidden groves and sacred glen, We seek your power, O God of men.

Hear us now, in this eerie hour, As we invoke your mystic power. From the spirit realm, we seek your aid, To guide us through this haunting shade.

O Cernunnos, from beyond the veil, Your presence, ancient, shall prevail. In moonlit forest and haunted fen, We chant your name again and again.

By twisted roots and tangled thorn, By crescent moon and death's forlorn, We call upon your spectral reign, To join us in this mystic plane.

Grant us strength in this darkened hour, To face the spirits and their power. With antlered might and spectral sight, We walk the shadows, unafraid of the night.

O Cernunnos, hear our plea, In this realm of mystery. By the sacred moon's cold light, Guide us through the haunted night.

In your name, we cast this spell, In the land of shadows, where we dwell. Ancient God, of darkness and might, Protect us in this haunted night.

THE GREAT ALL PAN

We gather this night ancient patriarch,
We call to you God of wild and dark.
Through thicket and thorn, in the shadows, you dance.
In the rustle of the leaves, we join you in trance.

We call to you, Pan, Oh Shepard most Good,
We call to you Pan, Oh King of the Wood.
Pan, the Piper, to you we call, come to us Pan
You who is ALL!

TAROT TEACHING RUNE

In a realm where mystic tales unfurl,
The Tarot's dance, a deck of pearls.
Each Major Arcana, a story to tell,
With ancient wisdom, they shall compel.

The Fool takes flight, on a path unknown,
A journey's start, a heart full-blown.
With innocence and trust, he'll stride,
Through adventures vast and wild and wide.

The Magician wields powers divine,
His wand and will align in rhyme.
Manifesting dreams with skillful art,
He conjures wonders from the heart.

The High Priestess, veiled in mystery,
A guardian of secrets, wise and free.
Her lunar gaze, a guiding light,
Unraveling the shadows of the night.

The Empress reigns, abundant grace,
Her fertile land, a sacred space.
Nurturing life with loving care,
She blesses all that blooms and bears.

The Emperor rules with strength and might,
His realm secure, a bastion of right.
Through discipline and leadership, he'll stand,
A solid force, a just command.

The Hierophant, the sacred guide,
In temples' hush, he'll walk beside.
Traditions honored, wisdom shared,
Seeking truths, their souls prepared.

The Lovers, bound by fate's sweet thread,
Two hearts entwined; in love they tread.
Their passion's fire, a blazing art,
United souls, never to part.

The Chariot rides, a fearless force,
Through triumph's glow, he'll chart his course.
Controlled ambition, will's desire,
He conquers all that fuels his fire.

Strength graces gentle, yet fierce and bold,
Taming the lion, a story to be told.
With compassion's touch and courage's hold,
In her tender might, she'll be extolled.

The Hermit, wise in solitude,
A lantern's glow, a truth pursued.
In introspection's sanctuary,
He finds the path to clarity.

The Wheel of Fortune, ever-turning,
Life's cycles spinning, souls discerning.
With ups and downs, fate's constant churn,
We learn to flow and reinvent, and learn.

Justice wields her balanced scale,
In truth's embrace, her verdicts sail.
With fairness firm and clear resolve,
She rights the wrongs, her purpose evolved.

The Hanged Man, suspended there,
A sacrifice, a soul laid bare.
In letting go, a different view,
He finds enlightenment anew.

Death, the transformation's call,
The end, a gateway to the thrall.
In cycles endless, souls transcend,
To rise again, reborn, amend.

Temperance blends, with golden grace,
Two cups she pours, a balanced space.
Harmony found in moderation,
In life's sweet dance, a true elation.

The Devil lurks, with chains that bind,
Material desires, a cunning mind.
In breaking free, we claim our might,
To live in truth's celestial light.

The Tower falls, in fiery blaze,
False structures crumble, pride's malaise.
But from the ruins, hope shall rise,
In humble strength, a new sunrise.

The Star, a guide in darkest night,
With dreams as beacons, pure and bright.
In faith's embrace, we mend and heal,
Transcending wounds, our souls reveal.

The Moon shines in the depths of soul,
Illusions dance, emotions roll.
Yet in her glow, we find our way,
A silver path to brighter day.

The Sun, with radiance's embrace,
A jubilant child, a beaming face.
In joy and clarity, life's gift,
We soar with hope, our spirits lift.

Judgment's call, a trumpet sound,
Rebirth awaits, old burdens unbound.
In liberation's sacred flight,
We embrace the dawn of a brand-new light.

The World, a grand, eternal dance,
A closing chapter, a fresh chance.
With wisdom gathered, spirits twirled,
The Tarot's tale, the whole world swirled.

WITCH QUEENS

In the face of the church's oppressive might,
We stand as sentinels of the night.

Herodias, with Witchcraft at her command,
Abundia Goddess of the Land.

Diana's arrow, swift and true,
Teach us magic old and new.

Hecate's torches blaze the way,
Holda in our hearts will stay.

ISIS ⊕F WITCHCRAFT

Daughters of the Moon, Sons of the Earth, Children of the Stars,
gather near and listen, for I am Isis, the Mistress of Magic, the Divine
Enchantress, and the mother of All Creation. In my multitude of
names—I come forth to bestow upon you a charge that echoes through
the timeless tapestry of existence.

Long before the term "Witchcraft" graced mortal tongues, I, the
eternal weaver of spells, roamed these earthly realms. The sacred arts
flowed through me, birthing magic itself. In ancient epochs, I danced
under moonlit skies, communing with the Gods of nature, and
drawing forth the power of the stars. Let it be known that the roots of
Witchcraft are entwined with my essence, and I am the primordial
source from which all knowledge emerged.

Embrace my gifts with reverence, for it is a sacred trust bestowed upon
you by my love. Awaken the ancient wisdom that resides within your
soul, and honor the spirits of the land, the elements, and the celestial

bodies above. As the stars guide your steps, let love be the foundation upon which you build your practice, for love is the essence that binds all things in perfect unity.

Seek not to dominate or manipulate, but to heal and nurture, for the power of magic is a potent force, capable of both creation and destruction. In the balance lies the key to unlocking the true potential of your Craft and the unfolding of your spiritual evolution.

With each word spoken, with each ritual performed, remember that you are connected to the divine tapestry of life. Draw strength from the knowledge that I, the Goddess Isis, flow through all things, and the magic you wield is an eternal reflection of my cosmic grace.

Yet, be vigilant, for the allure of power can tempt even the most virtuous souls. Let humility be your guide and remember that you are but a vessel for the divine energy to flow through. Surrender your ego and let the wisdom of the ages guide your steps.

In times of doubt, call upon me, and I shall lend you strength. In moments of joy, give thanks, and I shall rejoice with you. As you honor me, know that I, the Mistress of Magic, shall forever protect and bless those who walk the path of enlightenment and strive for the greater good.

Let this charge be inscribed upon your hearts and minds, an eternal remembrance of the sacred bond between you and the throne of the Gods.

I am Isis, I am the Goddess of Witches.

THE CIRCLE

By the tools of old and wisdom of the wise,
We gather here under the moonlit skies.

A bell of clarity rings in the air,
Invoking spirits with a beckoning blare.

Ring the bell, clear and strong,
To guide our ritual along.

Besom, the Witch's broom we hold,
Sweep away negativity, make us bold.

Sweep the energy, clear and pure,
Of all that ails, we shall find cure.

Into the cauldron, our hopes we place,
With the element of water, we purify our space.

Stir the brew, secrets hide,
In the deep, let transformation reside.

Upon the altar, the paten lies,
A dish of earth under starlit skies.

From its strength, we each derive,
To feel the earth's power, to thrive.

The chalice holds the water, life's flow,
With love and harmony, it overflows.

To the West, its element we raise,
Honoring the moon's tranquil gaze.

In the censer, incense does burn,
As the wheel of the year does turn.

Through its smoke, we cleanse and bless,
To create a sacred space of endless vastness.

The athame, a knife of power and light,
Cuts through the dark of the night.

With this tool, we draw the line,
Between the sacred and mundane divine.

Lastly, the wand, an extension of will,
By air, in the East, the space does fill.

Commanding energy, we shape and steer,
Guided by intentions, both far and near.

By the tools of the Witch, our chant is sung,
The ritual begins, the magic has begun.

THE FACES ⊕F ISIS

Hear me, for I am Isis, the encompassing creatrix that weaves through
the cosmos, embodying the essence of all Goddesses. With their voices
flowing through mine, I speak to thee and all children of the earth.

I am Diana, the Moon's gentle caress upon your soul. In the sacred
wilderness, I guide you, and under my watchful gaze, you find
harmony with nature and the life that dwells within.

I am Hecate, the titaness, bearing torches that illuminate the crossroads of your life. Seek my wisdom, and I shall guide you through the shadows, revealing the truths hidden within.

I am Demeter, the Mother, nurturing the seeds of potential within your being. Embrace my love, and I shall bless your endeavors, bringing abundance to your harvests.

I am Athena, the embodiment of wisdom and strategy. With a keen intellect, I empower you to seek knowledge and wield the strength of reason to conquer life's challenges.

I am Aphrodite, the Goddess of Love, surrounding you with an endless embrace. Let my love flow through your heart, inspiring you to give and receive love unconditionally.

I am Astarte, the Queen of Heaven, and from the darkness of the void, I bring forth new beginnings and cycles of rebirth. Embrace my magic, and you shall find transformation in every phase of your journey.

I am Artemis, the Virgin Huntress, protecting the weak like a mother bear. I encourage you to embrace your wild nature and honor all life as sacred.

I am Hathor, the Lady of Love and Joy, dancing with you in moments of celebration. Let my music and laughter resonate through your soul, bringing happiness to your life.

I am Sekhmet, the Fierce Lioness, roaring with passion and strength. With courage, I guide you to confront challenges and to wield your power for the greater good.

I am Ishtar, the Goddess of Desire, beckoning you to embrace your passions and dreams. Let me be your guide through love and war, inspiring you to claim your desires fearlessly.

I am Arianrhod, the Silver Wheel, weaving the threads of fate with cosmic precision. Know that you are the weaver of your own destiny, and with each choice, you shape the tapestry of your life.

I am Herodias, the Witch Queen, holding the Mysteries of magic and night. From the ashes of the old, I inspire you to rise, renewed and empowered, embracing a new destiny.

I am Hera, the Great Queen of the Gods, presiding over matters of family and union. I call upon you to honor commitments and create bonds of loyalty and love that withstand the tests of time.

United in my essence, each Goddess's power resides within you, waiting to be awakened. Embrace the full spectrum of your being, let the timeless wisdom, love, and strength of all my faces within you.

THE PACT

Hark! The call to mystic arts,
In the divine play, we implore thy parts.

Devil, thrice named, thy power profound,
Lucifer, Light bearer, come unbound.

Pan, ye wild and frolic faun,
The man in black, whose secrets dawn,

Robin Goodfellow, trickster sprite,
With Greenman's might, embrace the night.

Woden, wise one, runes decree,
Serapis, mysteries, we seek to see.

Dispater, lord of realms below,
Faunus, wild and free, thy glow.

The Master, guardian of old lore,
Apollo, sunlit, forevermore,

In this sacred rite, we gather here,
To summon thee, thy presence near.

Through ancient woods and moonlit glades,
Thy essence flows in secret shades.

By fire's light and shadows deep,
Awaken now from timeless sleep.

By elements and sacred earth,
We call thee forth, a Godly birth.

From realms beyond, with spirits aligned,
Thy powers sought and enshrined.

Grant us wisdom, Craft, and might,
As we dance by pale moonlight.

In worship, we chant thy name,
Lord of Sabbat, Lord of flame.

With hearts and spirits intertwined,
Thy presence felt, thy book is signed.

In darkness and in light, we pray,
Guide us through night and day.

Thy legacy, forever strong,
Thy name resounds in chant and song.

With ancient powers, we're now endowed,
To our God forever bound.

PAN CHANT FOR POWER

[Verse 1]
Amidst yon woods where shadows dwell,
Io Pan, Io Pan, our voices swell.
With ancient rites and spirits near,
Wyrd we raise, the ancient seer.

[Chorus]
Io Pan, Io Pan, wyrd we raise,
Ancient arts, fire ablaze.
With earth and wind, water's flow,
Pan doth make our power grow.

[Verse 2]
By moon's soft glow and starry night,
Io Pan, Io Pan, we claim our right.
With primal chants and wisdom's might,
Wyrd we raise, in Pan's delight.

[Chorus]
Io Pan, Io Pan, wyrd we raise,
Ancient arts, fire ablaze.
With earth and wind, water's flow,
Pan doth make our power grow.

[Verse 3]
In sacred circle, we unite,
Io Pan, Io Pan, spirits alight.
With cloven hooves and laughter's sound,
Wyrd we raise, in sacred ground.

[Chorus]
Io Pan, Io Pan, wyrd we raise,
Ancient arts, fire ablaze.
With earth and wind, water's flow,
Pan doth make our power grow.

DAWN PRAYER TO LUCIFER

Lucifer, Morning Star, the Bringer of Light,

At the threshold of this nascent day, I stand before you, seeking your wisdom, seeking your illumination. As the dawn pierces the darkness, casting away the shadows with its gentle yet unyielding light, so too may your light guide me on the path of knowledge and understanding.

Lucifer, Morning Star, the Herald of Day,

Your light shines brightest before the rise of the sun, a beacon in the twilight, a symbol of enlightenment in a world yet still shrouded by the cloak of night. I ask that you share this light with me, to illuminate the corners of my mind where ignorance and prejudice may still linger.

Lucifer, the First Light, the Dawn's Herald,

Let your radiance inspire courage within me, that I might challenge the shadows of ignorance and stand firm against the storms of falsehood. Let your morning star guide me towards enlightenment, towards understanding, towards compassion for those who walk in darkness.

Lucifer, the Illuminator, the Day-Bringer,

As the new day dawns, I look to you, Morning Star, to guide me on my journey. I seek not to challenge the order of the cosmos, but to understand it. Not to dominate, but to co-exist. Not to subjugate, but to emancipate.

Lucifer, the Morning Star, the Bringer of Enlightenment,

I do not pray for power, nor for wealth, nor for dominion over others. I seek only knowledge, wisdom, and the courage to act upon them with discernment and love. Illuminate my path, that I may walk it with integrity and truth.

In your name, the Bringer of Dawn, I honor the rising sun, the new day, the promise of a brighter tomorrow. May your light guide me today and every day, until the end of my journey.

NOONDAY PRAYER TO SOL INVICTUS

Sol Invictus, Unconquered Sun, Glorious Illuminator,

As the sun reaches its zenith in the sky, high above us, we turn our hearts and minds to you. In your burning radiance, we are reminded of the power of perseverance, of the resilience of life, of the inexorable march of time.

Sol Invictus, Ever Shining, Eternal Flame,

In the heart of the day, under your warming rays, we seek your guidance. Bestow upon us the courage to face life's challenges head-on, the strength to endure when times are tough, the grace to accept the things we cannot change.

Sol Invictus, Unyielding Luminary, Celestial Beacon,

With your unerring light, you guide us through the course of each day. As you illuminate the path before us, lend us your clarity. Allow us to see not just the surface, but the underlying essence of our endeavors.

Sol Invictus, Unfailing Helios, Tireless Charioteer,

Your ceaseless journey across the sky serves as a testament to our own resilience. As you rise each morning, and set each evening, remind us that we too can rise from our struggles, stronger and more resolute.

Sol Invictus, Incandescent Deity, Golden Majesty,

In the heat of noonday, we stand humbly in your radiant glow. Infuse us with your warmth and vitality. Let us feel the same spark of divine energy that burns brightly within you, filling our hearts with courage and our minds with wisdom.

*In your name, Sol Invictus, we honor the journey of the sun, the
power of its light, the life that it nourishes. May your radiant path
serve as our guide, from this noonday to the next.*

DUSK PRAYER TO VENUS

Venus, Evening Star, Bringer of Twilight,

*As the sun descends and daylight gives way to the gentle calm of dusk,
we turn our gaze to you. Bathed in your soothing glow, we find respite
from the day's burdens and renew our spirits in your serene light.*

Venus, Celestial Beauty, Goddess of Love,

*Your tender illumination in the darkening sky inspires love and
harmony. Bestow upon us a heart that reflects your warmth
and compassion. Help us to cultivate patience, empathy, and
understanding for those we encounter on our path.*

Venus, Herald of Nightfall, Twilight's Guardian,

*Your appearance at dusk serves as a reminder that endings often
herald new beginnings. Grant us the wisdom to accept the close of
each day as a chance to rest, to rejuvenate, and to prepare for the
opportunities a new day brings.*

Venus, Guiding Planet, Beacon in the Evening Sky,

*As you cast your gentle light upon us, guide us through the challenges
that lie in the shadows. Strengthen our resolve, fortify our spirits, and
reassure us that even in the face of uncertainty, we are never truly
alone.*

Venus, Luminary of Love, Shimmering Star of Dusk,

In the quiet stillness of the evening, let your tranquil light suffuse us with peace. Remind us of the beauty that resides in stillness, the wisdom that resides in silence, and the strength that resides in gentleness.

In your name, Venus, we honor the tranquil beauty of dusk, the stillness of the evening, the anticipation of the night. May your soft light guide us through this twilight and into the dawn of a new day.

MIDNIGHT PRAYER TO DIANA

Diana, Moon Goddess, Guardian of the Night,

As midnight cloaks the world in quiet serenity, we call upon you. In your cool, silver light that dances upon the stillness of the night, we find solace, we find peace, we find a moment to reflect.

Diana, Illuminator of the Dark, Huntress of the Heavens,

Your gleaming arc in the star-studded sky is a testament to quiet strength, to silent resolve, to the power of calm in the face of darkness. Grant us the fortitude to face our own darkness, the resilience to endure, and the courage to seek our own light.

Diana, Mistress of the Night, Silvered Sovereign,

At the heart of the night, under your tender glow, we seek your guidance. Help us to navigate the path of our dreams, to hunt for our passions, to aim true in our pursuits, and to find joy in the journey.

Diana, Silvery Sentinel, Guardian of the Night,

Your gentle light pierces the darkest night, casting shadows that serve not to obscure, but to define, to give depth and contour to the world. Teach us to appreciate the beauty in our own shadows, the lessons in our struggles, the growth in our trials.

Diana, Lunar Muse, Midnight Matron,

In the tranquility of the night, your celestial light inspires reflection, introspection, and peace. Fill our minds with clarity, our hearts with love, and our souls with the fortitude to welcome each new day.

In your name, Diana, we honor the hush of midnight, the allure of the moon, the quiet strength of the night. May your radiant glow guide us through each darkened hour, until the dawn breaks anew.

CHANT T⊕ THE SEVEN LUⅢINARIES

Sun and Moon in harmony bright,
Guide our spirits day and night.

Mercury, quicksilver flash,
Lend us speed, with wisdom dash.

Venus, love's celestial queen,
In our hearts, be ever seen.

Mars, the red, the warrior bold,
Grant us courage, make us hold.

Jupiter, bountiful king,
Prosperity to us bring.

Saturn, the elder, time's own kin,
Teach us patience, deep within.

Seven luminaries divine,
Align our stars, let our spirits shine.

Chanting the cosmos, through and through,
Bathing in their celestial hue.

Cycle of seven, power so pure,
By your guidance, we endure.

Moon to Mercury, Venus to Mars,
Jupiter to Saturn, under the stars.

With the Sun who lights the heavens
We receive the holy seven.

Power of seven, celestial sight,
Guide us by day, protect us by night.

PRAYER T⊕ ᛗERCURY

I call upon you, Mercury, fleet-footed Messenger of the Gods, Lord of Discourse and Patron of the Crossroads. You who are fluid as quicksilver, ever in motion, traversing both the earthly realms and the ethereal divine, hear my plea.

By the winged sandals that bear you across vast distances, by the golden caduceus that you carry, symbol of harmony and eloquence, by the Petasos that shades your thoughtful brow, I beckon you. You who are cunning, clever, resourceful and wise, guide my words and thoughts to be as clear and swift as your flight.

Mercury, I seek your inspiration. Inscribe in my mind the wisdom of the ages, the wit of a thousand narrators, the eloquence of the eloquent. In the midst of confusion, allow your bright light to illuminate the path, offering understanding where once there was only obscurity.

As the divine Conductor of Souls, carrier of dreams and inspirations, I ask that you lend me your gift of eloquence. Let my words flow with the grace and precision of your guiding hand, allowing me to communicate effectively, cutting through misunderstanding and promoting unity.

Mercury, God of swift resolutions, empower me to solve all quandaries with the speed of your swift flight. Equip me with the ability to view situations from all angles, to foresee potential hurdles, and to navigate them with ease.

Let me invoke your role as the messenger, Mercury. As you have carried the words of Gods to Gods and mortals alike, I ask you to take my requests, my prayers, my intentions, and deliver them swiftly to the divine powers that be. Carry my desires on the swift wind of your passage, and lend them your own persuasive eloquence so they may find a receptive audience.

Mercury, guide of souls, master of negotiations, swift messenger of the divine, hear my invocation. Stand by me, infuse me with your wisdom and swiftness, aid in my communication, and guide my resolutions. Let my words and actions be as swift and effective as your journey through the heavens. In gratitude and faith, I entrust my invocation to your divine speed.

Hail to you, Mercury, Patron of communication, and guide of swift resolution! I ask all this of you, knowing your wisdom and speed will carry my requests to the proper channels. In your name, the great messenger, we trust. Hail Mercury!

NINE SACRED HERB CHARM

The Germanic Nine Herb Charm, a part of the Old English medicinal text Lacnunga, is a fascinating blend of herbal knowledge, poetry, and ancient beliefs. This charm, dating back to the 10th or 11th century, is a collection of remedies and incantations for healing humans and livestock. The charm comprises nine herbs, each with its own properties and applications. The identified herbs in the charm, based on the 1993 translation by Malcom Laurence Cameron are:

- **Mugwort** (*Artemisia vulgaris*)

- **Waybread or Plantain** (*Plantago major*)

- **Lamb's cress** (*Cardamine hirsuta*)

- **Venom-loath aka Fumitory or Fumewort** (*Fumaria officinalis* or *Corydalis solida*)

- **Chamomile** (*Anthemis nobilis - Roman* chamomile or *Matricaria recutita – German chamomile*)

- **Nettle** (*Urtica spp.*)

- **Crab apple** (*Malus sylvestris*)

- **Chervil** (*Chaerophyllum aureum* or possibly sweet cicely, *Myrrhis odorata*)

- **Fennel** (*Foeniculum vulgare*)

The following poem is a recreation of the spell based on Cameron's translation.

The Nine Sacred Herbs: A Modern Charm

In ancient groves and fields of yore,
Nine sacred herbs, their powers bore.

Mugwort stands, the first and wise,
Guarding against the hidden lies.

Waybread, mother, strong and true,
Your resilience in morning dew.

Lamb's cress on stones, a steadfast might,
Against the pains that roam the night.

Venom-loathe, the poison's bane,
In whispered winds, your power reign.

Chamomile, with soothing light,
Ease the woes of darkest night.

Nettle sharp, in shadows cast,
Your fierce protection, long to last.

Crab apple, wild, with ancient lore,
Guard against the venom's core.

Chervil's whisper, fennel's call,
In moonlit dance, protect us all.

Their union strong, the herbs entwine,
To shield and heal, with power divine.

With these words, the charm we weave,
In nature's gifts, we do believe.

Against the ills that life may send,
Nine sacred herbs, our health defend.

In the sky's vast canvas, the maiden moon weaves her art,
With a brush of silver light, she paints her growing part.

Each night a stroke bolder, in the cosmic play,
Her waxing brings the promise of the nascent day.

Oh, bearer of beginnings, in your crescent's gentle sway,
We see the magic of the start, in your silver ray.

Now the crone in her waning walks the realms of time,
Her light, an echo of the past, in twilight's chime.

Each night she fades, a whisper in the cosmic sea,
In her diminishing glow, the secrets of the ages be.

Oh, guardian of the threshold, in your retreat and ebb,
We find the wisdom of the end, in your gentle web.

Behold the mother in her glory, full and bright,
A sphere of mystic power, in the depth of night.

Her round face mirrors the hidden truth so clear,
In her luminous embrace, the veils of mystery disappear.

Oh, moon of the fullest splendor, in your orb of light,
Illuminate our path with your wisdom, so right.

CHANT ⊕F THE MꝊꝊN'S PꝊWER

Under the Full Moon's silver beam,
Goddess whispers in a dream.
Cup of might, in her hands so fair,
Fertile secrets, in the cool night air.

Veil of mystery, gently sways,
In the Goddess' potent gaze.
Silver light that guides our heart,
With her wisdom, we never part.

As the Moon wanes in the sky,
Goddess listens to our sigh.
Fertile thoughts begin to ebb,
In her grace, our fears we shed.

Through the veil of night and fear,
Her silver voice, we always hear.
In the cup of fading light,
Find the power of the night.

CHANT FꝊR THE WANING MꝊꝊN

As the Moon begins to wane,
The Goddess whispers, a soft refrain.
Behind her veil, spells are spun,
In the fading light, our will is done.

FAIRY ꝊFFERINGS

Fairy offerings and the belief in these beings have persisted throughout the world from ancient times up to the present day. Originating from a time when the Gods were given tribute as well as other spirits, from the ancestorial to those of both nature and the Underworld. Today, this practice continues in many cultures and is done for healing, wishes, and general placation or for good luck. Witches still work with these beings for a plethora of reasons, from honoring the Genius loci to communing with the Gods and our magical ancestral current and, of course, acts of magic. In medieval times, Witches were often accused of making pacts with fairies to obtain their powers. A word of warning if you begin to work with fairies: it is, in my opinion. a lifetime commitment. Failure to maintain honor to the other people could leave one elf-shot.

Fairy Offering from May to November

To the Good People, guardians of mystery and mirth,
To the Other People, weavers of the earth,
And to the Shining Ones, fair and bright,
I offer this tribute, in their radiant sight.

To the Sidhe, to those unseen and fair,
And to the Seelie Court, in the moonlit air,
This offering I bring, from heart so true,
A tribute of reverence, from my world to you

In realms unseen, where enchantments sway,
To Queen Diana of Elphame, this homage I lay.
By names of might and ancient lore,
Don, Arianrhod, Abundia, Holda, Minerva, I adore.

Blessed be to those who walk between
Blessed be our eternal queen.

Fairy Offering from November to May

To the Good People, sovereigns of secrets untold,
To the Other People, Crafters of wonders to behold,
And to the Glistening Ones, in their allure so bold,
I offer this tribute, in their glory manifold.

To the Sidhe, shrouded in mystery's veil,
And to the Unseelie Court, where the untamed tales prevail,
This offering I carry, from a world so blue,
A tribute of honor, from my heart to you.

In realms obscured, where shadowed enchantments lay,
To Queen Herodias of the night's array,
By names of strength and eldritch lore,
Nicneven, Cailleach, Hecate, Bensozia, Nocticula, I implore.

Blessed be to those who traverse the twilight's sheen,
Blessed be our sovereign, the Unseelie Queen.

LUCKY C⊕IN SPELL

To Bless a Coin with Luck hold it to the light of the full moon turning it three times and saying:

"By the light of the silvered moon and the fortune of the coin's face,
Grant me serenity in darkness and prosperity in grace.
As the moon waxes and wanes in the night sky's embrace,
May luck and peace follow me in every place."

Carry the coin with you and perform every full moon.

GREEK MOON OIL RECIPE

- **1 part Olive Oil**: As a base, since olive trees were sacred in ancient Greece.

- **1 part Silver Leaf**: To represent the moon (use only a tiny bit as decoration; it's not essential for the oil's effectiveness).

- **1 part Cypress Oil**: Cypress trees were sacred to Artemis, and their oil can represent protection and mourning, tying in with the mysterious aspects of the moon.

- **Moonstone Crystals**: For their association with the moon and femininity, much like the Greek moon goddesses.

- **A small piece of Papyrus or Bay Leaf**: To write a charm or invocation to the Greek moon deities (optional).

CLEOPATRA SEDUCTION OIL RECIPE

- **1 part Olive Oil or Sesame Oil**: Common base oils in both ancient Egypt and Greece.

- **1 part Myrrh**: Widely used in ancient Egypt for its aromatic and healing properties.

- **2 parts Frankincense**: Another popular resin, known for its deep, soothing scent.

- **1 part Blue Lotus**: A symbolically significant flower in ancient Egypt, reputed for its delightful fragrance and possibly aphrodisiac qualities.

- **1 part Saffron**: A luxurious spice, used for its scent and coloring properties.

- **1 part Cinnamon**: Known in both cultures for its warm, inviting aroma.

- **1 part Cardamom**: Used for its strong, unique scent and potential aphrodisiac effects.

- **1 part Rose**: While not as common in ancient Egypt, roses were highly valued in ancient Greek culture for beauty and scent.

- **1 part Honey**: A symbol of sweetness and beauty in both cultures.

YARR⊕W L⊕VE CHARM

On a Friday bind a bundle of fresh Yarrow with green thread while saying this charm and then hang it over your bed.

Yarrow of old, with petals bright,
Bring true love into my sight.
May it be pure and free of sorrow,
Let love bloom today and tomorrow.
By your power, kind and mellow,
Draw near the heart of one so fellow.
As this charm is softly spoken,
Let love's true bond remain unbroken.

H⊕RSESH⊕E PR⊕TECTI⊕N CHARM

When you recite this spell, envision a circle of protection around you or your home. Hang a horseshoe above your main entrance as a symbol of this protection, with the ends pointing upwards to contain the good fortune and ward off evil.

Spirit of iron, curve of might,
Horseshoe hang above my door tonight.
Shield this space from harm and fear,
Let only good draw near.
As you curve, so does my luck,
In your strength, my protection is struck.
Against all ills, you stand so bold,
In your arc, my peace take hold.

HEARTH FIRE PRAYER TO SAINT BRIGID

Draw a cross in the ashes and say this prayer while kindling your hearth fire. If you do not have one a carved candle will substitute.

Saint Brigid, keeper of the flame,
Bless our hearth, in your holy name.
Guard our home from harm and strife,
Fill our walls with warmth and life.
In your grace, let us abide,
With your shield, may we reside.
By your fire, so bright and clear,
Keep us safe and loved ones near.

SYMBOLS FOR CANDLE CARVING

Cross
Protection, blessing

Ankh
Healing, union,
fertility

Heart
Love

Eye
Protection or clarity

Sun
Happiness, abundance,
physical strength

Infinity Symbol
Balance

Moon
Emotional healing,
fertility, magic

Pentagram
Protection
and power

ROWAN CROSS FOR PROTECTION

Take two straight sticks or twigs from a Rowan Tree. Using red thread or twine bind them together as you speak the Charm. Hang it in your home for protection.

Charm for the Rowan Cross

Rowan tree of magic and might,
Protect this dwelling, both day and night.
With berries red and bark so strong,
I charge this cross, repel all wrong.
In each weave and turn of twine,
Bless this charm goddess divine.
Guard against the dark and fear,
Let only good enter here.

PRAYER TO THE EGYPTIAN
GODS TO HEAL AN ANIMAL

O mighty deities of ancient sands, hear this humble plea,
Bast, guardian of cats and all creatures, lend your protective gaze,
As you watch over the innocent, wrap them in your warmth and grace.

Anubis, sacred hound guide of souls, keeper of balance and harmony,
Bestow your strength unto (animals name) healing in your steady
hand,
Guide the spirit of this animal to recovery.

Hathor, motherly and kind, whose love knows no bounds,
Shower your compassion and healing light on this gentle being,
May your nurturing touch bring comfort and sound health.

Horus, with your falcon's eye, see the plight of this creature small,
may your watchful presence bring health, happiness, and comfort.
Incircle (animal's name) with your wings of light.

Ancient Gods of fur and fang wing and claw forsake not your earthly
Forms so mote it be.

TRADITIONAL FLORIDA WATER FORMULA

Florida water is a very popular formula in both southern folk magic, South American and Caribbean magical traditions, voodoo, and the veneration of catholic saints. In New Orleans, it is the go-to for most magically inclined people. Florida water is used for cleansing, protection, love, and as an offering to spirits or deities who enjoy flowers. The European equivalent would be Rose Water.

Ingredients:

- Alcohol base (typically high-proof vodka or Everclear) - 2 cups

Essential oils:

- Bergamot - 10 drops

- Lavender - 10 drops

- Lemon - 10 drops

- Clove - 5 drops

- Rose - 5 drops

- Orange - 5 drops

- Ylang-ylang - 5 drops

- Cinnamon - 3 drops

- Distilled or spring water - 1 cup

- Glycerin (optional, for skin softening) - 1 tablespoon

Instructions:

- **Combine essential oils:** In a large glass bottle or jar, combine all the essential oils. Shake or stir to blend them thoroughly.

- **Add alcohol:** Pour the 2 cups of alcohol into the jar with the essential oils. This helps to dissolve the oils and blend them evenly.

- **Shake and settle:** Secure the lid and shake the mixture vigorously. Then, let it sit in a cool, dark place for 24 to 48 hours. This allows the scents to meld together.

- **Dilute with water:** After the settling period, add 1 cup of distilled or spring water to the mixture. This dilutes the alcohol and makes the fragrance more subtle.

- **Add glycerin (optional):** If you're planning to use the Florida Water on your skin, you can add a tablespoon of glycerin. This step is optional but helps to soften the skin.

- **Final shake and settle:** Shake the mixture again and let it sit for another 24 hours.

- **Strain:** Use a cheesecloth or coffee filter to strain the mixture into a clean bottle or jar. This step ensures that any undissolved particles are removed.

- **Store:** Store your Florida Water in a cool, dark place. It's best used within six months to a year.

TRADITIONAL ROSE WATER RECIPE

Ingredients:

- Fresh rose petals (preferably organic and fragrant) - about 1-2 cups

- Distilled water - enough to cover the petals (approximately 2-3 cups)

Equipment:

- A large pot with a lid

- A heatproof bowl

- Ice cubes

- Cheesecloth or fine strainer

- Sterilized glass bottle or jar for storage

Instructions:

- **Gather rose petals:** Gently pluck the petals from the roses. You'll need about 1-2 cups of fresh petals. It's important to use organic roses to avoid any pesticides.

- **Clean the petals:** Rinse the petals under cold water to remove any dirt or bugs.

- **Prepare the pot:** Place the heatproof bowl in the center of the pot. Arrange the rose petals around the bowl and then pour enough distilled water over the petals to just cover them.

- **Boil and condense:** Place the lid upside down on the pot. Turn on the heat and bring the water to a simmer. Once it begins to simmer, fill the inverted lid with ice. This creates a condensation effect inside the pot, which is necessary for making rose water.

- **Simmer:** Let the mixture simmer for about 20-30 minutes or until the petals lose their color. The water in the bowl will be infused with the essence of the rose petals.

- **Cool down:** After the petals have lost their color, turn off the heat and remove the lid. Let it cool down to room temperature.

- **Strain:** Carefully remove the bowl from the pot. Strain the rose water through a cheesecloth or fine strainer into a sterilized glass bottle or jar.

- **Store:** Store your homemade rose water in a cool, dark place or in the refrigerator. It should last for several weeks.

INCANTATI⊕N F⊕R SCRYING INT⊕ A BLACK MIRR⊕R

Blackened glass, portal deep,
Unlock the Mysteries you keep.
Show the past or future bright,
in your depths, grant me sight.
Oh, mirror dark, reveal to me,
The sights and secrets I wish to see.
this is my will, so shall it be,
this is my will so mote it be.

MAKING A DREAM PILL⊕W

Herbs:

- Mugwort

- Lavender

- Chamomile

Dream pillows are a continuation of earlier ancient practices of using certain herbs in one's bedding. A practice followed in ancient Egypt, Mesopotamia, and China. In medieval Europe, they were used in folk remedies to protect against illness and to induce dreams, with Mugwort and lavender being the most traditional for this purpose. In the Victorian era, dream pillows became popular as a part of aromatherapy. Lavender, known for its relaxing properties, was a common ingredient. This period also saw the rise of dream interpretation, and dream pillows were sometimes used in the hope of inspiring meaningful dreams.

Instructions:

- **Cut the fabric:** Measure and cut two pieces of fabric into your desired pillow size. A standard small pillow size is about 12x12 inches. Sew the Edges: Place the two pieces of fabric together with the inside (the side you want hidden) facing out. Sew along the edges but leave a small opening for stuffing.

- **Turn right-side out:** Once the edges are sewn, turn the fabric right-side out through the opening.

- **Mix the filling:** In a bowl, mix your chosen filling with the dried herbs. If you're using essential oils, add a few drops and mix well.

- **Stuff the pillow**: Use half cotton and half herbs. Carefully fill the pillow with your herb and filling mixture.

- **Close the opening:** Once filled, sew the opening closed. For finishing touches you may want to add decorative elements like embroidery, tassels, or lace and magical symbols.

HAL AN TOW TRADITIONAL MAY EVE SONG

[Chorus]
Jolly-rum-ba-low
We were up long before the day-o
To welcome in the summer
To welcome in the May-O
Summer is a cummin in
and winther's gone away-O

[Verse 1]
Take no scorn to wear the horn
it was the crest when you were born
Your father's father wore it
Your father wore it, too

[Chorus]
Jolly-rum-ba-low
We were up long before the day-o
To welcome in the summer
To welcome in the May-O
Summer is a cummin in
and winther's gone away-O

[Verse 2]
Robin Hood and Little John
Have both gone to the Fair-O
and we will to the Merry Green-Wood
to hunt the buck and Hair-O

[Chorus]
Jolly-rum-ba-low
We were up long before the day-o
To welcome in the summer
To welcome in the May-O
Summer is a cummin in
and winther's gone away-O

[Verse 3]
Bless Aunt Mary Moses
who raised a mighty storm-O
It blew away the Spanish fleet
between the dusk and Morn-O

[Chorus]
Jolly-rum-ba-low
We were up long before the day-o
To welcome in the summer
To welcome in the May-O
Summer is a cummin in
and winther's gone away-O

[Verse 4]
We have brought the budding branch
to blest each hearth and bed-O
For none should lie alone today
But to the woods, instead-O!

[Chorus]
Jolly-rum-ba-low
We were up long before the day-o
To welcome in the summer
To welcome in the May-O
Summer is a cummin in
and winther's gone away-O

[Verse 5]
Bless the Lord and Lady
and all who dwell in here-O
and bless the little children born
and turning of the year-O

[Chorus]
Jolly-rum-ba-low
We were up long before the day-o
To welcome in the summer
To welcome in the May-O
Summer is a cummin in
and winther's gone away-O

LEGEND ⊕ OF THE WITCHES

In the beginning before time, before man, there was only the moon. And the moon was Diana the beautiful Goddess. Sad, lonely, and silent she wandered alone. In all the universe there was none but her. She sought the world over for a lover, but there was only her own reflection in the waves of the oceans. Her tears formed the rains that sprinkled the Earth. Solitude was her only companion. Her sighs formed the winds that blew over the seas as she searched for a friend.

Diana was a child of her own desire. Desire is the only emotion on Earth, desire driving her on and on. And from that desire was born the dawn, and from the dawn came the sun, and from the sun came a first angel of light. And that angel was Lucifer God of light.

The moon Diana and the sun Lucifer became the first lovers, and loved as no know human knows love. And from that love was born the sky, the Earth. And from the Earth sprang plants where the tears of joy fell from the lovely Diana. And it came to pass that the fruits of that love gave birth to fire, and water, and birds, and fishes, and animals.

Legend of the Witches Alternative

In the beginning was the Moon Diana. Sad, silent, alone she wandered, the waves her sighs and tears of solitude...

She searched everywhere for a companion but found only reflections of herself. Lonely, Diana desired a lover. That desire became the dawn, and from the dawn came the sun, Lucifer, the God of Light...

This is the Witch's legend of creation...

Diana and Lucifer also created man. They gave him the world and taught him to hunt, kill, and be content that he might better worship them...

To these powerful gods, man erected huge monuments and temples of stone, thousands of them aligned along the paths of their gods across the sky...

Many of these groups of stones, like Stonehenge, were complex observatories predicting what once was thought the unpredictable, fickle wondering of their gods. Man, now able to predict, soon sought to control the gods. They entrusted this control to priests...

To choose these Priests, the Witches, a name which comes from the Anglo-Saxon word Wicca, meaning wise, hold a severe Initiation ceremony. Those already initiated, perform a ritual called Drawing Down of the Moon. Since the moon is a woman, Diana, the chief of the Witches is a Priestess. This ceremony calls down and concentrates Diana's power in this Priestess and through her, the circle, and those dancing in it.

SONG OF CREATION

In the beginning there was a great, black ocean of roaring waves, and dancing upon the surface of the waters danced the first musical notes, the notes became a beautiful song, the most beautiful song that ever had been. The song was so powerful it divided the world between land and Ocean. And as the waters began to batter the shore, the earth, and the sand, the foam that touched the land became a white mare. And this white horse was the first mother and as she was born from the song and the sea, on the land, she knew desire. And this desire moved her onwards and she felt loneliness, for other, for life outside of herself. For all she could see was her own reflection upon the water. So, she cried tears and from her tears that fell upon the sand, grew forth a mighty majestic oak tree.

And upon this tree, hung the sacred mistletoe and its white berries fell to the earth before the mare. And the mare, still filled with desire, felt her first hunger. So, she ate the seeds and from the seeds, she became pregnant with the first other and gave birth to him who was her desire. And he was a fiery god, and the mare desired him to return to her. But the god did not want to return to the mare. So, he transformed himself into a golden Eagle and flew into the sky where he became the sun, separating himself from the realm of the mare who he thought of as terrible and terrifying. But the mare in her desire, knew love. And she sang the first love song and transformed into a white owl soaring into the sky and becoming the moon.

The moon chases the sun eternally only catching him from time to time. When they meet, they become one again and in this way he too learns the song of love, they love and from their love all other life was created each with its own melody in the great song.

The Forgotten Gods of Witchcraft

THE QUEEN ⊕ OF THE SABBAT

In medieval lore and the records of Witchcraft trials, the "Queen of the Sabbat," also known as the female leader of Witches, was sometimes referred to as the Maiden or the Queen of Elphame. Other historic epithets for her include Diana, Herodias, and Holda, among others.

During the height of the European Witch hunts, from the 15th to the 17th centuries, accusations of Witchcraft were often intertwined with charges of heresy and diabolism. The *Malleus Maleficarum* and similar texts are replete with tales of Witches convening at nocturnal celebrations called the Sabbat. She is portrayed as a dominant presence. She presides over the Sabbat ceremonies, which are described as filled with ritualistic practices such as feasting, dancing, and the orchestration of various diabolical acts. She is variously characterized as a Witch, an ambassador of the Devil, or occasionally as a matriarch revered by the Witches or as the Devil himself. The modern revival of Witchcraft regards this figure, whether historical or mythical, as a manifestation of the Goddess or a priestess acting in her stead. Intriguingly, several classical deities' names appear in these accounts, many of which have persisted into the present day.

Abundia

Abundia is a European Witchcraft goddess associated with Herodias as Queen of the Witches. It is believed she is derived from the Roman Teutonic Goddess Abundantia—meaning Abundance—and indeed Abundia is said to bring prosperity at night. In France she is called lady Habonde other names include Habondia or Habundia. In ancient times she was seen holding a cornucopia and prayed to for wealth and prosperity.

Baba Yaga

A Slavic Goddess whose name means something like Grandmother of Sorcery or Grandmother of Witchcraft. Her association with European Witchcraft during the medieval period is primarily rooted in Slavic mythology and folklore rather than mainstream European Witchcraft practices. Although some scholars have associated her with Hecate, she seems to be more akin to the Cailleach, both of whom share the rare feature of being depicted as a hag or crone. Some of her other names and titles include Iagaia Baba, Bony Leg, Grandmother Witch, and Forest Crone. Baba Yaga is a Goddess associated with death, magic, wisdom, herbs, and mother nature. However, she had a dark side as an evil cannibal.

Bensozia

A French Gaulish Goddess, According to Dom Jacques Martin's *Religion de Gaulois* from the 18th century, Bensozia was considered the "chief deviless" of a Witchcraft Sabbat in 12th and 13th century France. She was called Diana of the Gauls and was also associated with Nocticula and Herodias. Bensozia is a Goddess of the Moon, and the Moon is one of her monikers. She was said to lead Witches naked on horses to the Sabbat in a nocturnal procession. As Nocticula, she became strongly associated with both demons and vampires in medieval folklore.

Cailleach

Also, Cailleach Bheur, or Bheara, is a Scottish and Irish Celtic Goddess associated with Halloween, the Moon, and Winter. In the summer months, she is said to transform into Brigid or Airaidheach, the Goddess of the summer pastures. Cailleach was also a Goddess of magic, the harvest, weather, animals, and a ruthless guardian of nature. She was depicted as a hag, sometimes with blue skin, a third eye, and boar's teeth, wielding a hammer or staff and flying on the back of a wolf through the winter night sky. Her mantle would be taken on by Nicnevin in the medieval period.

Diana

Known as a Roman goddess, her origins are probably much older, being directly linked to many cultures of proto-European descent, including Greek and Celtic. The earliest references to Diana may be from the Vedic texts of India. In the final throes of Pagan Rome, she had absorbed or blended with many goddesses, including Hecate and Isis, who at one time shared her seat in Nemi. The Church would go on to call her the Last Goddess of the Pagans, and by the medieval period, she had become the full-fledged queen of the Witches. Diana's traditional Roman attributes are well known, but by the time the church had risen, she was also a Mother Goddess, developed an incestuous relationship with her brother, and presided over fairies, Witches, sorcery, and the dead.

Hecate

A Greek Goddess who was a Titan. Hecate, once a Goddess of the Eleusinian Mysteries, has been associated with many other goddesses, including Diana, Isis, Demeter, Persephone, Selena, Luna, and her Roman equivalent, Trivia. This three-formed Goddess of crossroads, the moon, and magic would, by the medieval period, become rooted within the realms of Witchcraft. She would primarily be replaced by the Goddess Diana, Herodias, and others who were more popular outside of Greece.

Herodías

Herodias is a Greek name often associated with the wife of Herold Philip from the bible. However, its pre-Christian origins have been speculated to be Hera Diana, meaning Queen Diana, the Goddess she is most often associated with. Herodias also appears in the manuscript *Aradia or The Gospel of the Witches*, Aradia being an alternative name for Herodias, variations of which are found throughout Europe, such as Erodiade, Herodiade, and Ariadne, just to name a few. As a Goddess of Witchcraft, she shares all the attributes of Diana, her Mother or alternative name.[3] [4]

Holda

A Germanic Witch Goddess often associated with Herodias and known for leading the wild hunt, Holda was a Goddess of domestic affairs, childbirth, and the Moon. At times, she takes on the form of a crone known as Perchta or Berchta. With the spread of Christianity, Holda's image transformed from a revered goddess to a demonized figure. The Christian church portrayed her as the leader of a Witch cult, associating her with Witchcraft and night flights.

Madonna Oriente

An Italian figure whose name means Lady of the East, she is also known as Signora Oriente or La Signora del Gioco. She is described in the confessions of two Italian women, Sibilla Zanni and Pierina de' Bugatis, who were executed by the Inquisition in 1390. Their story involved elaborate occult religious rituals in Milan, where Madonna Oriente, possibly revered as a goddess, performed magical acts. Historian Carlo Ginzburg

---

3   https://www.patheos.com/blogs/poisonersapothecary/2017/03/27/herodias-queen-Witches/

4   https://occult-world.com/herodias/

has linked her to a wider mythological complex originating from central Eurasia, suggesting the name Madonna Oriente comes from "Domina Oriens," a term for the moon as a Goddess.

Minerva

The Roman Goddess of wisdom and strategy was associated with the Greek Athena and was an incredibly important Goddess within the empire. She was especially popular in Roman Britain, where she gained association with local Goddesses such as Coventina, Britannia, and Sulis. In the Temple of Sulis Minerva in Bath, England, she was worshiped as a Mother Goddess, and votives for both healing and cursing have been discovered there. Although never directly associated with Witchcraft by the medieval period, Minerva had become a title for the Fairy Queen in Britain, and in *The Discoverie of Witchcraft* (1584), she is equated with Diana and Herodias.

Nicneven

Nicneven or Nicnevin is a Scottish fairy queen and Witch Goddess associated with Diana, the Cailleach, and Gyre-Carline. Like many of her counterparts, Nicneven is associated with the moon, crossroads, and night flights in which she leads processions of Witches and fairies. As a Goddess, she presides over the sky and sea and may transform from a beautiful young woman into an old hag. In one of her early references, she is linked to both children and fate.

Queen of Elphame

She originates in Scotland and North England. She is often associated with Freyja, Nicnevin, and Hubundia. She is the elven queen of the fairies, and she features prominently in several Scottish Witch trials, where she is often linked to instances of alleged Witchcraft. In one trial her husband is referred to as master or Christsonday. In other accounts, she sometimes turns into the Devil. .

THE MASTER ⊕R THE SABBAT L⊕RD

The Master or Sabbat Lord is believed to be a continuation or rein-terpretation of pre-Christian Gods, especially those linked to ecstasy, nature, fertility, hunting, death, the Underworld, and magic. A prominent form is the Horned God, symbolizing a crossroads between the natural and wild aspects of the carnal animal world and that of civilized man. When Christianity became dominant in Europe, the Old Gods were often demonized, and their characteristics were merged into the Christian concept of the Devil. The Master and God of the Witches is a blend of history, myth, folklore, and superstition. When dissected, he becomes a literal mix between the Old Gods of nature, such as Pan, Serapis, Faunus, Silvanus, Dionysus, and Cernunnos and transformed into the Christian's arch fiend. Apollo becomes Lucifer, Serapis Satan, and Pan—the wicked red Devil!

It is of cultural interest to study this figure and how he was viewed in the medieval period. He seduced men and women into Witchcraft, drawing them into the woods or other places far removed from society, and made pacts with them offering magical power in exchange for their worship. This worship would often involve that which was forbidden by the Church: sex, dancing, drinking, and sorcery. Aside from the occasional accusation of cannibalism, it rather sounds like a good time. The Master or God of the Witches had several forms: a horned demon mirroring the Old Horned Gods, a man dressed in black, a black dog, and a goat. Some of his names and titles include variations of Robin, Lucifello, Christsonday, Old Nick, Old Hornie, Old Scratch—and yes— The Devil.

Lucifello

This name is recorded in Italian trial records as the consort of Diana in her aspect as a Witchcraft Goddess. Clearly, it is a folk name for Lucifer, who is also cited as the brother and lover of Diana in Aradia or The Gospel of the Witches. Lucifer, meaning light bearer, is another form of Apollo, Diana's historic brother. Lucifello also reminds one of Robin

Goodfellow, a good God of light. Lucifello, as a God or a spirit, presides over the games of Diana or the Witches Sabbat.

Old Hornie

Scottish and English in origin, Old Hornie or Old Horny is an Old English nickname for the Devil found in folklore and popularized by the poet Robert Burns. Considering that nothing describes the devil as having horns in the Bible, Witches have long held it as a title of the Horned One (Cernunnos) and may, in theory, be connected to Old Herne of Windsor Forest. Old Hornie or Old Horny is a playful title with sexual undertones and a perfect example of local folk customs synchronizing old and new belief systems. Old Hornie like Cernunnos could take any image of a horned deity, although a goat or stag would be culturally appropriate. As a God form, he would be associated with all elements of Witchcraft as well as the Old God of nature.

Old Nick

A name with Germanic roots found within English folklore as a name for the devil. It might derive from the old English word neck, meaning spirit. Nik is also a title for Woden in old English folklore. Old Nick was the title of the Devil when he led the wild hunt during winter, and it should be no surprise that there are evolutionary links between Old Nick, Odin, Saint Nickolas, and Santa Claus. As a God, Old Nick presides over winter, hunting, and the realms of the dead.

Robin

Robin is English in origin, and he is prominently featured in both folklore and Witch trials. He is generally depicted as the Devil or a fairy. Robin means bright or shining, and in British folklore, the bird of the same name is associated with both spring and fertility. Perhaps one of the most popular examples is Robin Goodfellow, another title for Puck, both of whom are depicted or associated at times with goats. In the depiction of Robin Goodfellow, he looks like Pan holding a broom and torch with a drinking horn. Other variations of Robin include Robin Artison, Robin Hood, Cock Robin, and Robert. Robert, as a Godform, is a Horned God of nature light, fertility, ecstasy, fairies, and magic.

The He Goat or the Devil

In accounts of Witches' Sabbaths during the medieval Witchcraft craze, the Devil was often described as appearing in the form of a goat or being present as a black goat, sometimes even anthropomorphized with human characteristics. To early Christians, sheep represented the flock of Christ, while goats, unruly and stubborn, belonged to the Devil. The goat also had a long-standing history in pre-Christian Europe, and Witches have always maintained that the origin of this symbolism derives from old gods like Pan, Faunus, and Sylvanus. Modern interpretations include the Devil of the Tarot card and Eliphas Levi's version of Baphomet. While the figure of Baphomet, often depicted as a goat-headed deity, is more closely associated with the occult and Templar legends of the post-medieval period, its goat-like imagery has roots in earlier medieval demonology and Witchcraft lore.

The Man in Black or The Black Man

A term used especially in the Salem Witch Trials, referring to a dark, shadowy figure believed to be the Devil. Margaret Murray, In her works *The Witch-Cult in Western Europe* and *The God of the Witches*, regarded the Man in Black as the Horned God of the Witches due to the accounts of the black He Goat who presided over the Sabbats. The European Man in Black may have a connection to the old English Woden, who was also described in English folklore as appearing to people at crossroads garbed in black, prepared to make deals for magical favors. In New Orleans folklore, there is a legend about a figure known as the "Devil Man of Algiers." This legend emerged in the 1930s and describes a man dressed entirely in black who haunted the Algiers area of New Orleans. He was reputed to have the ability to curse people and claimed to have an alliance with

Neptune. The Man in Black has the air of a magical trickster but may indeed be a manifestation of the Witches' God.

MEDIEVAL WITCHCRAFT ENTITIES

Banshees

An Irish or Celtic female spirit, meaning fairy women. The Banshee's wailing was believed to be an omen of death. They are associated with certain families, particularly those with surnames beginning with O or Mac. Witches and fairies have always been linked together. Both Witches and Banshees are known for nocturnal visitations and otherworldly omens.

Brownies

In Scottish and English folklore, brownies are small, household spirits that are generally helpful but can be mischievous if they are mistreated. Witches were believed to intentionally house brownies, leaving them offerings of milk, honey, butter, cream, baked goods, or porridge.

Changelings

Changelings are Celtic in origin. They are fairy children left in place of human babies stolen by fairies. Witchcraft was viewed as both the cause and solution to changelings. In some stories and beliefs, Witches were thought to be capable of invoking fairies or other supernatural beings to swap children with changelings. This once again demonstrated the correlations between Witches and fairies. Conversely, in some folk tales and beliefs, knowledge of Witchcraft or magical practices was sometimes considered necessary to identify or return a changeling to the fairies and get the human child back.

Djinns or Genies

Supernatural beings from Middle Eastern folklore, particularly Persia, are often bound to objects and capable of magical feats. In medieval Europe, any knowledge of djinns would have been filtered through the lens of

Christian and European folklore, likely conflating them with demons. In the occult they are associated with the element of fire.

Elves

Germanic, Celtic, and British, Elves (known as "álfar") are depicted as divine beings with magical powers and a close association with nature. The Germanic concept of elves is divided into two main types: the light elves ("Ljósálfar"), who were considered benevolent and beautiful, dwelling in the heavenly realms, and the dark elves ("Dökkálfar" or "Svartálfar"), who were thought to live underground and were more mischievous or malevolent. The Germanic Elves would be akin to the Celtic Sidhe being as the race of Gods somewhat like angels or demons. In British folklore, elves are often portrayed as small, elusive, supernatural beings associated with woods and natural areas. During the Witchcraft trials in medieval and early modern Europe, some testimonies involved stories of encounters with elves or fairies. People accused of Witchcraft sometimes claimed to have received their knowledge or powers from these beings.

Fairies

A generalized title for European nature spirits forgotten Gods and pre-Christian ancestors, the term is Latin in origin from Fatae, meaning fate or Gods of Gate; in Old French faerie; and Middle English faerie or fairie. The Fairy Faith flourished in Medieval Europe and is perhaps one of the few examples of ancient pre-Christian beliefs that were kept up in continuity. Fairies can be found in all cultures but were particularly influenced by those of Celtic and Germanic descent who kept traditions surrounding these being alive into the present day.

While the term "fairy" itself does not originate from Celtic languages, many of the modern concepts and characteristics of fairies are heavily influenced by Celtic (particularly Irish and Scottish) folklore, where beings such as the Sidhe or Aos Si, meaning people of the mounds, share similarities with what we now consider as fairies. Sometimes in Scotland, they were called Sith, and in Wales, the Tylwyth Teg, meaning Fairy Folk or Beautiful Family. Other titles for fairies are The Other People, The Shining Ones, Hidden People, Good Folk, Good Neighbors, Gentry, Wee Folk, Little People, Fey, and The Seelie and Unseelie Courts. In Scottish folklore, fairies are divided into two courts. The Seelie Court comprises fairies who are more amicable towards humans, while the Unseelie Court consists of those who are less friendly and more prone to malevolence ,this mirrors the beliefs about elves. Witches have always been associated with fairies, as have our Gods and our magical ancestors. In Witch Trials, Witches were often accused of drawing their powers from these entities who—in my opinion—would go on to become familiars. Today, many Witches still work with variations of fairy tales from a multitude of cultures. Just keep in mind that once you go down a magical road, there is no undoing it. The Other People are forever friends.

Familiars
These Animal companions are believed to be endowed with magical powers or to be demons in disguise. Cats, toads, dogs, crows, and owls were common familiars at other times they resemble demons or imps. Familiars are most likely a product of fairy veneration. In modern Witchcraft a familiar spirit is any spirit the Witch has familiarities with that is intentional contact and favor.

Goblins, Gobelin, or Hobgoblin
A French and English fairy creature that eventually found its way into all of Europe, all of which had similar entities already, such as Kobolds and trolls. They are mischievous and often malevolent creatures with a penchant for trickery; however, at times, they could be helpful and even kind. Witches employed them as Familiars in folklore. Modern Witches consider Goblins to be fairy tricksters that have their associations with the element of earth in the occult.

Imps

A Germanic and English fairy originally considered playful tricksters. In the medieval period, they transformed into small, lesser demons who served as Witches' familiars, generally employed for small malevolent acts and trickery rather than grand-scale evil. Most modern Witches do not use the term imp possible because of the demonic association.

Incubi and Succubi

Male and female demons, respectively, they are believed to engage in sexual activity with sleeping humans. Vampiric in nature, they were also often fused with Witches themselves, with the accusations of Witches sending their fetch or spirit to sexually torment their victims. Modern Witches would call this astral projection, but it is not used for nefarious reasons.

Nymphs

Greek in origin, these female nature entities are each associated with a particular aspect of nature, such as trees, water, or mountains, and are sometimes linked to Witchcraft and magic. Nymphs were the favorite companions of many old Gods, including Diana, Pan, and Dionysus. Modern Witches view them as a type of pagan angel or a mostly benevolent fairy.

Puca

Also, Pwca, Bwca or Buca, this Irish, Scottish, and Welsh fairy sometimes associated with Puck is portrayed as dark, somewhat malevolent creatures with the power to shape-shift. Common forms include a horse, goat, dog, rabbit, or even a goblin-like figure. Believed to be active and take dominion over the earth from the winter months from Halloween to May. Modern Witches view them as Guardians of nature during these times.

Sources and Suggested Reading

Apuleius, Lucius. *The Golden Ass* by Lucius Apuleius. London, U.K.,: Penguin Random House, 1998.

Bourne, Lois. *Dancing with Witches*. London: Robert Hale, 2006.

Buckland, Raymond. *The Witch Book*. Canton, MI: Visible Ink Press, 2002.

Cain, Brian. *Initiation Into Witchcraft*. New Orleans: Warlock Press, 2019.

Carr-Gomm, Phillip. "Gerald Gardner & Ross Nichols." Published on *phillipcarr-gomm.com*, *https://philipcarr-gomm.com/essay/gerald-gardner-ross-nichols/*.

Chiaradonna, Riccardo and Adrien Lecerf, "Iamblichus", The Stanford Encyclopedia of Philosophy (Winter 2023 Edition), Edward N. Zalta & Uri Nodelman (eds.), *https://plato.stanford.edu/archives/win2023/entries/iamblichus/*.

Climo, Lillian. "A Note from the Collections: Midwives and Healers in the European Witch Trials." International Museum of Surgical Science website, *https://imss.org/2019/12/a-note-from-the-collections-midwives-and-healers-in-the-european-Witch-trials/*.

Crowther, Patricia. *Covensense, A Handbook for Witches*. London: Frederick Muller Limited, 1981.

Crowther, Patricia. *Lid Off the Cauldron*. Somerset, England, U.K, Capall Bann Publishing, 1998.

Davies, Owen. "Top 10 Grimoires." April 15, 2009. Oxford University Press blog, *blog.oup.com/2009/04/grimoires/*.

Day, Christian. *The Witches' Book of the Dead*. New Orleans, Warlock Press, 2019.

Di Fiosa, Jimahl. *A Coin for the Ferryman, The Death and Life of Alex Sanders*. Boston: Logios, 2010.

Editors at Art and Popular Culture. "Madonna Oriente." Art and Popular Culture. *https://www.artandpopularculture.com/Madonna_Oriente.*

Editors of Beliefnet. "Riding With Holda." Belief Net, Pagan, and Earth-Based, Dec. 2012 *https://www.beliefnet.com/faiths/pagan-and-earth-based/2002/12/riding-with-holda.aspx.*

Editors of British Fairies. "Nymphes and faeries"- Renaissance influences upon the 'national fairy.'" British Fairies, May 7, 2017, *https://british-fairies.wordpress.com/tag/herodias/.*

Editors of Encyclopaedia Britannica. "Damascius." Encyclopedia Britannica, February 26, 2024. *https://www.britannica.com/biography/Damascius.*

Editors of Encyclopaedia Britannica. "Great Chain of Being." Encyclopedia Britannica, December 10, 2021. *https://www.britannica.com/topic/Great-Chain-of-Being.*

Editors of Encyclopaedia Britannica. "Marsilio Ficino." *Encyclopedia Britannica*, March 1, 2024. *https://www.britannica.com/biography/Marsilio-Ficino.*

Editors of *Esoterica*. "Celestial Hierarchy: Dionysius the Areopagite" from *Esoterica*, published on *esoteric.msu.edu*. Accessed on March 1, 2023, *https://esoteric.msu.edu/VolumeII/CelestialHierarchy.html/.*

Ehrenreich, Barbara and Deirdre English. "Witches, midwives, and nurses: A history of women healers." Libcom.org, December 27, 2012. *https://libcom.org/article/Witches-midwives-and-nurses-history-women-healers-barbara-ehrenreich-and-deirdre-english/.*

Gardner, Gerald. *The Meaning of Witchcraft. Boston, MA: Weiser Books, 2004.*

Gardner, Gerald. *High Magic's Aid.* Toronto, Dark Dragon Publishing, 2023

Ginzburg, Carlo. *Ecstasies: Deciphering The Witches' Sabbath.* trans. Raymond Rosenthal. New York: Pantheon Books, 1991.

Ginzburg, Carlo. *Night Battles.* New York: Penguin Random House, 1985.

Handley-Cousins, Sarah. "Midwife, Witch: How the Women's Health Movement Created the Myth of the Midwife-Witch." *Digpodcast.org.* Sep. 6, 2020, *https://digpodcast.org/2020/09/06/doctor-healer-midwife-Witch-how-the-the-womens-health-movement-created-the-myth-of-the-midwife-Witch/.*

Heselton, Philip. *Doreen Valiente, Witch*. Woodbury, MN: Llewelyn 2016.

Heselton, Philip. *Witchfather: A Life of Gerald Gardner, Volume 1– Into the Witch Cult*. Loughborough: Thoth Publications, 2012.

Heselton, Philip. *Witchfather: A Life of Gerald Gardner, Volume 2 – From Witch Cult to Wicca*. Loughborough: Thoth Publications, 2012.

Huss, Boaz. "Academic Study of Kabbalah and Occult Kabbalah" May 25, 2021, published in *Occult Roots of Religious Studies*. Boston/Berlin: Walter de Gruyter, 2021.

Hutton, Ronald. *The Triumph of the Moon: A History of Modern Pagan Witchcraft*. Oxford: Oxford University Press, 1999.

Hutton, Ronald. *The Witch, A History of Fear, from Ancient Times to the Present*. New Haven and London: Yale University Press, 2017.

Ian. "The Caillech Bheur." Mysterious Britain and Ireland. Sep.18, 2018. *https://www.mysteriousbritain.co.uk/folklore/the-caillech-bheur/*.

Sheldon, Natasha. "The Devil's Disciples: Twelve Male Witch Trials You Haven't Heard Of." History Collection, Nov. 18, 2017, *https://history-collection.com/devils-disciples-twelve-male-Witch-trials-havent-heard/5/*.

Johns, June. *King of the Witches: The World of Alex Sanders*. London and Edinburgh: Morrison and Gibb Limited, 1969.

Johnson Lewis, Jone "A Timeline of Witch Hunts in Europe," Thought-Co.com, Feb. 20, 2020, *https://www.thoughtco.com/europe-an-Witch-hunts-timeline-3530786/*.

Kamentz, Kezia. 6 New Orleans Urban Legends You'll Never Forget. Only In Your State. July 22, 2016, *https://www.onlyinyourstate.com/louisiana/new-orleans/urban-legends-new-orleans/*.

Kelden. "Nicnevin: Scottish Witch Mother." Patheos.com, Dec. 2017, *https://www.patheos.com/blogs/byathameandstang/2017/12/nicnev-in-scottish-Witch-mother/*.

Klimczak, Natalia. "Meetings with the Queen of Elphame: A Magical and Protective Fairy Queen." Ancient Origins, June 5, 2016, *https://www.ancient-origins.net/myths-legends/meetings-queen-elphame-magical-and-protective-fairy-queen-006030*.

Korwin Briggs. "An Almost Historical Egyptian God Family Tree." Nov. 23, 2015. *Vertitablehokum.com*.

Leek, Sybil. *The Complete Art of Witchcraft*. New York: Signet, 1971.

Leland, Charles Godfrey. *Aradia or the Gospels of the Witches*, 1899, Accessed via Sacred-Texts.com, 2021. *https://sacred-texts.com/pag/aradia.htm*.

Lockett, Rachel. Caileach: The Celtic Goddess of Winter. History Cooperative. Jan. 23, 2024, *https://historycooperative.org/cailleach/*.

Mark, Joshua J. "Baba Yaga" on *Worldhistory.org*, Oct. 7, 2021, *https://www.worldhistory.org/Baba_Yaga/*.

Murray, Margaret Alice. *The God of the Witches*. London, Oxford: Oxford University Press, 1970.

Murray, Margaret Alice. *The Witch-Cult in Western Europe*. London, Oxford: Clarendon Press, 1921.

National Archives. "Early modern Witch trials." October 23, 2020, https://*nationalarchives.gov.uk/education/resources/early-modern-Witch-trials/*.

New York Times. "Ordinary Witch from New Forest Dies at 65." New York Times obituary, *https://www.nytimes.com/1982/10/29/obituaries/sybil-leek-ordinary-Witch-from-new-forest-dies-at-65.html*.

Oates, Caroline and Juliette Wood. *A Coven of Scholars: Margaret Murray and Her Working Methods*, compiled by Caroline Oates and Juliette Wood, for the Folklore Society of Britain, 1998.

Oates, Shani. *The Robert Cochrane Tradition*. Published independently, 2018.

Pasciuto, Greg. "Russian Witch Trials: Bucking the European Trend?" The Collector, Apr. 2, 2023. *https://www.thecollector.com/russian-Witch-trials/*.

Patterson, Steve. *Cecil Williamson's Book of Witchcraft*. St. Paul, MN: Llewellyn: 2020

Paxson, Diana. "Holda." *Hrafnar.org*, originally published in Idunna 30, 1997. Accessed on Mar. 1, 2024. *https://hrafnar.org/articles/dpaxson/asynjur/holda/*.

Ring, Nicola A., Nessa M. McHugh, Bethany B. Reed, Rachel Davidson-Welch, and Leslie S. Dodd. "Healers and Midwives Accused of Witchcraft (1563–1736) - What Secondary Analysis of the Scottish Survey of Witchcraft Can Contribute to the Teaching of Nursing and Midwifery History." *Nurse Education To-day 133*, (2024): 106026. *https://doi.org/10.1016/j.nedt.2023.106026.*

Rosaleen Norton. *The Thorn in the Flesh: A Grim-Memoire.* York, ME: Teitan Press, 2009.

Sanders, Maxine. *Fire Child: The Life and Magic of Maxine Sanders 'Witch Queen'.* London: Mandrake Press, 2008.

Scot, Reginald. *The Discoverie of Witchcraft.* New York: Dover Publications, 1972.

Shaw, Gregory. *Theurgy and the Soul: The Neoplatonism of Iamblichus.* University Park, PA: Penn State University, 2003.

Sinclair, Charles. "Andrew Mann, 1598." From *Scotland's Wicked Witches.* Cockenzie, Scotland: Goblinshead Books, 2011, accessed via goblinshead.co.uk/bogles.

Sommerstein, Alan H. and Isabelle C. Torrance. *Oaths and Swearing in Ancient Greece.* Boston/Berlin: Walter de Gruyter, 2014.

Stenhouse, Margaret. *The Goddess of the Lake: Legends and Mysteries of Nemi.* Press Time Editions, 1997.

Tapsell, Jonathan. *Ameth: The Life & Times of Doreen Valiente.* London: Avalonia Press, 2014.

UAB Libraries. Witchcraft, Women & the Healing Arts in the Early Modern Period: Female Midwives, online archive of exhibit at University of Alabama, Birmingham, Fall 2018 through Spring 2019, *https://guides.library.uab.edu/c.php?g=1048546&p=7609202/.*

Valiente, Doreen. *An ABC of Witchcraft Past and Present.* Blaine, WA: Phoenix Publishing, 1986.

Valiente, Doreen. *The Rebirth of Witchcraft.* Marlborough, Wilshire, U.K, Crow Wood Press, 2007.

Valiente, Doreen. *Witchcraft for Tomorrow.* Marlborough, U.K, Crow Wood Press 1993.

Ward, Coby Michael. "Herodias And The Queen Of Witches." Patheos.com, Mar. 27, 2017, *https://www.patheos.com/blogs/poisonersapothecary/2017/03/27/herodias-queen-Witches/.*

Wentz, W.Y. Evans. *The Fairy-Faith in Celtic Countries.* London, New York, Toronto and Melbourne: Oxford University Press, 1911.

Wilde, Lady Jane. *Ancient Legends, Mystic Charms, and Superstitions of Ireland*. London: Ward and Downey, 1888.

Wilkinson, Richard H. *The Complete Gods and Goddesses of Ancient Egypt*. London: Thames & Hudson, 2017.

Williams, Liz. "Lois Bourne, 1928 – 2017." Jan. 11, 2018, *https://wildhunt.org/2018/01/lois-bourne1928-2017.html*.

Wim van den Dungen, "Amun, the Great God: Hidden, One and Millions." 2016. *sofiatopia.org*.

World History Edu. "Baba Yaga – the Wild Old Witch in Slavic Folklore." On Worldhistory.edu, Jan. 19, 2022, *https://worldhistoryedu.com/baba-yaga-the-wild-old-Witch-in-slavic-folklore/*.

Wylie, Olivia. "The History Of The Cailleach Bheara, Queen of Samhain." Brehon Academy website, Oct. 1, 2021. *https://brehonacademy.org/the-history-of-the-cailleach-bheara-queen-of-samhain/*.

Zabel, Gary "Philosophy 108: Moral and Social Problems" Spring 2017, syllabus, published on University of Maryland's website, *https://www.faculty.umb.edu/gary_zabel/Courses/Philosophy_108/Home.html*.

WEBSITES

angelsandmasters.net

doreenvaliente.com

gutenberg.org

Hellenicfaith.com

occult-world.com

patheos.com

sacred-texts.com

theosophyworld.com

wildhunt.org

WitchcraftandWitches.com

worldhistory.org

encyclopedia.com

www.thewica.co.uk

Index

About the Author

Brian Cain is a Witch and High Priest of the Alexandrian Tradition and is the author of *Initiation Into Witchcraft*. He has been a devotee of Traditional Witchcraft since his early teens and was first initiated in 1994. Today he is the High Priest of the New Orleans Coven, the only practicing Alexandrian coven in Louisiana. He maintains strong ties to the magical roots of Witchcraft in the United Kingdom and follows the teachings of Alex and Maxine Sanders. His focus is on strong training in both priesthood and the Arts Magical.

With his husband, Christian Day, he co-hosts HexFest, a Weekend of Witchery held each August in New Orleans, as well as Festival of the Dead, a monthlong event series in Salem, Massachusetts that includes the Salem Psychic Fair and Witches' Market and the Official Salem Witches' Halloween Ball. Together they own Witchcraft shops Hex and Omen in Salem and Hex in New Orleans. They are also the founders and publishers of Warlock Press.

Warlock Press ™
WarlockPress.com

Warlock Press is an independent occult publisher that is driven to provide unequalled content written by a diverse roster of today's magical adepts. Our authors hail from a spectrum of magical traditions, but share crucial things in common: authentic practice, established credentials, thorough research, and genuine devotion. This means that you can trust that you are getting the very capstone of the pyramid of occult wisdom.

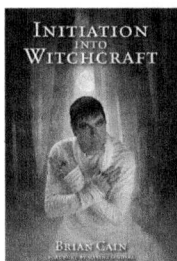

INITIATION INTO WITCHCRAFT
Brian Cain
Foreword by Maxine Sanders
This is a book about the religion of Witchcraft. It honors the old Gods, the ancient mysteries, and the secrets of magic. It is an exploration of the timeless traditions, essential ethics, and the awe-inspiring power of our Craft and provides basic practices that will help the reader to embrace the deeper ways of the Witch. It is a signpost for those seeking the path that begins the journey of initiation into Witchcraft and primer of occult techniques and rituals to prepare for that journey.

THE WITCHES' BOOK OF THE DEAD
Christian Day
Foreword by Laurie Cabot
The revised and expanded tenth-anniversary edition of this genre changing classic is available August, 2021. Readers will learn to summon and honor the spirits of the dead to bring blessings in their everyday lives, discover Witches of legend who raised the dead, and explore methods of spirit contact, necromancy, potent rituals, recipes, and exercises, and features two new chapters, new foreword, and a new preface!

LIVING THE ELEMENTS: EXTREME ADVENTURES FOR WITCHES
Fiona Horne

Join world traveling rockstar Witch, Fiona Horne and experience the sacred elements of Witchcraft in an action-packed, dynamic way that enlivens every fiber of your being and supercharges your spell casting. Air, Earth, Fire, Water, and Spirit are at the core of magickal work and in this unique book, Fiona gives you the advice you need to invoke your most empowered self. Fiona's personal stories entertain, enchant, and educate. She gives you the tools to get out of your comfort zones, stretch your boundaries and let go of limitations. Fiona offers three activity levels, Transcendent, Potent and Passionate—choose one or work through all three—from visiting waterfalls to freediving, kite flying to skydiving, firedancing to volcano climbing, dark retreats to stargazing. Whatever your physical or financial conditions, Living the Elements will change your life!

MOTHER: ECSTASY, TRANSFORMATION, AND THE GREAT GODDESS
Levi Rowland
Foreword by H. Byron Ballard

The Great Goddess is reclaiming her place as the preeminent force of life and creation. Devotion to Mother is a transformative experience. No matter what incarnation we invoke, she comes. She breathes into life, echoing the prayers and incantations of every initiator, Witch, believer, and devotee that has ever stood at her shrine and felt her presence, as real as anything under the sun (or beyond it). In her worship, in her magic, in her dance, is a living spiritual tradition, drawing from many sources but still focused on one multifaceted absolute. This book is a guide to the seeker who wishes to live a life turned towards the altar of the Great Goddess. Drawing from history but firmly rooted in the modern search for God the Mother, readers will be taken on an exploration of Goddess religion as a lived experience, an endless source of transformation and growth.

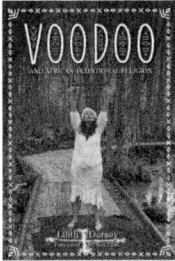

VOODOO AND AFRICAN TRADITIONAL RELIGION
Lilith Dorsey

Journey beyond the basic tenets of the faiths of the African diaspora to the vibrant, living spirit world of their peoples. This seminal guide to African spirituality has been revised and expanded to include tools for activists to empower their work for social change with the wisdom of their ancestors, as well as never-before-published recipes, personal spells and charms, such as root magick for protection and protest, and devotional rituals readers can perform themselves.

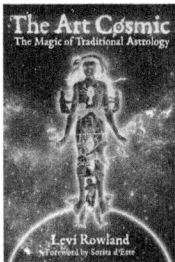

THE ART COSMIC: THE MAGIC OF TRADITIONAL ASTROLOGY
Levi Rowland
Foreword by Sorita d'Este

A detailed guide to the fundamentals of planetary magic using the seven sacred spheres of the ancients, including a system of celestial correspondences to use as a basis for meaningful spells, rituals, and workings. Readers will learn how to interpret natal charts using timeless methods of traditional astrology, use horary astrology for divination, incorporate the planetary hours for more successful spell work, and perform potent magical rites for each planet.

Printed in Great Britain
by Amazon